Advance Praise for *When Markets Collide*

"Mohamed A. El-Erian is one of the most gifted and successful risk management practitioners in the world. In this book he combines an academic's insight into advanced risk analysis with a portfolio manager's grasp of real world economics. This book is an essential read for those who wish to understand the modern world of investing."

—Alan Greenspan

"This extraordinary book portrays the future with a powerful and trailblazing illumination of the past. El-Erian takes aim at change at a wide variety of levels as the great dynamic, and I can assure you he hits the bull's eye."

—Peter L. Bernstein, author *Capital Ideas Evolving*

"Investors used to be content with getting the U.S. right—and then maybe Europe and Japan. Mohamed El-Erian argues why these tectonic economic continents are giving way to the emerging world. Brilliantly written, easy to understand—a forceful explanation of our changing global economy."

—Bill Gross, Managing Director, Founder and CIO, PIMCO

"Mohamed El-Erian, with his deep grounding in economics and his profound knowledge of financial markets, has written a book that no one else could write. From his vantage point atop Harvard Management Company and now PIMCO, he guides the reader through the great dislocations, extreme challenges, and exceptional opportunities generated amidst today's market tumult."

—Seth A. Klarman

"This book will certainly become an instant investment classic. Drawing on his extensive analytical knowledge of the academic literature, senior experience in policy circles, extensive knowledge of global financial markets and superior performance as an asset manager, Mohamed El-Erian has written a most excellent guide for investors, market practitioners, and policy makers for navigating the risks and opportunities of financial markets in this era of financial globalization and in these times of market volatility and turmoil.

This is a most sophisticated and comprehensive analysis from one of the deepest thinkers and foremost gurus of global investing. A must read for investors, policy makers and research analysts!"

—Nouriel Roubini, Professor of Economics,
New York University and Chairman of RGE Monitor

"Mohamed El-Erian's book is an important, wise, and insightful analysis of the way in which the changing global landscape and financial architecture, and the growing importance of developing nations, will change the nature of investing and risk management. It is fascinating reading.

His analysis of the importance of understanding policy responses on a global basis is persuasive and new. He foresees that we are entering a period unlike the past in which regulatory instruments and the level of international coordination will fall well short of being a match for the growing scope and complexity of the financial system. The result will be a bumpy ride, with attendant opportunities and risk."

—Michael Spence, Recipient of the Noble Prize in Economics (2001)

"I can think of no better guide to the terrifying yet exhilarating new world of global finance than Mohamed El-Erian. While others have been swept under by the upheaval of the credit crunch, El-Erian—who so brilliantly surfed the wave of emerging markets in the 1990s—more than weathered the storm while at HMC and is now poised to catch new waves back at PIMCO.

Not only has he managed to find time to dash off a book amid the market mayhem, he also turns out to have written the best account to date of the economic paradigm shift we are living through. It will be a rash investor who ignores his book."
—Niall Ferguson, William Ziegler Professor at Harvard Business School and author of *The House of Rothschild* and *The Cash Nexus*

"Mohamed El-Erian is a deep thinker of the global financial and economic scene. In *When Markets Collide* he brings to bear his unique investment, policy and academic experience in analyzing where we are heading and how we may get there. He does so in clear and logical fashion, and draws important lessons for policy makers and market practitioners. Read it and then study it, you will be rewarded!"
—Arminio Fraga, Founding partner, Gavea Investimentos and Former President, Central Bank of Brazil

"Mohamed El-Erian's book makes fascinating and instructive reading for policy makers seeking to understand the financial environment in which they are currently operating, as well as the major trends in the global economy and financial markets with which they will have to contend in the years ahead."
—Stanley Fischer, Governor, Bank of Israel

"Mohamed El-Erian is that rare creature: a skillful participant in financial markets who is also a brilliant analyst of them. He has written a book that is important and urgent, moving from the micro to the macro with equal ease. The result is a must-read."
—Fareed Zakaria, Editor, *Newsweek International*

"*When Markets Collide* is an extraordinarily powerful work on the evolution of the global economic and financial institutions, structures, and behavior—sharply defining how we got to where we are and where we will go in the years ahead, complete with wise counsel for both policy makers and investment professionals. To expand your knowledge and wisdom a mile wider and a mile deeper, this is a must read."
—Paul McCulley, Managing Director, PIMCO

"Mohamed El-Erian has created a road map to help us understand, navigate, and question the incredible and fundamental changes revolutionizing today's financial markets."
—Ken Griffin, CEO and Founder, Citadel Investment Group

"El-Erian is a doer and a thinker and someone who understands the risks of rare events. I never before saw such a combination in 20 years in the market. Read this book."
—Nassim Nicholas Taleb, author *The Black Swan*

WHEN MARKETS COLLIDE

INVESTMENT STRATEGIES FOR THE AGE
OF GLOBAL ECONOMIC CHANGE

MOHAMED A. EL-ERIAN

New York Chicago San Francisco Lisbon London
Madrid Mexico City Milan New Delhi San Juan
Seoul Singapore Sydney Toronto

1 2 3 4 5 6 7 8 9 0 DOC/DOC 0 9 8

ISBN: 978-0-07-159281-9
MHID: 0-07-159281-4

This publication is designed to provide accurate and authoritative information in regard to the subject matter covered. It is sold with the understanding that neither the author nor the publisher is engaged in rendering legal, accounting, or other professional service. If legal advice or other expert assistance is required, the services of a competent professional person should be sought.

> —*From a Declaration of Principles jointly adopted*
> *by a Committee of the American Bar*
> *Association and a Committee of Publishers*

This book contains the current opinions of the author but not necessarily those of Pacific Investment Management Company LLC. Such opinions are subject to change without notice. This book has been distributed for educational purposes only and should not be considered as investment advice or a recommendation of any particular security, strategy or investment product. Information contained herein has been obtained from sources believed to be reliable, but not guaranteed. References to specific securities and their issuers are for illustrative purposes only and are not intended to be, and should not be interpreted as, recommendations to purchase or sell such securities. PIMCO's clients may or may not own the securities referenced and, if such securities are owned, no representation is being made that such securities will continue to be held.

In memory of my father
To my mother, wife, and daughter

CONTENTS

PREFACE

When *Markets Collide* is about dynamics that are changing the global economy. Understanding these forces is consequential for investors, yet they appear to be difficult to fully identify and comprehend. They involve changes in both mature and emerging financial markets that will feature fresh opportunities wrapped in a complex and different configuration of risks.

I hope to share with you analysis and insights on what I refer to as a "new destination" for the global economy. In the process, I'll also talk about bumps along the journey, misleading diversions, and wild ups and downs as economies transform themselves and the world emerges from a period of disruption and confusion.

Long-term changes, what analysts refer to as "secular transformations," are inherently challenging. They involve significant realignments in economic power and tricky hand-offs in what determines economic growth, wealth, inflation, and investment returns. Newly influential actors and instruments emerge that are initially difficult to analyze. More generally, the secular transformation process triggers conflicts between the world of yesterday and the world of tomorrow—and in so doing, it makes a lot of noise.

As we move toward this new destination, existing infrastructures and systems will be pressured, including governments who must now address difficult policy challenges with incomplete information and outmoded tools. Individuals and institutions must adapt to new notions of actual and perceived entitlements. Previously dominant players on the global playing field must now accept the influence of those who were hardly considered to be serious competitors just a few years earlier. Meanwhile, these suddenly influential players must manage the challenges of success.

This book will help investors navigate the transformation of the changed global economy—a phenomenon that will seriously impact the potency of investment strategies and influence the effectiveness of risk management approaches. It will detail elements of an action plan and point to factors that can result in costly market accidents. It will argue that in navigating the transformation, investors must also take into account the actions of policy makers, on both the national and international (or "multilateral") levels.

I have had the privilege of having a career that has exposed me to both investment and policy issues, and I have come to recognize that it is impossible to discuss investment strategies for an age of global change without specifying how investors *and* policy makers should and will react. Whichever group one is in, successful endeavors require the understanding of how the others should, and are likely to, behave.

Investors who wish to maintain strong performance and reduce the risk of sudden and large losses will, I hope, find the insights and framework in this book useful in understanding the context, outlook, and implications of the new global landscape.

When Markets Collide covers the following topics:

Following the Introduction, Chapter 1 details some of the aberrations, conundrums, and puzzles that have dominated the economic and financial landscape in recent years. At their most basic level, these phenomena signal ongoing secular transformations.

Chapter 2 illustrates that, despite the growing difficulties of understanding the changing landscape, investors have been assuming significant risk; and they have been doing so in ways that have not always come under the purview of the traditional oversight bodies that possess the needed sophistication. As a result, a significant disruption hit the nerve center of the financial system starting in the summer of 2007. The result has been a series of high-level institutional losses that fueled the risk of a global credit crunch, and triggered emergency policy responses around the world.

With these developments as background, Chapter 3 discusses more generally why it inevitably takes investors time to understand ongoing structural transformations. In distinguishing between noise and signals, the discussion presents tools drawn from traditional economics and finance, behavioral science, and neuroscience. These tools help explain the causes behind market inconsistencies and shed light on how and why they resolve themselves over time.

This leads to Chapter 4's discussion of the new secular destination for the global financial system. It illustrates actual and prospective changes in the drivers of four variables that impact the robustness of virtually all the approaches taken by market participants—namely, growth, trade, price formation, and capital flows. The outcome will be nothing less than a regime change in which the next stage in globalization and integration is characterized by more diversified engines of global growth, a reduction in global trade and payments imbalances, the return of more pronounced inflationary pressures, and a more diversified allocation of investible funds around the world.

A destination is relevant only if you can navigate the journey to it. Accordingly, Chapter 5 analyzes the road ahead, potholes included. It details the drivers of nonlinearity occasioned by the risk of *market accidents*—that is, dislocations caused by unsustainable behavior on the parts of investors and intermediaries. It also looks at the compounding influence of potential *policy mistakes* on the part of national governments and international organizations.

The next three chapters speak to how market participants should position themselves to benefit from the upside and better manage the downside. For the global system as a whole, the challenge is to tip the dynamic balance—away from large structural and financial imbalances in industrial countries (and in the United States in particular) and toward the underlying stability associated with the coming on stream of emerging economies as important determinants of global growth and capital flows.

The challenge has two distinct components that investors need to understand and optimize simultaneously and consistently with their level of expertise. The first speaks to designing and implementing an asset allocation plan that is consistent with the forward-looking (as opposed to the historical) secular realities. In technical terms, the focus is on the appropriate specification of the *belly* of the distribution for global outcomes. The second component involves managing the *tails* of the distribution and, in particular, partially protecting the portfolios against the vagaries of the journey to the new secular destination.

To this end, Chapter 6 starts with an analysis of the main drivers of superior long-term investment performance, focusing on asset allocation and effective implementation vehicles. Since investors will excel only if they adequately understand the policy context, Chapter 7 focuses on the outlook for national policies. It points to changes that are needed to traditional approaches to make them supportive of investor adaptations. It also offers an action plan for multilateral institutions that can play an important role in enhancing the international consistency of national actions and but currently have the wrong set-up.

Chapter 8 supplements the analysis by looking at the risk side. By detailing the asymmetrical nature of risk mitigation in the international financial system, the emphasis is on approaches that long-term investors can adopt to appropriately navigate the journey. The conclusions of the book are contained in the final chapter.

I faced several choices as I endeavored to write this book. I wondered about the target audience and approach. Should I speak primarily to investors or to colleagues in policy circles and the research community? How about the tools of analysis? Should I rely on just one approach, or should I incorporate a broader mix?

After giving these questions considerable thought, I decided to take an eclectic approach notwithstanding the risk of ending up in the "muddled middle." Specifically, I am addressing both investors and national and international policy makers. I've adopted a multidisciplinary approach that combines traditional tools of analysis with newer ones. And throughout the process, I have linked the analytical discussion to historical and modern-day situations, including my own experiences.

To a considerable extent, these choices have been shaped by a career that, I believe, has been enriched by the opportunities afforded to me to cross the boundaries between research, policy making, and investing. These choices also reflect the intellectual stimulation I experienced during my undergraduate years at Cambridge University where the teaching of the traditional (neoclassical) approach to economics was brilliantly combined with other approaches (such as Keynesian, neo-Ricardian, and Marxist). This cocktail of approaches helped in training the minds of undergraduates to think. It also served as a great illustration of the importance of looking at issues from different perspectives, with explicit recognition of the merits and limitations of each approach.

So much for what I thought desirable for this book; what about feasibility? The contributions of others—past and present—facilitated my ability to draw on insights from different approaches. And whenever I stalled, I drew encouragement from some recent books—such as *Freakonomics*,[1] the two volumes by Nassim Nicholas Taleb,[2] Peter Bernstein's *Capital Ideas Evolving*,[3] and Richard Peterson's *Inside the Investor's Brain*[4]—that illustrate the advantages of exploiting the synergies between different disciplines.

Finally, in choosing an eclectic approach, I was also influenced by the more general insight provided by John Maynard Keynes, perhaps the most influential economist ever (and certainly my favorite). Keynes reminded us that economics is "a method rather than a doctrine, an apparatus of the mind, a technique of thinking which helps its possessor to draw correct conclusions."[5] As such, it can and does benefit from appropriate interactions with other disciplines. Moreover, the interactions act as sensible checks and balances against the risk that an individual analytical tool or approach will be hijacked by some oversimplifying assumptions or incomplete applications.

It is my hope that readers will find the eclectic nature of this book helpful in understanding an ongoing global phenomenon that is consequential to so many and in so many ways. Indeed, there may be no other alternative for understanding the emergence of this new economic age. The complexity of the regime shift is such that it warrants the use of the most appropriate tools from the most applicable disciplines.

I finished writing this book in January 2008. Since then, the global economy has experienced a series of previously unthinkable developments, including the demise of Bear Stearns, an iconic U.S. investment bank, and frantic policy attempts on the part of the U.S. authorities to contain the damage of the financial market turmoil. These developments are consistent with the analysis in this book. Indeed, the analysis predicts such disruptions, reinforcing the importance of its findings for those who wish to end up on the beneficial side of significant global changes rather than be victims of the inevitable turmoil that accompanies such changes.

INTRODUCTION: FINDING SIGNALS WITHIN THE NOISE

By the standards of the financial markets, I entered the investment world late. I was 39 years old when I left the relative predictability and stability of a career at the International Monetary Fund (IMF) at the end of 1997 for the rough and tumble world of Salomon Smith Barney in London. A fascinating journey followed during which I had the privilege of witnessing at close hand the slow but steady transformation of the global economic and financial landscape.

At first, the changes impacted relatively small areas of the investment and policy world—essentially, the specialized segment of emerging market investing and the even more specialized and arcane world of derivative instruments and risk transference. But the phenomena—and the related good, bad, and ugly that came with them—gathered momentum, and they are now critically relevant to a broad spectrum of investors, policy makers, and international institutions.

By discussing these phenomena in some depth, *When Markets Collide* seeks to shed light on how the ongoing economic and technical shifts, what I refer to throughout the book as "transformations," are impacting the world we live in—present and future. The book offers analytical anchors for identifying the key elements of what, for some, have become drivers in an unusually fluid environment. In so doing, I will uncover many of the understandable reasons that otherwise rational and well-informed investors can be late in recognizing important turning points and, subsequently, be prone to mistakes. In some cases, such mistakes have resulted in market turmoil, liquidity sudden stops,[1] institutional failures, and emergency policy responses—and they will continue to do so.

The information in this book has important practical implications for investment strategies, business approaches, and policy making. It provides readers with insights on how best to exploit new opportunities and minimize exposure to changing patterns of risks. Or in market jargon, the aim is to minimize the left (that is, unfavorable) tail of the distribution of outcomes while simultaneously exploiting the right (that is, favorable) tail.

In this new economic and financial age, both tails are fatter.

Transformations: Inherently Tricky

Transformations are not easy to recognize or navigate, especially when they are initially unanticipated and evolve rapidly. By challenging conventional wisdom and historic entitlements, transformations feed a dynamic that is inevitably uneven and, at times, unpredictable. Indeed, the phenomena accentuate in an important manner the difficulties that people face in the run-up to the more familiar long-term (i.e., secular) turns.

2

Here, the issues tend to revolve essentially around the timing and the orderliness of the turn as opposed to the secondary considerations that pertain to time and system consistency.

As transformations in individual markets are gathering momentum, it becomes evident that the market and policy infrastructures cannot yet adequately support the emerging realities—at either the national or international levels. Activities that have been newly enabled by the transformations tend to outrun the ability of the system to accommodate and sustain them. The result is a series of blockages and other "plumbing problems" whose prevalence gives rise to an initial bewilderment, turmoil, a blame game, and a subsequent realization that some type of change is needed.

Then when the needed refinements are being undertaken, market participants—investors and national and multilateral policy makers—face uncertainty and worry about the prospect of further turbulence. The market turmoil that started in the summer of 2007 illustrates the type of overshoots and dislocations that are likely to continue to occur. I would go so far as to say that the turmoil will shake the foundation of our global financial system. What started as a problem peculiar to the subprime segment of the U.S. mortgage market has morphed into a series of collapses whose impacts are being felt on both Wall Street and Main Street.

The responses of both the private and public sector market participants were initially undermined by their lack of understanding of the causes and consequences of the turmoil. Too many observers were quick to dismiss it as transitory and of limited impact. Investors, particularly in the equity markets, regarded it as an isolated event that would not prove contagious.

Policy makers initially remained on the sidelines, also influenced by the understandable desire to allow greedy borrowers and unscrupulous lenders to suffer the consequences of their actions.

However, it did not take long for all this to change as elements of the financial industry and the economy as a whole fell with a loud thud. Wider recognition triggered a catch-up process involving massive injections of emergency liquidity by central banks around the world. When such injections failed to halt the collapse, the U.S. government was forced to adopt a large fiscal stimulus package and directly support the housing sector. Meanwhile, senior executives of major western investment banks headed to Asia and the Middle East in a massive capital raising campaign—one that was described on the front pages of the financial media as involving "lifelines" (*Wall Street Journal*),[2] "bailouts" (*Financial Times*),[3] and the "invasion of the sovereign wealth funds" (*The Economist*).[4]

To some of us, the financial market turmoil that started in the summer of 2007 reflects the secular transformation of the global economy. There are now economic and financial forces in play whose impacts are of great consequence but that cannot as yet be adequately sustained by the world's current policy and market infrastructures. As such, the efficiency gains that they bring are associated with higher risks of short term disruptions. Indeed, one of the important messages of this book is that *the present turmoil is neither the beginning nor the end of the transformation phase.*

A series of inconsistencies and anomalies, which will be detailed throughout the book, acted as early *signals* of the growing tension between what participants or actors on the global finance stage were pressing for and what could be reasonably and safely accommodated by the existing systems in order to minimize the risk of turmoil. The signals also indicated the extent to which cross-border wealth hand-offs were empowering a new set of actors and products when it came to global influence.

As you read this book, it is important to realize that the forces behind the recent financial crises have not gone away. Instead, underlying global transformations will play a major role in defining and influencing the investment and policy landscape for years to come.

When Noise Matters

This bumpy process is nothing less than a collision of markets, in which *the markets of yesterday collide with those of tomorrow.* The underlying dynamic is one of hand-offs being made between actors, instruments, products, and institutions. In this environment, the basic challenge is to understand the inevitable bumpiness of such hand-offs and to manage them appropriately without losing sight of the nature and implications of the new destinations.

Market participants first become aware of transformations through what is commonly known as "noise." This noise comes initially from the sudden emergence of anomalies to long-standing relationships that participants take for granted. The typical human inclination is to treat the anomalies as both temporary and reversible. People tend to dismiss the noise as containing no meaningful information. Consequently, they believe there is little point in thinking about the longer-term implications for investment strategies, business models, or national and multilateral policies. But a careful reading of history and theory suggests otherwise. Noise can matter in so far as it contains signals of fundamental changes that, as yet, are not captured by conventional monitoring tools.

During my first year as an analyst on the Salomon Smith Barney trade floor in London in the late 1990s, I learned through observations a simple but powerful lesson about how to approach market noise. Rather than automatically dismissing it, one should ask whether there are *signals within the noise*. This lesson came from observing a smart colleague—a trader in his early twenties—who was working on the emerging markets bond desk. His name was Edward Cowen. I remember Edward as a talented trader and a diehard supporter of Arsenal in the English football league.

Edward was particularly well versed in one of the three qualities that Bill Gross, PIMCO's founder and widely respected "Bond King," argues are essential for an ideal portfolio manager or, more realistically, an ideal portfolio management team: street smarts. And to the outsider, Edward seemed to know it and be proud of it—so much so, I am told, that at one stage early in his career, he preferred to be seen walking to his desk in the morning with a tabloid under his arm as opposed to the *Financial Times* or the *Wall Street Journal*.

Edward's market instincts were so sharp that they more than complemented the other two qualities that Bill Gross had identified: a rigorous training in economics and a command of finance mathematics. These qualities made Edward a moneymaker for the firm at a young age. Indeed, he illustrated back then what work, particularly in behavioral finance and neuroscience, has confirmed: The importance of instincts, especially during periods of market stress. This was most visible in the manner he would treat analysts like me. On some occasions, he would step back from the markets to listen to our views—in fact, he aggressively sought them. In the process, he would push us hard on whether the turmoil reflected a potential realignment of fundamentals. On other occasions, he would ask us (mostly politely, but not always) to stay away from his desk lest we confuse him with some fundamental analysis that bore no relationship whatsoever to the realities of that day's market action.

This lesson—and specifically the discipline to think about potentially different interpretations of market noise—stayed with me as I moved from analyzing markets at Salomon to directly investing in them at PIMCO and at the Harvard Management Company (HMC). And over the years, I have found validation for this approach from thoughtful academic work on imperfect and asymmetrical information, market failures, and behavioral finance.

Most of the time, I have applied the lesson to specific strategies and trades. Early in my investing career, I was lucky to be involved in an asset class (emerging market bonds) inherently prone to noise and investor overreaction. After all, it was still in its early maturation phases. The challenge was to identify the causes of the noise and derive their implications. And the outcome was often good—not only through the calls that PIMCO made on Argentina's bond price collapse in 2000 to 2001 and on Brazil's sharp bond price recovery after the summer of 2002 but also in the contrarian positions taken vis-à-vis smaller market events (for example, the manner in which the markets was extrapolating in early 2002 the impact of Argentina's default on Mexico and the impact of Zimbabwe's unstable political situation on South Africa).[5]

The methodology was a simple one: Observe and analyze the underlying causes of the noise; see how those causes relate to a separate and distinct analysis of valuations based on economics and financial fundamentals and market technicals; test the initial findings against the views of experts in the markets; and derive short- and long-term implications for the impacted financial asset valuations and those that are connected through common ownership or other drivers of correlation.

In many instances, the right answer was to "fade" the noise—that is, treat it as a temporary and reversible deviation. But in some important cases, the correct response was to interpret the noise as containing signals—that is, pointing to meaningful changes in parameters governing both absolute and relative prices in certain market segments. Always, the right approach was to resist the initial temptation to simply dismiss, and therefore ignore, the noise.

With time, I inadvertently documented the process through a regular publication that I wrote for PIMCO and in op-ed pieces for the *Financial Times* and *Newsweek*.[6] The articles had a simple objective: to explain recent market developments and trends, including how they impacted investment strategies and policies going forward. In the process, I ended up compiling a body of evidence suggesting that the noise was signaling the emergence of deep and, as yet, little-understood changes impacting the global economic and financial landscape.

A shift in the nature of the noise coming out of the markets supported this evidence. Starting in 2004 and 2005, we moved from a world where noise was generally associated with *sequential* inconsistencies in markets to a world where *simultaneous* inconsistencies were notable. In other words, rather than just being inconsistent *over time*, the progressively louder signals coming from various market segments also became increasingly inconsistent *at the same time*.

Some Recent Inconsistencies

There are many examples of recent anomalies, several of which are discussed in detail in Chapter 1. Perhaps the most vivid public illustration of this change came in early 2005 when Alan Greenspan, the former chairman of the U.S. Federal Reserve, described as a "conundrum" the fact that successive and meaningful upward moves in short-term interest rates (the federal funds rate) had been accompanied by downward moves in long-term interest rates in the United States.[7] Indeed, for what seemed an eternity for investors (many of whom feel that a week is a long time), the U.S. bond market provided signals about the economy that conflicted with those coming out of the other most liquid market in the world, the U.S. equity market.

This inconsistency was accompanied by a rather peculiar situation among Fed watchers, that group of economists and analysts on Wall Street who make their living from predicting the course of the most influential interest rate in the world—the fed funds rate. In the middle of 2006, with the rate at 5¼ percent, the vast majority of Fed watchers fell into two distinct and opposite camps. One confidently predicted rate *hikes*—to

6 percent; the other equally confidently predicted *cuts*—to 4 percent. I remember noting several times that I could not recall such divergence in sign and size among such credible market observers.

Yet, despite such divergent views and inconsistent signals from the two most liquid financial markets in the world, the traditional indicators of market volatility and uncertainty (or market fear) continued to reach new lows. Too many market participants started to confuse the decline in market volatility with a decline in overall risk. This led them to make ever riskier trades. Questionable loans were made, and, with financial alchemy working over time, a host of balance sheets were excessively leveraged (including those of U.S. homeowners) using overly complex investment vehicles, products, and instruments.[8]

The work that I carried out with colleagues at PIMCO and HMC to explain the economic and financial inconsistencies pointed to three structural forces. As these factors played out, they emitted unusual signals on both a standalone basis and through their interactions. In the process, they confused existing models and the accepted rules of thumb. And while they were not the only factors in play, they were influential enough to explain much of what puzzled investors and policy makers.

Missing the Signals

The increasing prevalence of unusual signals was not accompanied by an adjustment meaningful enough on the part of market participants. Rather than seek out new analytical and operational anchors to better understand developments, too many investors went full steam ahead, taking on more risk and heavily engaging in new activities with backward-looking approaches. Policy makers expressed some discomfort, but they seemed either unwilling or unable to take much action. Indeed, along with the majority of market observers, policy makers shifted to becoming "data dependent" as their long-standing and seemingly robust models failed to explain modern-day realities. This data dependency was adopted notwithstanding the recognition that high-frequency economic and financial information is inevitably volatile and subject to important ex post revisions.

Such a situation begs for a disorderly unwind. Indeed, one problem of navigating markets without robust analytical anchors is the potential severity of the consequences when there is a sudden turn in the high-frequency data and/or prices. This phenomenon was, of course, vividly illustrated starting in the summer of 2007. In the intense period that followed, the financial system suffered a tremendous amount of damage. As the smoke initially started to clear, the media's first estimate of $18 billion in losses for the "big banks"[9] was subsequently revised up to $400 billion by analysts at Deutsche Bank.

An $8 billion write-off by Merrill Lynch was followed by the resignation of its CEO, Stan O'Neil. The CEO of Citigroup, Chuck Prince, followed after an additional $8 to $11 billion in losses. More was to come. A few weeks later, both institutions announced another round of losses that stunned Wall Street; yet another round followed a few weeks after that. They were not the only ones.

An initial upbeat assessment by UBS gave way to a multi-billion-dollar, subprime write-down that would lead to an overall loss for the year. A similar series of events happened at Morgan Stanley and elsewhere on Wall Street and in Europe. Indeed, Goldman Sachs seemed to be the only large investment bank that managed to navigate well through the turmoil.[10] And it also stood out as one of the few large institutions not forced to embark on an urgent capital raising campaign to safeguard its balance sheet.

The turmoil in the banking system was only part of the story in the financial markets. Several mortgage companies went bankrupt. AAA companies that insure bonds issued by municipalities and others faced large losses and the prospect of downgrades, forcing them to also look for emergency injections of capital.

The damage in the financial markets pushed governments and central banks into crisis management mode. This was vividly illustrated in the dramatic interest rate cuts in the United States and the U.S. government's emergency fiscal stimulus package. Yet the credibility of the official sector (i.e., governments, central banks, and regulatory agencies) suffered, including the Bank of England, which was forced into a very public U-turn on policy. Indeed, virtually every regulatory and oversight body in the major industrial countries came in for some criticism, as did the rating agencies.

Let us not forget Main Street. The turmoil in the financial markets raised legitimate concerns about collateral damage in the economy. References to a "credit crunch" multiplied, which drew the attention of politicians and acted as a catalyst for multiple legislative hearings, particularly in the U.S. Congress. Questioning went well beyond the nearest trigger (namely, the debacle in the subprime mortgage market) and the potential consequences (higher actual and expected foreclosures). It also encompassed the breakdown in consumer protection and financial regulation, the role of fraud, the near paralysis of money markets, the fragility of interbank activities, and the activities of credit rating agencies. And, in looking at the potentially stabilizing role of the fresh and patient capital waiting on the sidelines, some politicians questioned its motives rather than welcoming its involvement.[11]

No wonder observers have started to question the long-term impact of this episode. Instead of a cyclical hiccup, some have expressed concern that it will pull the legs out from under the globalization process and, more precisely, derail the integration of markets across geographical boundaries and financial instruments.

The New Secular Reality

The reaction of some observers in the recent past—in particular, the once-eager supporters of financial globalization who are now willing to ditch it—reminds me of the way five- to seven-year-olds play soccer: Players on both teams tend to chase the ball in the manner of a noisy herd. They are, in effect, totally data dependent. Their approach stands in sharp contrast to the behavior of older kids. Anchored by a better understanding of the game and more of a strategic mindset, the older players seek to maintain positions on the field and rely more on letting the ball do the work.

So, you ask, what are the structural factors that help explain the noise, and why has it been so difficult for market participants to develop appropriate analytical tools and approaches?

I am sure you have come across these three factors under various labels:

- The first is a fundamental realignment of global economic power and influence, including a gradual hand-off to a set of countries that previously had little if any systemic influence.
- The second is the pronounced accumulation of financial wealth by a set of countries that includes some that were previously more used to being debtors and borrowers than creditors and investors. This has fueled the systemic influence of sovereign wealth funds (SWFs),[12] reinforced the natural desire to diversify the allocation of their capital, and attracted the attention of politicians in industrial countries.
- The third is the proliferation of new financial instruments that have deeply altered the barriers of entry to many markets. For some, such as Greenspan, they are an important source of risk transfer and risk diversification; for others, such as Warren Buffett, the well-known value investor, they constitute "time bombs" akin to weapons of financial mass destruction.[13]

The interaction of these three factors has resulted and will continue to result in deep changes to the drivers of key global economic and financial relationships. Markets collide as new actors, instruments, products, and institutions assume greater systemic importance and do so in a manner that is different from that exercised by the previous sets. No wonder it has been difficult for market participants to adapt quickly and effectively.

These phenomena are being seen in the appearance of new, and in some cases previously unimaginable, drivers for such basic variables as global economic growth, trade, price formation, and capital flows—variables that investors should take seriously because they carry enormous weight in selecting appropriate investment strategies, business models, and policies. They are also seen in the stress faced by previously dominant players in the financial industry, some of whom are adjusting more quickly than others. Witness as well the way in which the interlinkages among markets are changing. As a result, diversification no longer delivers for investors the same amount of comfort as it once did. And all this inevitably leads to excessively large swings in the *production and consumption* of new, complex "structured products" and related investment vehicles, with the resulting need for costly "clean-up" operations.

Plumbing Problems Arise Out of the New Reality

There is another reason history tells us that such fundamental structural changes are not easy to navigate. It is not just because the recognition of risks is delayed and the risks are configured differently. It is also because the changes are yet to be accompanied by a retooling of enabling functions, including the "pipes" and infrastructure of the financial markets. Yet many investors feel compelled to jump in, either willingly or otherwise.

This combination results in a typical plumbing problem: The pipes are simply unable to handle the flow of new and old transactions. This is true at the level of the individual firm, where the willingness of the portfolio managers to use new strategies is yet to be accompanied by the ability of the middle and back offices to adequately process and maintain them. It is true at the level of the financial system as a whole where basic parameters—such as valuations, price discoveries, transparency and adequate supervision—risk being overwhelmed. It is also true at the level of policy where traditional instruments are less potent.

Like plumbing problems that you may experience at home, the result is a cleaning process that is often unpleasant. The costs can also be significant since they relate not only to the problem itself but also to the collateral damage. Indeed, investors face more than just the difficult challenge of understanding the new *destination* (or "steady state"), including what it implies for institutional and organizational set-ups. They also have to understand and navigate a *journey* that is inevitably turbulent and nonlinear. And with that comes the probability of *market accidents and policy mistakes*.

Due to the difficulties in being able to rapidly identify and adapt to multiple structural changes, it is inevitable that some investors (including previously successful investors) will trip, some firms will fail, some admired policy makers will be slow in reacting, and some international institutions will lose relevance. As long as the numbers remain contained, they will constitute only "flesh wounds" for a generally robust secular transformation. But if few become many, the world faces the prospect of a disorderly adjustment characterized by disappointing economic growth, higher unemployment, greater poverty, trade wars, capital controls, and financial market instability.

A Framework for Understanding the New Reality

Against this background, the purpose of this book is to document and detail the fundamental structural changes that are now in play—both their individual impacts and the manner in which they come together in defining a new secular destination. In doing so, the book also sheds light on the journey. This combination offers the readers analytical anchors—mental models, if you will—that can help in the formulation and implementation of strategies for an age of economic and financial change.

I would view this book as meeting its objective if it helps readers better understand the nature and implications of the emerging global secular realities. To this end, it details the challenges that face market participants and suggests ways to address them. The focus is on the ability to address both the most likely secular results (that is, the results that anchor the belly of the distribution of outcomes) and potential major disruptions (that is, the fat left tail of the distribution).

In attempting to meet this objective, I also provide a framework for explaining developments in the financial industry and the policy world, including the recent market turmoil and liquidity disruptions that started in the summer of 2007. I demonstrate that these developments share a common root:

the tendency of structural transformations to enable activities that initially outrun the ability of the system to accommodate and sustain them. This mismatch will continue to play out in the period ahead pending what is likely to be a protracted phase of reconciliation at the level of individual firms and nations and the multilateral system as a whole.

The analysis thus sheds light on such factors as the recent large-scale migration of financial activities beyond the purview of traditional regulatory and supervisory jurisdictions; the virtual 180-degree turnaround in the sources and victims of systemic disruptions; the difficulties that exist in valuing certain instruments; the proliferation of structured investment vehicles (SIVs) and other off-balance-sheet conduits; and the new influence of SWFs.

Finally, the analysis also speaks to the unusual spectacle of seeing the most sophisticated banking system in the world come under significant pressure. It sheds light on what was previously thought to be a highly unlikely and, for some, unimaginable shutdown of the vibrant market for commercial paper lending. It explains why investors have suddenly had to worry about the stability of their money market funds and long-standing financial institutions. And it details why authorities in countries with highly developed market mechanisms have been forced into crisis management and emergency policy actions.

CHAPTER 1

ABERRATIONS, CONUNDRUMS, AND PUZZLES

In the Introduction, I noted that over the last few years, economic and financial issues have arisen that could not be explained using existing models, mindsets, or prior experiences. As a result, they came to be called "aberrations," "conundrums," and "puzzles," and many in the marketplace dismissed them as being just "noise" and, as such, devoid of meaningful information. But these issues were, in fact, signals of underlying shifts or transformations that have proven to be of great consequence—in particular, as illustrated in the crisis that shook the foundation of the international financial system starting in the summer of 2007. These signals remain significant to investors now and will continue to be so in the future.

Perhaps the most famous reaction to the phenomena of anomalies and inconsistencies was contained in then Fed chairman Alan Greenspan's semiannual monetary report to the Senate. In the February 2005 report, he noted that "for the moment, the broadly unanticipated behavior of world bond markets remains a conundrum." I still remember the reaction on PIMCO's trade floor when Greenspan used the word "conundrum." Many were struck by how the most-respected, well-read, and influential policy maker of the day did not have an explanation for something as basic as the shape of the U.S. interest rate curve (that is, the "yield curve").

Greenspan was far from alone. Later in 2005, *The Economist* ran a cover story about the puzzling global economy. A few months later, Larry Summers, the Harvard professor and former secretary of the U.S. Treasury, referred to "an irony of our time" when reflecting on the configuration of global payments imbalances. He was commenting on the large flow of capital from developing to industrial countries, or from the poor to the rich—a flow that runs completely counter not only to what is predicted in economic textbooks but also the logic of rich-poor relationships. Summers observed: "To my knowledge it was neither predictable nor predicted and the implications are large and have not yet fully been thought through."[1] The finance minister of New Zealand was similarly perplexed when asked to comment about the actions of investors in his country. In a September 2006 interview with the *Financial Times*, he described these investors as "irrational," noting that their investment behavior was consistent with "someone [who] would have to be slightly strange."[2]

For me, the biggest puzzle of all centered on the reaction of investors—particularly the ability *and* willingness of the financial system to overconsume and overproduce risky products in the context of such large systemic uncertainty. Like others, I was struck by how two phenomena that you would expect to be negatively correlated ended up being positively correlated for so long—namely, on the one hand, the significant fall in the premiums that investors were paid to assume risk and, on the other hand, the investors' desire to assume even more of this mispriced risk.

The dynamics behind this positive correlation, which I will discuss in greater detail in Chapter 2, went something like this: Some investors were hesitant to accept the lower expected returns associated with the generalized decline in risk premiums. Accordingly, they tried hard to squeeze out additional returns. Leverage served as the best way to do so: By borrowing, they could put more money to work in their best investment idea; and this seemingly made sense as long as the expected return was higher than the cost of borrowing. In turn, the leveraged positions pushed risk premiums even lower, encouraging another round of leverage.

That cycle is just one illustration of the amazing sense of calm and self-confidence that prevailed despite the abundance of things that could not be explained. Rather than stay on the sideline until proper explanations emerged, many investors rushed into ever riskier trades and even higher leverage. Wall Street responded by putting the production of ever-more-complex products into overdrive. Many of these products offered investors "embedded leverage," playing directly into the hands of those looking to magnify what would otherwise be for them, low expected returns. And while national and multilateral policy makers expressed a mix of concerns and bewilderment, no meaningful actions were taken to "take the punch bowl away."

A few months later, the world economy found itself in the grip of significant market turmoil. Unlike the majority of the global financial crises of the preceding 25 years, this one was triggered by events in the world's most sophisticated economy, the United States. It impacted segments closest to the monetary authorities—namely, the interactions among banks. The results were bizarre to say the least.

Consider the highly unusual intraday swing in interest rates of over 100 basis points that occurred in the U.S. Treasury bill market, that on at least one occasion, was associated with highly unusual erosions in liquidity and market flows. You would expect such a systemwide event to cause collateral damage or be contagious, perhaps even envisioning people lining up outside banks to pull their money out. Based on recent history, you might also expect the casualties to be in an emerging economy with a weak banking system and not in another industrial country with a sophisticated financial system.

There was indeed a bank run, but it came from the United Kingdom. The event panicked the government into guaranteeing all bank deposits and triggered an amazing turnaround in the publicly stated policy of a highly respected central bank—the Bank of England. And there was collateral damage to an extent that in years past would have resulted in job losses on the part of ministers of finance and central bankers in emerging economies and in some cases, prime ministers and presidents. But this time, the high-profile casualties were the CEOs of some of the most influential banks in the world and other senior corporate officials.

The list of aberrations goes on. Interestingly, the numerous instances did not involve just one market, one country, or one set of actors. They pertained to several. Also notable was that the more usual tendency of inconsistencies occurring *sequentially* gave way to the emergence of inconsistencies occurring *simultaneously*.

It is therefore no surprise that, in the presence of so many anomalies, some conventional approaches to making investments have become less effective. Conventional strategies and business models are no longer adequately capturing the real dynamics that exist in the global economy; and the dominant industry players are being challenged by competitors who once seemed to be undertaken only lower-value-added activities and, as such, were not viewed as influential market participants. At the same time, policy measures and coordination mechanisms increasingly lack relevance and effectiveness.

In the following sections, I will discuss the nature of the aberrations, conundrums, and puzzles that have recently emerged. By focusing on topics that relate to market and policy issues, it will be clear that these inconsistencies contained important signals about underlying global transformations. In the process, I will shed light on the future evolution of the fundamentals that influence expected returns and risk—namely, global growth, trade, price formation, and financial flows.

Global Payments Imbalances and the Role of Developing Economies

Economics textbooks agree that the baseline expectation for the natural direction of capital flows across borders in the global economy is from developed countries to those countries still in the process of developing. The presumption is that because they are capital scarce, developing countries can offer a potentially higher expected return on a unit of invested funds than that offered by developed countries. The argument is based on the relative cheapness of labor in developing countries, as well as the relative lack of sophistication in their financial markets. Both factors serve to enhance the expected return on a unit of capital coming from developed economies.

This natural flow can be interrupted or even reversed by certain risk factors. For example, concerns about barriers to exit—such as capital controls or outright nationalization and confiscation—will discourage the flow of capital to developing countries. After all, why invest in a foreign country if you cannot repatriate the dividends, profits, and remaining capital as appropriate? For those reasons, the overall flow of capital can change directions—often so much so that there are outright large reversals in conjunction with episodes of capital flight as nationals of these countries also seek to protect or disguise their holdings.

As illustrated in Figure 1.1, the last few years have seen a sharp and sustained change in both the expected and historical trends. For example, at the end of the 1990s, the trend of developing countries' registering account deficits over time turned as these countries began to run up sizable surpluses— that is, they saved more than they invested. These surpluses have been large and persistent, resulting in a significant accumulation of international reserves. For example, as of 2007 China's reserve growth had been running at around 10 percent of its gross domestic product (GDP) for three straight years.

Another unusual aspect to these surpluses is that they have been accompanied by a pickup in economic growth and imports, not a decline. This is in stark contrast to past episodes when developing countries had to resort to highly

Figure 1.1 A Dramatic Transformation in Developing Countries' External Accounts, Billions of U.S. Dollars*

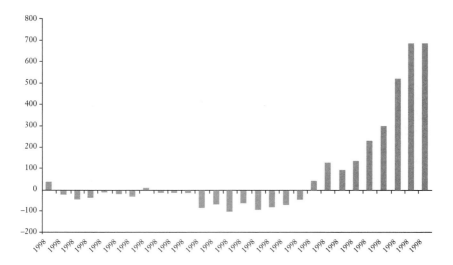

*Includes developing countries and newly industrialized economies.

Source: IMF's WEO, October 2007.

restrictive economic policies in order to generate a surplus. Specifically, in the past, governments would have had to cut spending, raise taxes, and devalue their currency to generate the types of surpluses that have materialized in recent years.

In short, the last few years have been *different*. Developing countries have run persistent surpluses, and they have done so in a manner that suggests economic strength rather than weakness. And they have saved in a lasting manner an important portion of the surpluses. This unusual phenomenon has caused a ripple of other irregularities. One of the most visible

Figure 1.2 A Highly Asymmetrical Distribution of Payments Imbalances, Billions of U.S. Dollars

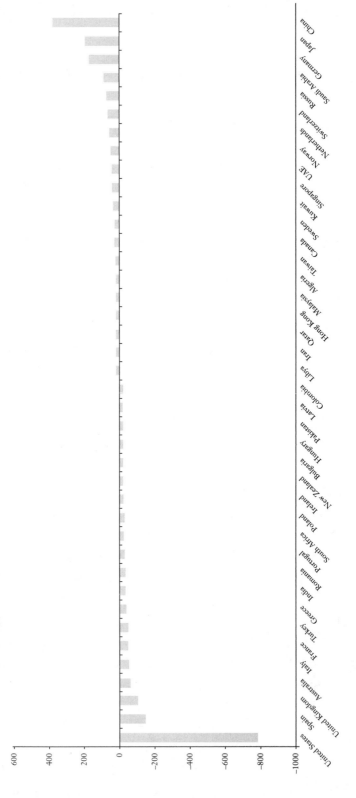

Source: IMF's WEO, October 2007.

was, of course, the ability of the United States to run a counterpart and large current account deficit that, at one stage, consumed over 90 percent of the world's savings. While this burden on global savings has declined, the country distribution of payment imbalances remains highly skewed; and the United States is the notable exception in the international line-up (Figure 1.2).

At PIMCO, we used the term "stable disequilibrium" to characterize this highly unusual configuration of global payment imbalances. The size of the U.S. deficit constituted a clear signal of disequilibrium. The willingness of developing countries to fund this deficit cheaply made it stable, at least in the short term. This situation led to a set of emerging economies[3] becoming creditors to the United States (Figure 1.3). Imagine that: The poorer countries were lending to the rich country, which meant that they were accumulating large claims against this rich country. As they grow in importance as holders of industrial countries' assets, whatever the emerging markets say about how they allocate their funds can and does influence markets globally. Their impact is felt in the pricing of bonds, in the valuing of specific companies, and in the movements of exchange rates.

These are just some indications of the extent to which the shift of developing countries from operating in *debtor regimes* to *creditor regimes* is leading (and has led) to a gradual change in how investors perceive the role of these countries within the world economy. And the transformation has been enormous, aided in some cases by large inflows of funds on the capital account that have turbocharged the reserve accumulation dynamics, including through inflows of portfolio and foreign direct investments.

Figure 1.3 The Accumulated, Substantial Holdings of U.S. Treasuries by Emerging Economies*

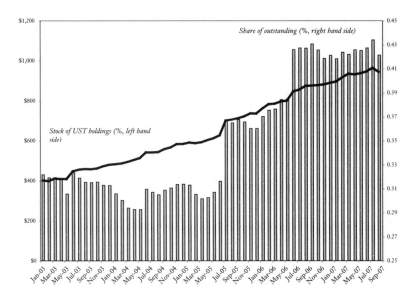

*Includes China, Taiwan, OPEC, South Korea, Hong Kong, Mexico, Singapore, India, Brazil, Thailand, Poland, Israel, and Turkey.

Source: U.S. Treasury, Treasury International Capital (TIC) data.

Just a few years ago, developing countries were viewed as *the* predominant sources of economic disruptions, and for good reasons. After all, there was Latin America's lost decade of the 1980s during which the damage to the global economy went beyond the period of stagnant growth, higher poverty for the region, and deteriorating social conditions; the well-being of the money center banks in the United States and elsewhere was threatened by the region's debt restructurings. We had the 1994 and 1995 Mexican "tequila crisis," which required massive emergency assistance, partly in response to concerns that millions of Mexicans would come across the border into the United States trying to escape a severe economic crisis and high unemployment at home. And who could forget the 1997 and 1998 Asian crisis and the 1998 Russian default that contributed to the demise of Long-Term Capital Management (LTCM)—a hedge fund collapse that was seen to threaten the stability of the global financial system?

More recently, developing countries have been viewed less as a threat of systemic disruptions and more as a source of global stability. This shift was unimaginable just a few years ago. Yet this new view has developed deeper roots and is being felt through several channels. And the view has found support in the emerging countries' contributions to global economic growth and their willingness to provide massive amounts of cheap financing to the U.S. government, banks, brokerage companies, and other private sector entities.

The global financial market disruptions that started in the summer of 2007 highlighted the change in the international standing of emerging economies. To the surprise of many, the emerging markets showed enormous resilience in the face of market turmoil so severe that it shut down segments of the credit markets and paralyzed interbank activity in industrial countries. Even more surprisingly, some of these emerging markets were seen as playing a critical role in trying to safeguard the viability of such western financial icons as Citigroup, Merrill Lynch, Morgan Stanley, and UBS.

In addition to showing resilience, some emerging markets acted as de facto market stabilizers. As an example, consider the November 27, 2007, announcement that ADIA, the investment arm of the Abu Dhabi (a member state of the United Arab Emirates [the UAE]) government, would inject $7.5 billion of capital into Citigroup. In the process, ADIA's holdings of convertible stock would, upon mandatory conversion into common stock, make the institution the largest single Citigroup shareholder (at just under 5 percent). This announcement came on the heels of a sharp drop in Citigroup's share price as investors reacted negatively to the news of large write-offs. The stock had closed the previous day at a price of $29.80, representing a decline of over 40 percent since the start of the year (and compared to a positive return of 4.4 percent for the Dow). The ADIA news helped the stock recover by 12 percent in the next four trading sessions and by 4 percent more the next week. It also helped the Dow record what constituted at that stage as the biggest two-day rally in the last five years (in excess of 500 points).

A few weeks later, UBS coupled the announcement of a $10 billion subprime loss with indications that it too would sell a stake to sovereign wealth funds (SWFs) led by Singapore's Government Investment Corporation (GIC). As in the case of Citigroup, the mechanism for this capital injection was a bond issuance that would convert into equity stakes. And again, the markets responded favorably to indications that inflows from a pool of large and patient capital would materialize and act as a stabilizer. Finally, Morgan Stanley combined its announcement of large losses in December 2007 with the news that it had obtained a $5 billion injection from Asia. China, through the Chinese Investment Company, bought mandatory convertibles that gave them a stake of almost 10 percent in Morgan Stanley.

In short, we have and will continue to witness a complete transformation in the systemic role of developing countries in the world economy, which is part of the broader phenomenon occurring in the financial industry that was unthinkable just a few years ago. Martin Wolf, the economics editor of the *Financial Times*, captured well the switch in the roles between the developed and emerging economies when describing the causes behind the market turmoil of 2007: "Its origin lie with credit expansion and financial innovation in the U.S. itself. It cannot be blamed on 'crony capitalism' in peripheral economies but rather on irresponsibility in the core of the world economy."[4]

The Interest Rate Conundrum

These historical aberrations were part of a larger phenomenon. And who better than Alan Greenspan to describe the interest rate "conundrum" that took hold of the largest bond market in the world?

In his 2007 book, *The Age of Turbulence*, Greenspan shared the following scene: "What is going on? I complained to Vincent Reinhart, director of the Division of Monetary Affairs at the Federal Reserve Board. I was perturbed because we had increased the federal funds rate, and not only had yields on ten-year treasury notes failed to rise, they'd actually declined. . . . Seeing yields decline at the beginning of a tightening cycle was extremely unusual."[5]

In his February 2005 testimony to Congress, Greenspan provided some details about this phenomenon, noting that "long-term interest rates have tended lower in recent months even as the Federal Reserve has raised the level of the target federal funds rate by 150 basis points." He went on to observe that "this development contrasts with most experience, which suggests that, other things being equal, increasing short-term interest rates are normally accompanied by a rise in longer-term rates." Greenspan suggested that the conundrum impacted the full range of market-determined interest rates. Referring to the longer-dated bonds, he stated, "Historically . . . even these distant forward rates have tended to rise in association with monetary policy tightening. In the current episode, however, the more-distant forward rates declined at the same time that short-term rates were rising. Indeed, the ten-year [bond], which yielded 6½ percent last June, is now about 5¼." Finally, Greenspan observed that this conundrum went beyond the United States. It was also apparent in other industrial countries.

The phenomenon Greenspan described played out to such an extreme that the yield curve inverted; that is, the long-term interest rates fell below those on shorter-term maturities (Figure 1.4). Put another way, by receiving initially lower interest rates, savers were apparently penalized (rather than rewarded) for their willingness to invest their money for longer periods of time.

Many hypotheses were offered to explain the conundrum. Some dealt with the unusual flow of capital around the world; others with institutional considerations. A good example of the first argument was the "savings-glut" hypothesis put forward by Ben Bernanke (when he was a Fed governor and before he came back from the Council of Economic Advisors to replace Greenspan as chairman of the Federal Reserve).[6] This argument suggested that the large U.S. current account deficit was more sustainable than the experience of other countries would suggest.

Figure 1.4 The U.S. Yield Curve Inversion that Occurred as the Fed Hiked Rates

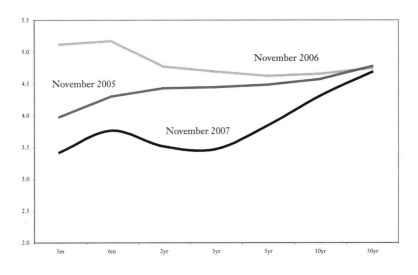

Source: Bloomberg.

The reasoning was simple. Faced by the largely unexpected improvements in their current account described earlier, central banks in developing countries (and in the newly formed SWFs) did what was both prudent and expected: They bought the least risky and most liquid financial instruments that they could buy (that is, U.S. Treasuries) pending a better understanding of the permanency of the improvement, as well as the development of a more sophisticated approach to wealth management. Their focus was initially on short maturity instruments, but, as the dynamics for building reserves gained momentum, their focus expanded to include longer maturity and other instruments.

This type of buying is driven by safety and liquidity consid- erations rather than strict profit-maximizing interests. Put another way, the U.S. Treasury was being rewarded for its deep and liquid markets, the predictability of its debt manage- ment policy, and a history of respect for property rights and the rule of law; and not for the yields that were on offer. The purchases by emerging economies put upward pressures on the prices of Treasuries, reducing the yields further—even though the Federal Reserve was hiking the federal funds rate. Since they appeared not to be pursuing the most profitable commercial opportunities, the markets referred to this behav- ior as being "noneconomic" and "noncommercial."

Sovereign wealth funds were not the only investors acting in a way that others would regard as noneconomic from a narrow profit maximization perspective. Certain pension funds also bought U.S. Treasuries in order to "immunize their liabilities." Since the claims of pension holders are long dated, it made sense for them to engage in "liability-driven investments" (LDIs) whereby they underpinned part of their future payouts by buying "risk-free" long cash and derivative instruments that closely matched the maturity of their liabilities. Again, the buying of Treasuries was not driven strictly by value consider- ations but rather by the desire to match liabilities. A similar phenomenon occurred in the United Kingdom. The result in both countries was to depress the long end of the yield curve as compared to what would have occurred otherwise.

Others pointed to the possibility that the markets were much better predictors of the economic outlook than the offi- cial sector. So while the Federal Open Market Committee (FOMC) repeatedly warned about inflation, the market signaled the prospects of a significant economic slowdown—thereby pushing longer-term interest rates below those maintained by the Fed in anticipation that the monetary authorities would have to cut rates aggressively. Interestingly, the equity markets' view was different from the bond markets' view—an issue that I will return to shortly.

Ultimately, the curve normalized, but it required a major financial market disruption to do so. Spreading concerns about the impact of the subprime mortgage debacle and related worries about a credit crunch, including difficulties faced by numerous financial institutions, forced central banks around the world to inject significant liquidity. In addition, the FOMC cut interest rates by 50 basis points (bps) in September 2007 and a further 25 bps in October and December, followed by cuts of 125 bps in January 2008 (including a dramatic 75-bps intermeeting action).

Simultaneously, the Fed took aggressive measures to close the gap between the higher discount rate and the fed funds rate, and it directly injected large liquidity through the introduction of a term auction facility (TAF). This facility allowed banks to liquify their holdings. Testifying before the U.S. Congress, Bernanke stated, "The goal of the TAF is to reduce the incentive for banks to hoard cash and increase their willingness to provide credit to households and firms."[7]

The Most-Liquid-Markets Puzzle

What was also unusual about the interest rate conundrum is that the inversion occurred at a time when the U.S. equity

Figure 1.5 U.S. Equities Registered Successive Record Highs While the Yield Curve Inverted

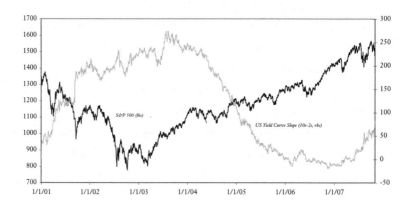

Source: Bloomberg.

markets were experiencing a period of robust price appreciation consistent with a period of strong economic growth that was forecast to continue. As Figure 1.5 suggests, the U.S. stock market (as measured by the Dow Jones and S&P 500 indexes but not the technology-laden Nasdaq) surged to a series of new historical records while the U.S. yield curve inverted.

Consider this: The U.S. bond and stock markets are the two most liquid markets in the world. As such, economists regard them as also being the most efficient markets in the manner in which they process and price information. Yet these markets had sent conflicting signals about the prospects for the largest economy in the world. And these conflicting signals were occurring *at the same time.*

Again, several explanations were offered, but none garnered a meaningful consensus. Some cited the strength of the equity market as signaling the robust state of companies' balance sheets. With companies' holding so much cash, there is always the possibility of higher dividend payments and share buyback programs. Others pointed to the health of the global economy *as a whole* and the growing extent to which U.S. corporations were booking earnings from foreign sales.

A third view stressed the "private equity put." This notion was based on the correct observation that private equity firms were attracting a ton of cash and had access to extremely accommodating debt financing (in terms of both interest rates and covenants). As such, they were able to step in at the slightest sign of a price downturn and buy public companies in a "public-to-private" transaction. As this behavior became noticed and understood by investors, some rushed in to front run the private equity bids, and others repriced whole market sectors on the basis of private equity funds' interest in a particular company.

We will never be able to determine with certainty what caused the U.S. equity market to behave so differently from the bond market, and for such a prolonged period of time. However, what is clear to me is the importance of not dismissing the phenomena as simply "market noise"—especially when these aberrations were accompanied by other puzzling events. Fortunately, all these previously unthinkable developments are now finally being recognized for what they really were—indications of a sea change. Indeed, what began as noise for many investors and policy makers became a signal of a major redefining of the global financial system. And it quickly became clear that certain parts of the international monetary system and market infrastructure were particularly ill prepared for this change, which had costly consequences, as I discuss in the next chapter.

CHAPTER 2

HOW TRADITIONAL RESOURCES FAILED US

Institutions that are one step removed from the immediate action and that are staffed by professionals charged with "surveillance" of the international system are particularly well placed to correctly identify when signals are something more than noise, perhaps even to predict them. Moreover, due to a universal membership and the power granted to them by their articles of agreement, they should play a role in facilitating welfare-enhancing changes in the global landscape. After all, they are built to reconcile domestic and international considerations. In actuality, however, these institutions have often found themselves better equipped to deal with the challenges of yesterday rather than with those of today and tomorrow.

The International Monetary Fund (IMF) has traditionally been considered the most influential of the existing multilateral institutions that are operating at both the country and cross-border levels. Consider some of its attributes:

- It has a virtually universal membership, with 185 member countries as of the end of 2007.
- Through its international staff, it assembles one of the world's largest populations of economics Ph.D.s to work under one roof, and it exposes them to real-world policy challenges.
- It has unmatched access to countries because, under its articles of agreement, members agree to a number of obligations that include subjecting themselves to a periodic (usually annual) check-up by IMF staff.
- By mandate, it complements its "surveillance" of national policies with multilateral responsibilities.

With these attributes, you would expect the IMF to flourish in the scenarios that have played out among nations in the last few years—namely, lots of national policy uncertainties, new and unusual forms of cross-border flows, and the inability of any one country to deliver an *orderly* global outcome. Instead, it has languished.

The Challenges Facing the International Monetary Fund

In commenting on the challenges facing the IMF, its then managing director, Rodrigo de Rato, observed in 2005 that "there is the question of whether the Fund is fully prepared to meet the great macroeconomic challenges that lie ahead."[1] He went on to note that the institution faces "the imperative to stay relevant in a changing world." Others were more direct.

Barry Eichengreen, professor of economics and political science at the University of California, Berkeley, described the IMF as "a rudderless ship adrift on a sea of liquidity."[2] Tim Adams, the former U.S. Treasury undersecretary for international affairs, publicly characterized the IMF as "asleep at the wheel" while he served in his official post.[3] Jim O'Neil, chief economist at Goldman Sachs, asked, "Which of the big countries in the developing world needs the IMF or really cares what they think?" Adam Lerrick, economics professor at Carnegie Mellon University, added, "Heads of state no longer tremble at the approach of the IMF because they no longer need its money."[4] This echoed a *Financial Times* editorial that argued, "Since the world's foreign currency reserves will shortly be 20 times the resources of the Fund, the day when it could dictate to important countries are past."[5]

Sensing the increasing awareness of the IMF's weaknesses, a growing number of parties have joined the ranks of those taking potshots at the institution. Those ranks have included the two extremes of the political spectrum in industrial countries: those who believe that the IMF is an instrument of western imperialism and postcolonialism and those who believe that the fund interferes with the efficient functioning of markets and the related disciplinary mechanisms. And don't forget those who feel that national prerogatives should never be ceded to a multilateral body. Those groups have been joined by those—primarily in Asia and Latin America—who still resent the conditionality that they believe the IMF imposed on them.

A vivid illustration of this comes from the ads that ran on Argentine television in October 2007 ahead of that country's presidential elections.[6] In one ad financed by the leading candidate, a group of children is asked about the IMF. They respond in a way that is familiar to any parent but has nothing to do with the institution: The IMF is a horse; no, a satellite; or is it a country? An offscreen voice then emerges to reassure those watching that "we're making sure that your children, and your children's children, have no idea what the IMF is."

Problems at All Levels

The IMF's problems go beyond its inability to respond to the types of challenges that, on paper, speak strongly to its attributes. Like many other entities and activities in both the public and private sectors, the business model of the IMF is ill equipped to deal with the changes that are occurring in the global economy.[7] Indeed, the highly visible and documented case of the IMF contains important insights for many financial firms around the world.

First, and foremost, the IMF has to deal with global issues that reflect the growing interaction between traditional economic issues, where the IMF is strong, and financial innovation, where it lacks sufficient expertise. As such, the IMF is not seen as a credible and knowledgeable "trusted advisor." The resulting loss of influence is compounded by the fact that, as suggested in Figure 2.1, the institution is no longer called upon to lend, given the above-noted sharp improvement in developing countries' external accounts. As a result, the IMF is no longer able to impose the same degree of policy "conditionality" that it did in the past.

Second, the IMF is facing internal budgetary problems. The institution relies on an income model that assumes a high

Figure 2.1 Few Countries Now Accessing IMF Financing: IMF Credit Outstanding, Billions of IMF Special Drawing Rights (SDRs)

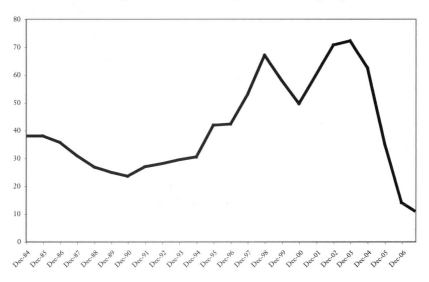

Source: IMF.

level of lending activity.[8] Consequently, its income has fallen sharply as countries have repaid it. The fund is now running an annual and growing deficit that is slowly eating into its reserves. The result is that just when it needs to learn how to better respond to the new global realities in economics and finance, it must do so in the context of a constant or contracting budget—not an easy endeavor.

Third, the outlook for the global economy is that it will be increasingly dependent on the policy actions of countries that are underrepresented at the IMF. Indeed, it is now widely recognized that the fund's governance structure is outmoded and feudalistic.[9] How else would Belgium, with a population of just over 10 million, have almost the same voting power (2.13 percent of the total) as China (2.94 percent, population of 1.3 billion), Russia (2.74 percent, population of 141 million), and Brazil and Mexico combined (2.61 percent, and almost 300 million)?[10] These inconsistencies are stark regardless of what comparison indicator one uses—GDP, trade, reserves, or virtually any other.

Legitimacy and Representation Deficits

The deficit in legitimacy and representation is also apparent in the approach taken to selecting the head of the institution—a position that has been always "reserved" for a European national. (Under a similar arrangement, the president of the World Bank has been "reserved" for a U.S. national since the institution's creation in 1944.) Over the last few months, a meaningful consensus has emerged seeking to do away with the feudal selection process. It was bolstered by a less-than-genuine attempt by western European countries and the United States to advocate "an open and transparent system" for the 2007 change in leadership at the two organizations while in fact maintaining the old system based on nationalities.

The cries of foul are now heard almost as commonly in official circles around the world as they are heard in the media, seminars, and conferences on the topic. At the end of September 2007, after the choice had been made for the new European head of the IMF, the deputy prime minister of Russia published a strong criticism in the *Financial Times*. Commenting on the IMF and the World Bank, he noted: "A prerequisite of their success is trust from the world community and agreement from the overwhelming majority of states with the rules by which they operate. It is not difficult to understand that if one or other structure is seen by a significant part of the world as ensuring the domination of one country or group of countries over others, it will lose its legitimacy. It will cease to be an effective instrument."[11]

All this speaks to a simple but powerful observation: The ongoing changes in the global economy are so powerful that they have taken an institution that was once at the center of the international monetary system to a peripheral position where it risks being further marginalized. The underlying dynamics are similar to those that face many other institutions that operate in both public and private sectors around the world.

The Volatility Mystery

You would expect that traditional measures of market uncertainty would have registered some uptick as the aberrations began multiplying and the inadequacy of the international system became more apparent. Yet the contrary occurred. For a few years leading up to the summer of 2007, several measures of market volatility actually pointed to a *reduction* in uncertainty, as opposed to an increase. This was part of a broader tendency for market participants to romance what became known as "the great moderation"—that is, the belief that the world's economies had entered a period of reduced fluctuations in both economic and financial indicators.

The trend of declining market volatility was evident in the measure that attracts the most attention in the financial media:

the VIX. Often labeled as Wall Street's "fear index," the VIX is short for the "Chicago Board Options Exchange Volatility Index." It is a measure of implied volatility based on the weighted average of prices for various options on a diversified basket of stocks.

While the mapping is far from perfect, sustained moves in the VIX carry important information about the underlying extent of uncertainty in the markets. And as many investors use similar approaches to determining an important component of risk management strategies (essentially those approaches based on *value at risk*, or VAR), you would be right to expect that a decline in the VIX would be accompanied by an increase in many investors' willingness to assume risk.

As Figure 2.2 illustrates, there is no question as to how the VIX behaved while aberrations were all strongly in play. Contrary to expectations (and I would argue intuitive logic), it steadily declined and did so in an impressive fashion until the summer of 2007. In other words, investors preferred to take more risks at a time when growing and simultaneous inconsistencies dominated the marketplace.

The VIX is not the only variable that behaved in this way. The same happened in measures of volatility for the fixed-income and foreign exchange markets. Indeed, the graphs for those markets, as well as those for intramarket equity volatilities, all looked similar. They were also consistent with a more general observation: a notable increase in correlations among different asset classes, different geographies, and different fundamental drivers.

Changes in investor behavior accompanied the decline in the VIX. The most visible was the encouragement of all sorts

Figure 2.2 A Counterintuitive Decline in Market Volatility until Summer 2007 as Seen in the VIX Index

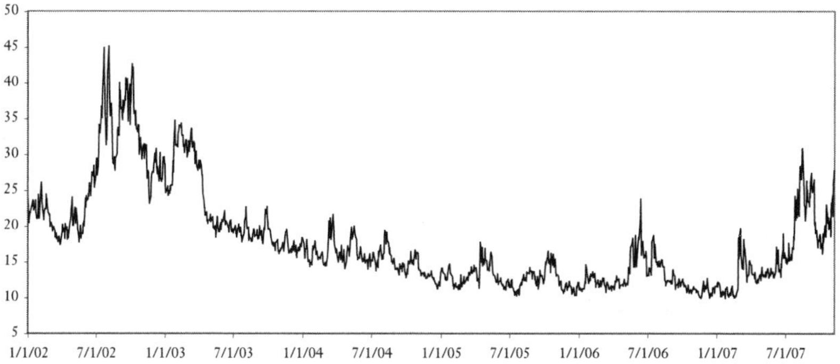

Source: Bloomberg.

of "carry trades" (that is, borrowing at a lower rate and investing at a higher rate, thereby earning the "positive carry"). These trades were particularly prevalent in foreign exchanges where investors borrowed the currency of countries with low interest rates and invested in the currency of countries with high interest rates.

Over the last few years, the favorite funding currency has been the Japanese yen since short-dated interest rates there are below 1 percent. And the related investments occurred in countries such as Brazil, Iceland, New Zealand, and Turkey.

Figure 2.3 provides a simple example of the extent of the phenomena. The value of the New Zealand dollar against the Japanese yen rose sharply despite two notable issues: First, New Zealand was running a large and growing current account deficit—traditionally a signal of upcoming currency weakness

Figure 2.3 So Much for Interest Rate Parity: The New Zealand Dollar versus the Japanese Yen

Source: Bloomberg.

rather than strength; and second, the prevalence and profitability of this carry trade defied for a long time the logic of uncovered interest rate parity, a widely accepted economic theory that postulates that interest rate differentials between two countries are equal to the difference between the current and future exchange rates. No wonder then that New Zealand's minister of finance questioned the "rationality" of those investing in his currency. Yet these investors made money for quite a prolonged period.

All these developments were associated with some notable structural shifts that will be discussed in more detail in a later chapter. The significant increase in overall risk taking by the marketplace was accompanied by a migration of activities to the oversight of supervisory agencies that were ill equipped for the task. They lacked the sophistication, tools, and the proper mindsets. We also witnessed a proliferation of new products, as well as heightened interest on the part of banks to use newly created conduits that did not reside on their balance sheets— what PIMCO colleagues Bill Gross and Paul McCulley elegantly labeled "the shadow banking system."

Structured investment vehicles (SIVs) and other conduits were "off balance sheet" in their formal definitions and accounting treatments. Indeed, they enabled banks to take advantage of what was perceived at the time as an attractive "regulatory arbitrage." Specifically, the activities undertaken through the conduits did not necessitate the type of regulatory capital backing that would have been required if they had been kept on balance sheet. But the theoretical hands-off formulation proved less so in practice. The links to their "parents," particularly the large banking institutions, came in the form of contingent funding lines, partial guarantees, and reputational risk.

In practice, many large financial institutions were ultimately forced to take directly onto their balance sheets heavily hemorrhaging SIVs at a time that was particularly inopportune in terms of their capital robustness and reputational standings. On November 26, 2007, HSBC announced that it was explicitly taking onto its balance sheet some $45 billion of holdings that resided in two SIVs connected to the bank.[12] At full risk weighting, the impact reduced the bank's regulatory capital ratio by around half a percentage point to just under 9 percent. Other banks followed HSBC. A few weeks later, Citigroup announced that it would bring on balance sheet assets that were residing in its large SIV program.

Credit rating agencies, particularly Moody's and Standard & Poor's, were also a factor in facilitating the migration of complex instruments to institutions and balance sheets that lacked the expertise to understand and assess the risks. Benefiting from their designation as "Nationally Recognized Statistical Ratings Organizations (or NRSROs), these agencies act as de facto gatekeepers for investors that use rating restrictions to control risk exposures.[13] Investment guidelines typically postulate that no instruments with a rating below a threshold level can be bought. As it turns out, the agencies were rather active in the rating of tranches (i.e., slices) of structured products as AAAs, thereby affording these products entry to the portfolios of a very large set of insurance companies, pension funds, and other major investors.

With the market eventually trading these tranches as BBBs or worse, questions have multiplied about the robustness of agencies' rating methodologies, as well as the potential conflict of interests given that the agencies are paid by the producers of the structured products. All this has reopened the old concern as to "who rates the rating agencies"—an issue that we will return to later in the book.

The end product went beyond an overproduction and overconsumption of complex risk configurations, some of which had not yet stood the test of time. In the process, we also saw the financial system of the United States assume a degree of maturity mismatch that is highly unusual in such an advanced and sophisticated economy. Indeed, the massive maturity gap that emerged due to the use of short-term funds to finance long-term commitments reminded me of the situations that had given rise to deep crises in developing countries (for example, Mexico in 1994, Thailand in 1997, and Turkey in 2002).

Gillian Tett captured the situation well in the *Financial Times*, where she remarked that "not only have financiers created these vehicles on a startling scale this decade but they have also done so using an appalling funding mismatch." She added, "What is truly shocking is that the risks posed by this funding mismatch have gone so unnoticed, for so long. . . . Until recently it appears that few policy makers, bankers, or investors had ever factored the prospect."[14]

Think of it: At a time when the world's economies seemed more difficult to understand (which is the logical consequence of the widespread emergence of aberrations) *and* multilateral financial regulation mechanisms were failing us, the marketplace ended up willingly taking on greater risk exposures through the alchemy of new structured products, off-balance-sheet conduits, and other vehicles that lie outside the purview of the sophisticated oversight bodies, be they private or public. In the process, too many investors mistakenly assumed that a technically driven reduction in volatility implied that risk had actually declined. And in the process, rather than truly spread risk throughout the global system, financial innovation enabled an excessive concentration of risks in some of the most sensitive parts of the system and in some of the most unstable balance sheets.

The then CEO of Citgroup, Chuck Prince, summarized the situation well in a now famous interview featured on the front page of the *Financial Times* on July 10, 2007: "When the music stops, in terms of liquidity, things will be complicated. But as long as the music is playing, you've got to get up and dance. We're still dancing."[15]

I doubt that many people, including Prince, envisaged the scene that would play out for Citigroup (and other financial institutions) when the music stopped. By January 2008, Citigroup was scrambling to raise new capital from institutional and retail investors. It had lost its CEO and several other senior executives. It was further embarrassed by the downgrading of its credit rating to AA–, with the added insult of a negative outlook.

Driving home from work on a January evening, I was struck by how Citigroup's historic loss led the news bulletin of the *BBC World Service*. A few days later, the *Wall Street Journal* conveyed the depth of the "pool of red" phenomenon in a simple yet powerful table, part of which is reproduced here as Table 2.1. The table listed the $108 billion, yes *b*illion, of writedowns taken by "banks, brokerage firms, and others in the subprime mortgage downturn."[16] And that was just an interim (January

---

Table 2.1 "Pool of Red"

Company	Writedowns, in Billions of U.S. Dollars
Merrill Lynch	$22.4
Citigroup	19.9
UBS	14.4
Morgan Stanley	9.4
HSBC	7.5

Source: Susanne Craig, David Reilly, and Randall Smith, "More Zeroes for Investors," Wall Street Journal, *January 18, 2008.*

2008) report that, as yet, did not capture the enormity of the phenomenon.

More generally, the pressure to assume greater risk, especially through complex structured finance instruments and buyout loan commitments, combined with overconfidence in a "just-in-time" risk management paradigm led to the trio that would (and should) keep any trustee, shareholder, or policy maker awake at night: a set of institutions taking risk beyond what they can comfortably tolerate; another set of institutions taking risk beyond what they can understand and process; and a third set of institutions doing both!

The Changing Nature of Risk and Contagion

Given the lead-up to the market turmoil that started in July 2007, it is perhaps not surprising that the disruptions differed significantly from what had been the norm in the previous 25 years. Nevertheless, there were many unusual things about the trigger for the systemwide dislocations, the impacted market segments, and the collateral damage.

Markets had been led to worry about emerging economies when it came to economic and financial shocks with universal consequences. After all, these economies lack the financial sophistication of more advanced countries; their institutions are structurally weaker; hedging and other insurance possibilities are more limited; and the populations, which have experienced past crises that resulted in large losses and some confiscation of capital, are more likely to panic and contribute to capital flight.

Not surprisingly, therefore, very few people expected the source of the 2007 disruptions to originate in the United States. And even fewer people expected the disruptions to paralyze the nerve center of the U.S. financial system. Yet for a few days around August 17 in particular, the world's most sophisticated financial system appeared close to paralysis. Market participants, including me, cut short our summer breaks to meet with colleagues and talk about "capital preservation." And these discussions did not just extend to the usual suspect of risk assets (such as equities and commodities). They also focused on where the cash was held.

Cash Management

I remember cutting an attempted holiday short and rushing back on August 14, 2007, to discuss with my colleagues at Harvard Management Company (HMC) our cash management approach. We had entered the summer's dislocation defensively positioned, including having raised significant cash. The question on the table went beyond where we had placed our cash (the answer being money market funds managed by well-established financial intermediaries); it also concerned how these money market funds were investing.

After assessing the information available to us, we decided to transfer an important part of our cash holdings to one- to three-month U.S. Treasury bills. In doing so, we applied the old saying that there are times when you have to worry about the return *of* your capital and not the return *on* your capital. Little did we know that these bills would subsequently rally the way they did as risk aversion and a general flight to quality took hold of the markets; and little did we know that a number of money market funds would register losses that, absent the injection of capital by their sponsoring institutions, would have forced them to "break the buck."

Harvard Management Company was clearly not the only place where such discussions were taking place. The related concerns vividly played out in what is usually regarded as the most boring of all markets—the very front end of the U.S. Treasury market.

It is a common view on Wall Street that this segment is populated either by novice traders looking for a gradual manner to gain experience or by 30-year veterans looking to live a less stressful life as they edge toward retirement. Yet, suddenly in mid-August, Treasury bills started fluctuating widely. There were equally unusual swings in the London Interbank Offered Rates (the LIBOR—that is, the rate that governs activities among financial institutions) as banks hoarded cash, as well as in other similar market segments (Figure 2.4). And trading virtually stopped in many segments of the credit markets as buyers stayed on the sidelines (which became known as the "buyers' strike").

An insight into the July and August turmoil may be obtained from the writings of Hyman Minsky or Irving Fisher's influential work on the dynamics of a debt-deflation spiral.[17] At the heart of the spiral is the decline in the value of the collateral that is underpinning various creditor-debtor relationships. As the value declines (or becomes uncertain), lenders become more cautious with respect to both existing and future commitments. The process becomes particularly dangerous if the spiral impacts the banking system, as it did during the summer of 2007.

Figure 2.4 Disruptions at the Heart of the Financial System

(a)

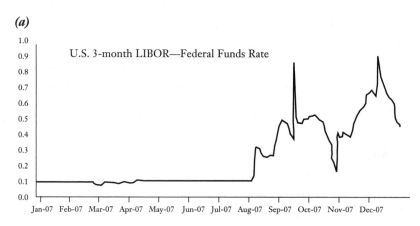

U.S. 3-month LIBOR—Federal Funds Rate

(b)

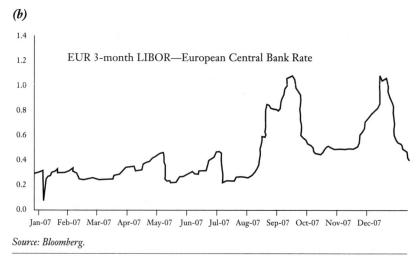

EUR 3-month LIBOR—European Central Bank Rate

Source: Bloomberg.

Collateral Damage

How about the collateral damage? Surely if the crisis is so deep as to impact the heart of the U.S. financial systems, then the emerging economies would face significant disruptions. After all, the conventional wisdom is that whenever the indus-

Figure 2.4 Disruptions at the Heart of the Financial System *(cont'd.)*

(c)

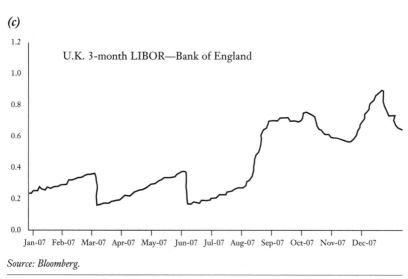

Source: Bloomberg.

trial countries sneeze, the emerging economies catch a cold, if not something more serious.

Once again, something rather unusual took place. Emerging markets held up well. Indeed, notwithstanding their traditionally higher sensitivity to global disruptions, emerging market risk spreads outperformed expectations, as did emerging market equities (Figure 2.5). Moreover, as I noted earlier, rather than be a victim of contagion, some emerging economies exploited the situation by buying industrial countries' assets at reduced prices.

Such resilience was less evident in industrial countries. The Federal Reserve and the European Central Bank (ECB) were forced to provide emergency liquidity to the markets. The ECB's bold response was particularly notable in terms of its urgency and magnitude, earning Jean-Claude Trichet, its

Figure 2.5 Emerging Markets: No Longer the Most Vulnerable to Global Shocks, July 2007 = 100

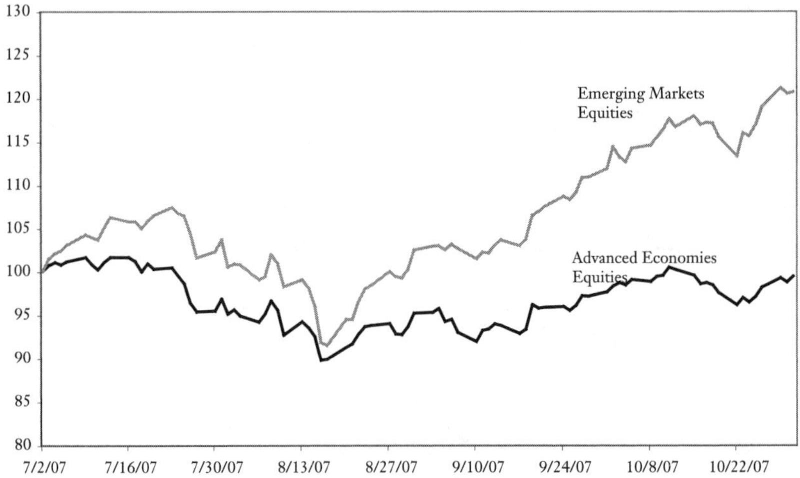

Source: Morgan Stanley Capital Investment (MSCI) Index. (EAFE [Europe, Australasia, and Far East] free for developed countries and EM free for emerging markets, both in local currency.)

president, the *Financial Times'* award of "person of the year" for 2007.

As it became obvious that the Federal Reserve's policy responses were failing to halt the cascade of falling economic and financial dominos, the federal government was pushed into designing a major fiscal stimulus package. The emphasis was on a package that would provide immediate help but without adding to the budget's structural weaknesses—an approach that, after a Larry Summers' article, was known as dictated by "the three Ts": targeted, temporary, and timely.[18] At the same time, action started to be taken to directly support the housing market, albeit in a muted manner initially.

Individually driven policy measures were accompanied by attempts at coordinated actions by major industrial country central banks. One of these actions saw the Federal Reserve and the ECB being joined by the Bank of Canada, the Swiss National Bank, and the Bank of England. The Bank of England's participation was particularly notable: It had initially dismissed such operations as weakening market discipline, encouraging "moral hazard," and risking to "sow the seeds of future financial crises."[19] But shortly after taking such a public stance in the summer of 2007, the bank was forced into an embarrassing volte-face as it injected liquidity in the context of efforts to rescue Northern Rock, a bank facing panicked withdrawal by depositors. Periodic liquidity injections followed.

The comments by the chairman of Northern Rock are particularly illuminating on the concept of a sudden stop in liquidity. In a letter to *The Economist*, Matt Ridley wrote: "We were repeatedly advised that liquidity in wholesale markets depended on lending quality: good loan books would continue to attract funding when bad loans began to default. Instead, from August 9, liquidity has dried up across all wholesale markets, making no distinction between loans of different quality, for much longer than even the most extreme forecast."[20]

Writing in the *Financial Times*, Martin Wolf observed that the Northern Rock episode caused Meryvn King, the governor of the Bank of England, to lose "a game of chicken with the world's most irresponsible industry."[21] Moreover, fearing a more general run on the U.K. banking system, Alistair Darling, the chancellor of the exchequer (the finance minister), informed the public that the government would guarantee all deposits. As one observer at a conference noted, this "opened the door for banks and others to gamble with guaranteed deposits."[22]

There is another reason why central banks prefer not to be called on for emergency liquidity injection to counter disruptions in the financial sector. They realize that such injections could run counter to the type of domestic liquidity management needed to sustain low inflation and contain inflationary expectations. As a result, the injections can undermine a hard-won effort to lower real interest rates, enhance policy credibility, and contribute to noninflationary long-term growth.

Columbia University Professor Guillermo Calvo popularized the concept of "sudden stops" in liquidity. His work during various emerging markets crises and thereafter offers important insights for the more recent type of market turmoil. Note in particular two findings: First, in most cases, "external factors" were the major trigger of sudden stops (that is, the cause did not originate in the entity facing the dislocation occasioned by the sudden stop); and second, the severity of the impact depended on the extent of internal financial vulnerability.[23]

These two lessons played out in the disruptions. Consider the cases of statistical arbitrage ("stat arb") and capital arbitrage hedge fund strategies that had particularly difficult situations: The causes of the disruptions came from outside these market segments. Those funds that were most impacted were vulnerable on account of one or several of the following factors: leverage, maturity mismatches, lack of term financing, and client redemptions.

The collateral damage was also clear in other institutional arenas. Hedge funds had difficulties, with some closing down altogether. The volume of political rhetoric rose as the crisis had all the makings of a political drama: irresponsible financial behavior, unscrupulous lenders, greedy borrowers, fraudulent activities, conflicted institutions, and collateral damage for households that could least afford it (including those facing tragic foreclosures).

Charlie McCreevy, the European Union commissioner for internal market and services, captured the mood in the opening speech to the Wachovia Bank International Conference in Ireland in October 2007. "Irresponsible lending, blind investing, bad liquidity management, excessive stretching of rating agency brands and defective value at risk modeling pose questions for a much wider audience. . . . Now that the tide has gone out, the state of undress of many participants in financial markets is there for all to see—bare bottoms all over the place. Nobody can be proud of some of the ugliness that this credit crisis has exposed."[24]

The Bottom Line

So where does all this leave us? It leaves us with four important observations that I believe warrant further investigation and shed light on the future opportunities and risks confronting investors.

First, we are coming from a period of significant and simultaneous historical aberrations. They have been widespread and have posed quite a puzzle for long-standing models, strategies, and conventional wisdom.

Second, too many investors rushed to dismiss these aberrations as noise rather than considering whether they were signaling something consequential about underlying forces. As a result, and despite the deep and wide market inconsistencies that were prevailing, many investors' initial reactions were to assume greater risk, consistent with the decline in implied volatility. At the same time, policy makers ended up taking a rather laissez-faire attitude in reaction to the migration of risk away from official and private supervisory bodies that had the expertise to conduct the necessary oversight.

Third, the systemic failure to distinguish signals from noise undercut the ability of both investors and policy makers to understand the nature and implications of the underlying transformations—transformations that were not only changing the secular destination for the global economy but also making for a rather bumpy journey.

Finally, when the inevitable adjustment came, it caught many off guard. The result was a major shock to the traditional parameters that underpin the smooth functioning of the market system. Yet industrial countries, rather than emerging economies, experienced the bulk of the collateral damage.

CHAPTER 3

SEPARATING WHAT MATTERS
FROM WHAT DOESN'T

The easy thing to do when confronted with the types of anomalies noted in the previous chapters is to ignore them! For a few years leading up to the summer of 2007, that is what some of the sophisticated institutions and economic thinkers chose to do, treating the anomalies as having no meaningful information content. Others identified the proximate causes of the noise but then viewed them as both *temporary* and *reversible*. The investing and policy reaction, if any, was therefore to fade the noise. This approach can be summed up by the notion of "mean reversion" or the more mundane "business as usual."

There is a second dimension of human reaction worth noting that has to do with the dynamics associated with the simultaneity of the anomalies. In addition to treating them as temporary and reversible in and of themselves, the conventional approach assumes that these abnormalities will not create feedback loops that will further change risk and return patterns in the marketplace. This approach is not just intellectually and operationally straightforward; it is also supported by the majority of historical experiences. In many instances the correct and wise reading of history suggests that it is best to dismiss the notion that "things will be different this time around."

Change runs counter to what makes most people feel comfortable in their day-to-day lives. A large part of our lives is based on the peace of mind that comes with predictability and repetition. Whether we know it or not, most of us draw comfort from the ability to use existing constructs or mental models to explain historical developments, to govern our present-day activities, and to predict our future actions. As John Maynard Keynes said, "The difficulty lies, not in the new ideas, but in escaping from the old ones, which ramify, for those brought up as most of us have been, into every corner of our minds."[1]

All this suggests that there is a meaningful risk that investors will be late to recognize and react to structural transformations, turning points, and regime shifts. In fact, a unifying theme for this book is that today we are living through such an episode—an age of global change—that is yet to gain sufficient recognition and understanding. As a result, many investors have not fully appreciated the impact inconsistencies and aberrations will have on a range of market, policy, and institutional factors.

This chapter offers a straightforward framework that you can use to recognize and understand turning points in the markets so that you have a way to identify and think about *signals within the noise*. With this in your back pocket, you will be able to better navigate and manage the implications appropriately. The chapter then discusses why it is difficult to look for signals within the noise and why finding signals may not to be easy despite the enormous consequences of overlooking them. To this end, I use a multidisciplinary approach that draws on insights from traditional economics and finance, as well as the newer behavioral disciplines and neuroscience.

In addition to addressing issues of delayed recognition and related costs, this approach sets the stage for how best to think about the potential for damaging feedback loops. Such loops give rise to the possibility of "multiple equilibria" and pose interesting questions regarding the design and implementation of optimal solutions.

These issues are attracting attention beyond the world of finance. There is growing talk about the importance of reducing noise lest it adversely impact quality-of-life indicators. How often, for example, do vacationers ruin their holidays by keeping in touch with their offices through "real-time" e-mails and voicemails—an awful habit that I must admit being guilty of. You have no doubt come across the image of Blackberries on the beach—and now iPhones! An interesting analysis of this trend can be found in a recent book by Stuart Sim, professor of critical theory at the University of Sunderland in the United Kingdom.[2] Sim's book *Manifesto for Silence: Confronting the Politics and Culture of Noise*, advocates that greater emphasis be given to developing and maintaining quiet areas lest the ever increasing noise tear at the fabric of society.

A Simple Framework

I'll start with the basic observation that noise is an inevitable consequence of a complex world. After all, economic, political, and social relationships are hardly ever frictionless. Nor do they proceed in a linear fashion. And then there is always a host of unanticipated developments that need to be internalized. And our personal lives are no different. Consider the challenges facing first-time parents. They have to deal with the unfamiliar expressions and sounds of their baby. And most do so without having the knowledge or experience to evaluate, with sufficient confidence, what is truly noise and what signals something more fundamental that requires parental action.

Noise is all around us, and because it is so prevalent, we are tempted to go to extremes and ignore it completely or to obsess over each and every component of it. In certain circumstances, going to either of these two extremes can prove quite risky. If we ignore the noise, we might miss an important change; if we obsess over it, we might be overwhelmed (and potentially paralyzed) by minutiae. So how do we strike the right balance?

Some Reverse Engineering

Being an economist by training, I am inclined to seek frameworks to help me think about various issues. The context that I use here has its origin in observing the emerging markets trader Edward Cowen whom I worked with at Salomon Smith Barney in London in the late 1990s, as I mentioned in the Introduction. In working with him, I came to reference a model that I had previously resisted when I first came across it at the university—a model made famous by an analogy used by Milton Friedman, the Nobel-winning economist.

Friedman argued that the actions of a pool player may be largely predicted by a model constructed on the assumption that the player possesses high-level mathematical and other skills. These skills enable the player to compute quickly and accurately the angles and deflections that determine the best shot at any specific time. Friedman's approach was part of a more general, and highly controversial, debate about proper scientific method.[3] There were strong proponents on both sides of the debate. Indeed, if one existed, the bumper sticker for this controversy would read something along the lines of "Whose side are you on: falsifiability or verifiability?"

Taking a cue from the work of Karl Popper, a highly regarded philosopher, Friedman argued that the best test of a model is to compare its predictions with actual outcomes. To this end, it was defensible to construct the model on the basis of simplifying assumptions (as in the case of the approach used for the pool player). While one may bicker with this approach—and I would still do so today—it is nevertheless useful for thinking about how to reverse engineer a type of behavior that leads to specific outcomes. And whether they know it or not, many of today's hedge funds that use "black box" models are effectively applying Friedman's approach.

Today, the question is whether we could reverse engineer the reaction of Edward Cowen, the Salomon trader, by assuming that, as a starting point, he was anchored by a systematic approach to analyzing market noise and reacting accordingly. This in no way denies the fact that, in reality, sharp "street smarts" drove Edward's ability to decipher signals within the market noise. Instead, it is an attempt to reverse engineer his behavior on the basis of an analytical model.

In doing so over the years, I have come to the conclusion that such an exercise would yield the following six key steps:

1. Identify the source of the noise that creates an unusual market dislocation.
2. Be disciplined in treating each episode of such noise as potentially containing important signals.
3. Assess the actual signal content through an evaluation based on the a priori modeling of the economic or market phenomenon.
4. Differentiate between factors that influence the destination and those that influence the journey when assessing the content.
5. After you have gone through this process, and not until then, you should actively pursue the views of the experts and the talking heads.
6. Be open to finding not only cyclical influences but also secular ones.

An Elaboration

The first step—identifying the source of the noise—is perhaps the hardest one. It is similar to the challenge that hundreds of airline pilots face every day before they pull their planes out of the gate. Typically, as passengers board and settle into their seats, the pilots are busy going through a checklist. They use visual methods and rely in part on a very busy instrument panel. In doing so, they are trained to look for anomalies.

Good investors often do the same thing. They observe the mass of market data with a view to picking out anomalies. The best have developed an effective way to sidestep the enormous quantity of high-frequency data that simply confirm what they already know.

For some, including Edward Cowen, the Salomon trader, this process comes easily. But, as I suspect is also true of most pilots starting their training, for others the process requires practice and discipline. This ability is best developed on the basis of an initially small set of market priors. In my case at Salomon in the late 1990s, it involved starting each morning with the preparation of a small note that listed my expectations for the data releases scheduled for that day. And once a week, typically on a Sunday, I would write down a set of ex ante hypotheses for potential economic and market trends in the coming week.

To make sure that I disciplined myself to do this, I entered into an implicit contract with my colleagues. I circulated my daily note to the traders and sales force, thereby providing them with updates on our expectations. They viewed it as a service. The daily note also served as a vehicle for developing something that did not come easily to me—an ability to efficiently interpret the signal within the large amount of data releases that face market participants.

I continued this practice at PIMCO at the emerging markets desk. Both the Salomon and PIMCO daily notes grew in scope and complexity to include the very valuable and critical direct inputs of hard-working colleagues stationed in many different time zones. The result was a broad characterization of the international market organism in which we were operating. Because it was a dynamic approach, it helped us identify the emergence of aberrations and other forms of noise.

Once able to carry out the initial screening, investors are then well positioned to move through the next five steps. Specifically, they are able to analyze episodes of noise, recognizing that there will inevitably be "false positives" when look-ing for signals within that noise. They are making this evalu-ation against the background of a prior specification of the economic and market phenomena, which allows them to iden-tify the anomalies relatively quickly.

In analyzing an anomaly, it is important to be open to the fact that it can be related either to the destination (the "steady state") or to the journey (the process of getting to the steady state). And the latter need not necessarily be straightforward. Specifically, by impacting the journey in a meaningful way, an anomaly can trigger a set of dynamics that end up altering the journey itself.

Once they have taken these steps, and only then, should market participants seek the views of experts and talking heads. After all, it is probable that many of these pundits have not as yet gone through the in-depth type of analysis that is required to identify signals within the noise. Who can blame them? They are expected to react quickly and be among the first to communicate effectively. Accordingly, once they come up with a story line, they must move decisively away from thinking about the substance and toward developing the most effective method of delivering the story line (or, if you wish to be less charitable, the marketing approach).

The final step is to think and ask about the potential depth of the underlying factors that gave rise to the anomalies. Most often they will be *cyclical* in nature. But once in a while they will have a long-term, or secular, character and thereby fun-damentally impact the robustness and future effectiveness of approaches that had previously withstood the test of time.

Skepticism Is Understandable

At this point, I would expect some readers to be rolling their eyes. After all, even if you accept my adaptation of Friedman's controversial approach, some of you will no doubt refer me to more traditional theories that minimize the possibility that market noise may contain meaningful signals that are not quickly internalized by investors. And when there are mispricings, arbitrageurs step in quickly to take advantage of the situation. This is, after all, a highly competitive and well-remunerated industry!

In this context, remember the story that economists reportedly like telling each other during lighter conversational moments. They cite the case of the person who comes across a dollar bill lying on the street. The person *rationally* refuses to pick it up on the argument that, if indeed it were a genuine dollar bill, it would not have been left on the ground. Someone else would have already gotten it! Sounds silly? Well, let me share with you a more personal experience. In August 2007, I was holding a meeting in my office at the Harvard Management Company (HMC) when a colleague—Mark Taborsky, the head of the External Management Group—pointed out a fire on the bridge hosting the now-closed Tea Party Museum—a bridge that can be easily observed in its entirety from HMC's sixteenth-floor windows. I dismissed the possibility, noting that the people crossing the bridge were doing so in a very normal and relaxed fashion. Surely they would be showing some greater sense of urgency if there were indeed a fire. Well, Mark was right. Within a few minutes, the fire was spreading and people were no longer walking normally across the bridge. Fire engines appeared on the scene as billowing smoke rose into the sky.

The *Boston Globe* reported the next day that "sparks from a bridge construction site ignited the century-old Boston Tea Party Ship and Museum yesterday, scorching the popular tourist attraction." It went on to note that "the black skies the fire caused over the Financial District yesterday drew hundreds of spectators."[4] Yet, based on seemingly good logic, I had initially dismissed the event!

Rational Fools

I can be described as a "rational fool"—a term used by Amartya Sen, the 1998 Nobel Prize–winning economist and a Harvard professor, to illustrate some of the problems that arise from the traditional economic characterization of human behavior.[5]

There are good reasons why we risk misdiagnosing an event even when we believe we have a clear perspective. The reason is not that market participants, as a group, are "irrational" (even if some are). Instead, there are other reasons that we know about because of influential work that has been done in areas such as the economics of asymmetrical information and market imperfections. Equally important, the reasons relate to more recent work analyzing fat tail events, as well as studies that blend insights from psychology and neurology.

It is important to stress that the basic issue here is not whether market participants are irrational—a possibility that is strongly dismissed by the dominant neoclassical school of economics and its close sibling in finance, the efficient-market school (traditionally associated with the University of Chicago). Indeed, the idea that market participants are irrational is also counterintuitive for an industry that attracts its share of sharp people looking for opportunities to pounce on.

Recall the speech of Gordon Gekko, a character played by Michael Douglas in the 1987 movie *Wall Street*, to the Teldar Paper shareholders. Gekko tells the group, "The point is, ladies and gentleman, that greed—for lack of a better word—is good. Greed is right. Greed works. Greed clarifies, cuts through, and captures the essence of the evolutionary spirit. Greed, in all of its forms—greed for life, for money, for love, knowledge—has marked the upward surge of mankind."[6] Whether you agree with or are disgusted by Gekko, it is hard to deny that the financial industry is influenced by many who share his view. As such, irrational behavior is hard to sustain and can prove costly. The rational players pounce, driven by a desire to make money in an industry that rewards the winners astoundingly well.

So the issue is not one of irrationality. Rather, it is whether predominantly rational market participants are occasionally impacted by *distortive* influences, and, as a result, valuation and liquidity dislocations emerge as markets adapt slowly to the new realities. For outsiders, the characterization is one of rational fools. If the answer is yes—and it is—we need to consider two additional issues: First, should such situations arise, will they give way to *further* distortions; and second, does the desirable reaction by rational and well-informed investors entail *further* deviations from equilibrium conditions?

The distortions can be as intuitive as information failures and can signal breakdowns; they can be as complex as those associated with emotional and intellectual biases, including the inability to internalize the possibility and nature of fat tail events. And all this fundamentally interacts with the natural temptation to take intellectual shortcuts that use the past as a guide to the future.

A Cocktail of Approaches

The next sections aim to give you a general feel for the underlying forces of these phenomena. I start with one of my favorite findings in economics—that pertaining to "The Market for Lemons," which originated more than 25 years ago. I have found it valuable in explaining why outcomes may differ at times from what would be deemed likely. I follow that with a discussion—albeit highly abridged—of factors that lead to such outcomes, and I draw on a true cocktail of economics, finance, behavioral theory, and neurology. I conclude with discussing the implications of investors' reactions, doing so by drawing on the insights of the literature on "multiple equilibria" and the "theory of second best."

Let me preface this discussion, however, by mentioning the important insights made by Thomas Kuhn in his influential writings on the history and philosophy of science.[7] Kuhn stressed the nonlinear and, at times protracted nature of scientific advances. Inevitably, paradigm shifts involve fits and starts. Those clinging to the old paradigm await insurmountable evidence, including prolonged inconsistencies. At first, the inconsistencies are attributed to the researchers as opposed to the deficiency of the paradigm. And the difficulties are compounded by the difficulties of viewing the new paradigm through the lens of the old paradigm. The result is a delayed and bumpy journey from old to new.

Why use a mix of disciplines and insights to encourage you to look beyond the noise in seeking signals? One reason is that the ability to draw on several disciplines also minimizes the risk that this analysis will be inadvertently hijacked by a particular set of oversimplifying assumptions. Such oversimplified assumptions often drive theories and models, and they can also undermine their application if the user loses sight of the fact that these assumptions were oversimplified to begin with. In contrast, the greater the number of disciplines used to support a hypothesis, the greater the probability that accuracy and applicability will be achieved.

I was deeply struck by something I heard over 25 years ago. In a seminar series at Oxford, the late John Hicks, a highly respected economist, insisted that, for insights to be convincing and firmly established, they needed to be presented in words, symbols, and charts. While I will not be so comprehensive here, I will draw on many different and complementary perspectives to reinforce the argument that it is a deep and natural temptation for market participants to ignore the signals within the noise, and, because of that, they face difficulties in recognizing (and reacting to) important turning points on a timely basis.

Decomposing the Noise

Insights from the Market for Lemons

The traditional theoretical approach to explaining seemingly abnormal market behavior and outcomes relies on "market imperfections"—that is, the notion that markets would have behaved perfectly if it were not for a breakdown in a key enabling condition. The most recurrent breakdowns are associated with the process of compiling and disseminating information that is critical to the proper and smooth functioning of a market system. As these breakdowns occur, the traditional concepts of neoclassical economics and efficient-market finance must be supplemented by notions of signaling confusion, bounded rationality, and structural uncertainty. Thus information failures can cause discontinuities that, in the extreme, can inhibit buyers and sellers from coming together and interacting in a constructive manner. The result is a series of market disruptions, including sudden stops in liquidity. This was certainly the case in the summer of 2007.

One of the most useful tools I know of goes by the name of the "market for lemons" (MFL). I have used the MFL numerous times to inform what have turned out to be sound investment strategies in a world of technical fluidity. The MFL originated in a 1970 paper by George Akerlof, a professor at the University of California at Berkeley who won the 2001 Nobel Prize in economics.[8] Akerlof used the example of the secondhand market for cars to illustrate the impact of information and signaling asymmetries and breakdowns. In the process, he showed why in extreme cases these may result in markets behaving badly, including ceasing to operate altogether.

Cars with hidden defects are called "lemons." Now consider what happens when a buyer does not have sufficient information to distinguish the lemons from the good cars. The outcome will most likely be a situation in which the market prices of the good cars are contaminated by the known presence of lemons among the cars on sale. Bottom-up signals are too weak and are easily overwhelmed by top-down concerns. Normal market signals are unable to close quickly the informational gap with the result that the market unravels—and such unraveling includes the withdrawal of higher-quality suppliers who react to the decline in the perceived average quality of the market.

Do you recall from Chapter 2 the comments made by Matt Ridley, the chairman of Northern Rock? The assumption that had been made prior to Northern Rock's liquidity crisis and supported by traditional economics and finance was that, in his words, "good loan books would continue to attract funding when bad loans began to default." Yet in periods of market turmoil, the MFL consideration suggests that this is often not the case. Instead, the high-quality part unravels. Again using Ridley's words, "Liquidity has dried up, . . . making no distinction between loans of different quality, for much longer than even the most extreme forecast."

How can investors identify MFL situations? By evaluating individual prices against the fundamentals and by seeing how these prices have moved relative to those in competing and complementary asset classes. In this way, they stand a chance of identifying and benefiting from situations in which asset prices have been impacted by herdlike behavior driven by market imperfections. Most typically, investors end up buying cherries for the price of lemons. In the process, they are able to take advantage of circumstances in which the markets are not behaving optimally due to imperfections in information and signaling.

Beyond Traditional Market Imperfections

Information limitations are not the only imperfections that lead to market breakdowns that are characterized by mispricings, inefficient allocations, and seemingly abnormal investor behaviors. In less mature economies, they can also occur as a result of a weak governance system, fluid property rights, and the uneven application of the rule of law. Indeed, the litany of possible market imperfections helps to explain the emergence of anomalies and subsequent derailments. But it does not go all the way in explaining why sophisticated investors who are operating in mature and deep financial systems wind up making big mistakes. Moreover, since these mistakes may be repeated over time, there is also the question of how investors develop biases that are not corrected—biases that lie beyond the awareness of sophisticated and well-informed investors.

To complement your understanding of the issues, you need to go beyond traditional economics and finance thinking and draw on insights that come from behavioral science and neuroscience.

Black Swans

Think back to the contrast Chapter 2 drew between the multiplicity of market aberrations and the initial inclination of many investors to continue operating confidently with their existing models—so much so as to assume even greater risk. This contrast speaks directly to a more general historical observation: Investors tend to underestimate extreme events.

Nassim Nicholas Taleb provides important insights on this issue, particularly in his 2007 book, *The Black Swan: The Impact of the Highly Improbable*. His analysis deals with the human inability to internalize, ex ante, an event that combines "rarity, extreme impact, and retrospective (though not prospective) predictability."[9] This "blindness to Black Swans," as he labels it, results in a universal bias in favor of dismissing the possibility of major developments even though they can have great consequences.

Taleb provides lots of examples of Black Swans, reminding us that they are not limited to financial change, natural disasters, and major wars (such as World War I). Indeed, the "Harry Potter" phenomenon fits the definition of a Black Swan, as does the emergence and impact of Google.

Despite the periodic occurrences of Black Swans in many areas of life, human beings remain resistant to fully grasping the phenomenon of the Black Swans' existence. At a general level, this bias is influenced by a deep human desire to see the world as a structured and understandable place. And even when this comforting bias contradicts some of the world's complexities—especially in the context of the recurrence of what should be extreme events (or tails of the distribution)—the human tendency is to seek shelter in ex post explanations that often reduce the tails to nothing more than a reconstitution of previously held views.

Taleb believes that many people fall victim to the "triplet of opacity." Specifically, there is a natural tendency to over-simplify current events, distort historical developments, and exaggerate the ability to interpret data. The results are, first, an inherent underestimation of what are viewed as rare events and second, an excessive reliance on interpretation of the past to predict the future. This inevitably amplifies the effects of rare events.

In one of several instances that have triggered quite a controversial exchange of views, Taleb has complained that these general biases are inherent in the traditional financial working models that are taught to students of modern finance, many of whom end up as investors. He argues that "the environment in financial economics is reminiscent of medieval medicine . . . [which] used to kill more patients than it saved."[10] His writing takes particular aim at the normal (bell curve) distributions that underpin many of the financial instruments used in the marketplace, noting that they tend to obfuscate the magnitude of an event by focusing excessively on a "predicted probability" that, by definition, is badly specified and will underestimate the likelihood and consequences of the event's occurrence.

Howard Wainer, a research scientist at the National Board of Medical Examiners and a faculty member of the Wharton School at the University of Pennsylvania, arrives at a similar conclusion even though he takes a different route. In his 2007 article "The Most Dangerous Equation," he notes that human beings have a tendency to focus on the average and ignore the variations (that is, the standard deviations around the mean), which has been "perilous" for so many fields.[11] He points to "the extreme length of time over which ignorance of it has caused confusion, the variety of fields that have gone astray, and the seriousness of the consequences that such ignorance has caused." By looking at some historical examples that go back as far as 1150, he argues that the ignorance has "led to billions of dollars of loss over centuries yielding untold hardship."

Especially when combined with those of other disciplines, these insights speak directly to our hypothesis on the uneven impact of structural hand-offs and the related clash between the world of yesterday and that of tomorrow. Furthermore, they highlight why it pays to think about exceptions to the norm, including the signals that may reside in the noise of the financial system. Also, as I will discuss in Chapter 7, these insights give further support to the importance of protecting yourself against fat tail events, particularly in the context of a wild ride to a new secular destination.

Behavioral and Neuroscience Dimensions

A slowly expanding number of investors are starting to pay attention to the professional literature on how intelligent people—including those in the investment world—make the same mistakes repeatedly. This research, which is usually grouped under the heading of "behavioral economics and finance," draws heavily on insights from psychology, and it is increasingly being accompanied by insights from neuroscience.

Behavioral and neuroscience dimensions complement more traditional approaches in explaining the evolution of asset prices, the behavior of investors, and developments in corporate finance. I have found them useful in helping me understand common (and inefficient) investment phenomena such as the manner in which some investors repeatedly chase historic (as opposed to expected) returns. In addition, they shed light on the herding behavior among investors, as well as the seemingly asymmetrical sensitivity to gains and losses.

They have also proven informative for analyzing initial public offering (IPO) activities, as well as some investors' inclination toward passivity, procrastination, and home bias. They help explain the persistence of home bias in portfolio construction and the related lack of diversification. Indeed, later in the book I will share some ideas on how market participants can position themselves for the ongoing structural shifts. I will be drawing on this relatively new literature in suggesting approaches that are not just appropriately designed but that can also be implemented in a manner that overcomes traditional biases.

The fuel for this increasingly influential literature has come from repeated observations that are seemingly inconsistent with the notion of rational human behaviors that dominates the traditional economic and finance approaches. The literature cites a host of examples. They include our tendency to display time-inconsistent preferences, as well as our propensity to not follow through on a course of action that we know will be good for us. They also cover our willingness to walk away from "free cash" (for example, in the context of company-matching pension plan contributions),[12] our "narrow framing" of choices (that is, our interpreting them in isolation even though we end up implementing them as a package), and the excessive influence that "sunk costs" have on our future decisions.

To help explain these observations, the behavioral literature has sought to apply and model certain psychological traits that influence market behavior.[13] For example, it has looked at the extent to which investors are influenced by perceptions of confidence, optimism, belief inertia, and excessive anchoring by market-arbitrary considerations. It has also identified the middle ground between "the automatic operations of perception and the deliberate operations of reasoning."[14]

Most of us would recognize our own sensitivity to one of these considerations, if not to more than one. The explanations for these behaviors differ from the traditional "market failure" insights noted earlier in this chapter in that the "irrationality" can occur in the context of both complete information and the potential for learning from "repeated games" (that is, the frequent recurrence of the same phenomenon). Specifically, these explanations draw on the role of emotions in decision making.

Given the focus of my book, it is important for readers to note the existence of yet another behavioral phenomenon: "the disposition effect"[15]—that is, the hesitation of investors to sell assets whose prices have fallen below the prices at which the investors bought them. Indeed, one often hears really successful investors, such as Bill Gross, the founder of PIMCO, warn colleagues against the human tendency to hold on to their losers and to sell their winners. Behavioral finance suggests that the disposition effect reflects what is essentially an excessive and distorted belief in mean reversion that is easily accentuated by the narrow framing of the investment decision. This is also related to the sunk cost effect.

These explanations are complemented by insights on how various parts of our brains work together.[16] Neuroscience researchers will explain to a layperson like me that our brains have evolved over time through a building block process— that is, new facilities are added to existing ones in the context of natural evolution. As such, our actual behaviors and decision making are driven by the fusion of different systems that, at times, are subject to inherent tension and conflicting outcomes. To illustrate this point, researchers speak to the conflict that often exists between the limbic system (which most of you and I would label the "emotional brain") and the lateral prefrontal cortex (the "analytical brain").

Robert Shiller, the Yale professor who has been a pioneer in the field of behavioral finance and who attracted international attention with his book *Irrational Exuberance*, summed it up well in a recent interview: "The human mind is incredibly powerful; it is capable of computations that can dazzle you, but can also be very blundering and foolish at times."[17]

No Wonder Change Is Hard

Those who are really interested in the scientific details and their application to a host of real-life examples should refer to the interesting work that has been conducted by researchers at places such as Carnegie Mellon, Harvard, and Princeton. The work at these institutions includes the use of functional magnetic resonance imaging to assess how the brain goes about dealing with choices between immediate and delayed rewards.[18] For the rest of us, the takeaway is a simple yet powerful finding: Our ability to identify and adapt quickly to structural transformations faces many headwinds that go well beyond the traditional notion of "market imperfections"; they relate to some basic considerations as to how our brains operate. Indeed, it is both probable and likely that, in the context of the aberrations discussed earlier, the analytical segment of an investor's brain will be so crowded as to allow it to be fairly easily overcome by the emotional segment.

These insights also speak to the phenomena of people's generally limited openness and slow adaptation to change. Indeed, structural changes fall outside the comfort zone of many. After all, by definition, such changes are hard to identify because we tend to use backward-looking frameworks. In turn, the delayed recognition amplifies the turmoil occasioned by the changes.

At her October 2007 inauguration as the new president of Harvard, Drew Faust talked about how universities deal with change. Through their emphasis on research in addition to teaching, universities are, almost by definition, hardwired to target knowledge expansion. And such expansion inevitably involves some type of change to priors, entitlements, and conventional wisdom.

President Faust reminded me, along with thousands of others sitting out in the rain on that windy October afternoon in Harvard Yard, that change does not come easily—even for a university. Here is the relevant passage from her speech:[19]

> By their nature, universities nurture a culture of restlessness and even unruliness. This lies at the heart of their accountability to the future. Education, research, teaching are always about change—transforming individuals as they learn, transforming the world as our inquiries alter our understanding of it, transforming societies as we see our knowledge translated into policies. . . . The expansion of knowledge means change. But change is often uncomfortable,

for it always encompasses loss as well as gain, disorientation as well as discovery. It has, as Machiavelli once wrote, no constituency. Yet in facing the future, universities must embrace the unsettling change that is fundamental to every advance in understanding.

For those of us who find it useful to complement academic insights with more mundane illustrations, consider one of the many great scenes in the 1984 hit film *Amadeus*, directed by Milos Forman. A young Mozart is presenting one of his new compositions to Emperor Joseph II. On completing the wonderful rendition of music, Mozart turns to the emperor to see his reactions, as do others attending this royal demonstration. Looking befuddled by the novelty and complexity of Mozart's brilliant composition, the emperor responds politely, "My dear young man, don't take it too hard. Your work is ingenious. It's quality work. But there are simply too many notes, that's all. Too many notes!"

The emperor did not have the ability (and perhaps also lacked the willingness) to distinguish brilliance from noise, or what he labeled "too many notes." Indeed, left to his own devices, he would have inadvertently repressed what proved to be a major advancement in the history of music. Fortunately, there were others that recognized the change and, in their own ways, enabled it to develop lasting roots.

As such, the question facing investors today is not why otherwise efficient markets can be late in adjusting to structural transformations; nor is it why investors may differ in their reaction functions. Rather, the key issue is what happens as a result of them.

Multiple Equilibria

Having established the possibility of investors' missing turning points and therefore delaying their responses, the question arises as to how the world evolves in such circumstances. Does it simply reset at the new equilibrium, albeit in a delayed manner, or is the adjustment process itself subject to certain vagaries? And if the latter is a possibility, what does that mean for investors in the interim?

Economists who have studied the actual (as opposed to theoretical) evolutions of financial markets have resorted at times to the concept of *multiple equilibria*. This concept eschews unique, one-to-one mappings in favor of more complex interactions and consequences. The notion of multiple equilibria has found support in some of the recent work conducted in behavioral finance—specifically, the "limits-to-arbitrage studies" that show how markets often deviate for a considerable length of time from equilibrium conditions. This occurs even though there are "rational" participants who interact (and therefore can offset) the impact of their "irrational" counterparts. The phenomenon is most evident in the failure of markets to arbitrage obvious structural mispricings.[20]

A notable feature of multiple equilibria is that they incorporate feedback loops and path dependencies as important drivers. Simply put, a "threshold-crossing event" triggers a reaction that prompts and activates yet another set of reactions that otherwise would have remained dormant. You can easily see how this process gets even more interesting when it occurs in the context of imperfect and asymmetrical information of the type discussed earlier in this chapter.

Sounds complicated? Not if you think of how a small event can cause massive shifts in sentiment. Sports fans will recognize this phenomenon because they have seen games in which there was a big change in momentum caused by a relatively simple occurrence that eventually altered the evolution of the game through cascading dynamics. In American football, a single play can "turn the tide," "bring the crowd back into the game," "energize the team," or "act as a wake-up call."

The cascading dynamics of multiple equilibria can also be evident for parents building a sand mountain with their children on the beach. For a while, the excessive grains of sand simply roll off the sides of the growing mountain. At some stage, however, just a handful of grains can collapse the mountain. Mountain climbers will tell you that just a little shift in snow can cause an avalanche. And there is always the image of the straw that broke the camel's back.

At the heart of all this is a phenomenon that provides a common link throughout this book: a catalyst that ends up fueling a regime change.

Contagion

The multiple-equilibria phenomenon also explains why, when faced with the possibility of cascading liquidity problems, policy makers will *rationally* overreact. After all, the shift in framework from single-equilibrium dynamics to multiple equilibria means that the precise sequencing of outcomes is much harder to predict. As such, the downside risks of policy makers' underreacting become substantive.

As I mentioned earlier, there were two vivid examples of this phenomenon following the liquidity disruptions that started in the summer of 2007. The first example came from the United Kingdom. The bank run on Northern Rock caused the British government to guarantee all deposits in U.K. banks. Put another way, a problem specific to the maturity mismatch at a particular bank prompted the guarantee of all deposits in the banking system—and this was in full knowledge of the moral hazard risk. In multiple-equilibria jargon, the government was keen to minimize the possibility that the Northern Rock regime change would cause other disruptions fueled by self-fulfilling expectations that initially had no fundamental anchors.

The second example came from the United States when the Federal Reserve surprised the markets in September by cutting interest rates more than expected. This was repeated by a series of other cuts that included a highly unusual and dramatic intermeeting reduction of 75 basis points on January 22, 2008. Again this was motivated by a desire, albeit unsuccessful, to stop a specific market dislocation from developing into a general credit crunch that would undermine economic activity, raise unemployment, and cause undue distress to many segments of the population.

This move was accompanied by a signal from the Fed that it would look for "insurance" in designing its policy response. As Federal Reserve Chairman Ben Bernanke stated to Congress, "We stand ready to take substantive additional action as needed to support growth and to provide adequate insurance against downside risks."[21] In his remarks, he also stressed that the Fed's policy-making body "must remain exceptionally alert and flexible." Again the motivation was a desire to stop a specific market dislocation from developing into something more general. This monetary policy response was accompanied by fiscal and quasi-fiscal actions aimed at forestalling a wave of home foreclosures and a related sharp drop in house prices and consumer confidence.

The concepts of multiple equilibria and contagion shed light on a number of topics ranging from business cycles to the dynamics of climate change and ecosystems. I first came across these concepts some 25 years ago when I was observing markets in emerging economies. Specifically, I saw that there is a tendency of a crisis in a specific country and/or region to impose collateral damage on other countries that do not necessarily share the same initial conditions.[22]

At the time, the world of emerging markets was particularly prone to contagion effects and multiple equilibria through three distinct transmission channels:

- *Economic:* The need for emerging economies to access industrial countries through exports in order to generate earnings to meet high debt service payments
- *Funding:* The reliance of emerging economies on being able to mobilize new funding to de facto roll over maturing debt obligations
- *Technical:* The importance for emerging economies of accessing tactical investors in order to go beyond what was at that stage an insufficient set of narrow and small *strategic* (that is, specialized and more stable) investor flows.

These channels involved enormous correlations. After all, they were themselves correlated: An economic dislocation could slow the overall flow of cross-border funds and, in the process, also scare tactical investors out of their emerging market exposures. In addition, each of the factors involved a significant degree of correlation across individual emerging economies.

My first practical introduction to the effects of emerging markets took place in the summer of 1982. I had traveled from Oxford to Washington, D.C., for a three-month internship at the International Monetary Fund. At the time, the phrases "emerging markets" and "emerging economies" had not as yet entered the public domain. Instead, the talk was mostly of "developing countries," though the older labels of "less developed" and "third world" countries were still very much in evidence.

My internship that summer on a "currency substitution" project was supplemented by exposure to daily global financial occurrences through a wonderful daily publication known at the time as the *Blue Sheet*. The tone and coverage of this daily, which is a summary compilation by IMF staff of major economic and financial stories appearing around the world, changed dramatically in August. The shift was triggered by Mexico's announcement that it was no longer in a position to meet its scheduled international debt obligations.

What started as a story about Mexico evolved into a major global event. Concerns mounted about the health of the major U.S. banks (such as Chase Manhattan and Citibank), especially the "money center" giants whose loans to Mexico and its regional neighbors exceeded the institutions' capital.[23] Lending to other Latin American economies was disrupted, exposing virtually every one of them to a cycle of debt moratorium and restructuring. Multilateral institutions were forced into crisis management operations on a scale that was simply unthinkable prior to the Mexican announcement.

I remember vividly how I internalized the operational implications of contagion. A few years later, and in what constituted an unusual step at that time for the IMF (but is now routine), a group of us visited banks and investment managers in New York to obtain information on private sector flows to developing countries. When we asked about their immediate reactions to hearing about the Mexico news, many told us that they had stepped back from making any new loan commitments to countries such as Chile and Colombia and that they had decided to only partially renew existing credit lines if at all.

The actions of the banks and investment managers seemed illogical to us as IMF economists. After all, Chile and Colombia had stood out from other countries in the prudent manner in which they had run their economies and their finances. Yet the technicals were such that this fundamental analysis was inapplicable. These two countries were faced with an increased degree of credit rationing because of something occurring well beyond their purview. Luckily, they were both able to navigate this period of general credit crunch for developing countries without resorting to a debt restructuring.

As it turned out, the Mexican announcement constituted the beginning of what became known as Latin America's "lost decade" of the 1980s. The region's growth plummeted and trade shrank. Poverty went up as several governments were forced to cut expenditures in a paniclike manner that inadequately protected the social sectors (e.g., education and health) and infrastructure.

For the industrial countries, concerns about growth and welfare in Latin America were essentially overshadowed by a major effort aimed to recapitalize the banking system. The key was to gain time to enable the banks' capital base to withstand the restructuring of loans made to developing economies around the world. The IMF and World Bank were provided with greater flexibility to respond. Concurrently, new phrases entered the operational vocabulary such as "debt overhangs" and "Brady bonds." The latter—which originated with a push by U.S. Treasury Secretary Nicholas F. Brady to securitize and sell banks' defaulted claims on emerging economies—marked the beginning of a more optimistic phase in global finance.

During this phase, emerging economies gradually saw the restoration of their access to international capital markets; and that access resulted in the proliferation of a new set of financial instruments and investing activities.[24] By being willing to assume higher credit risk, investors had the potential to buy the restructured bank loans in the form of bonds. The yield on the bonds involved a significant premium over the interest rate available on the obligations issued by governments and corporations in industrial countries. But as this new, more optimistic phase was gaining momentum, the world was quickly reminded of the widespread impact of emerging economies. And, once again, this impact was disruptive.

Global markets were shaken again in December 1994 and the first quarter of 1995. Once again Mexico served as the catalyst: Its debt maturity mismatches accentuated the risk that a sovereign country could enter default status. I still remember the look of shock on the faces of some executive directors of the IMF when they were informed by Managing Director

Michel Camdessus of the extent of the required financing and the funding burden that the IMF would have to carry. The crisis was averted through a major international financial rescue package that came in two steps. The first injection of emergency funds did not suffice; the funding package had to be replenished in March 1995.

A couple of years later, the world was abruptly reminded that Latin America did not hold a monopoly on the ability to cause disruptions to global financial markets. The summer of 1997 marked the beginning of the Asian crisis that saw a spectacular implosion of the financial systems in countries such as Indonesia, South Korea, and Thailand—economies that were previously viewed at the center of the much-celebrated "Asian miracle."

By August 1998, the wave of disruptions had migrated west and now engulfed Russia. On August 17, Russia announced that it would default on a set of liabilities. The process contributed to a major dislocation in markets that, by September, saw some parts of the global financial system on the verge of collapse. This was most vividly illustrated by the demise of the highly leveraged hedge fund Long-Term Capital Management (LTCM) and by subsequent efforts by policy makers, led by the United States, to facilitate an orderly unwinding of LTCM's position and to reliquify the financial system.

The Theory of the Second Best

Considerations of multiple equilibria and contagion lead naturally to the insights provided by the "theory of second best," which dates back to the 1956 work of two economists, Kelvin Lancaster and Richard Lipsey. Their analysis considered how best to react to situations in which one (or more) "optimal condition" is not met. Intuitively, you would think that the best approach would be to continue meeting the *other* optimal (or "first best") conditions. Based on their findings, however, Lancaster and Lipsey caution against doing that. Indeed, they found that there are situations in which, once a first best condition is violated, the best outcome involves violating other first best conditions.

To illustrate to students the insights of this important theory, I have often referred back to a popular activity of mine during my university days—that of playing the game of Risk. This simple board game involves a competition among players to take control of the world by conquering and securing countries and continents. The movement of "armies" is based essentially on rolls of the dice, which means that players who tend to win are those who use a probability-based approach to forming their strategies, particularly since the games can last for many hours, if not days.

Over time I found that the optimal, probability-based approach needed tweaking in certain circumstances. For example, and to my great frustration, I found that adhering strictly to a probability-based approach was inadvisable when some of the people I was playing against were not influenced by probability-based considerations. I found that the more my opponents deviated from a probability-based approach, the greater was the likelihood that I would have to depart from my normal probability-based strategy to counter his or her influence on the game. In fact, my opponents in these circumstances ended up changing the game's initial best dynamics and what constituted optimal behavior for other players.

The theory of second best has important application to financial markets. It lies at the heart of a quote that has been attributed to Keynes that "markets can remain irrational longer than you can remain solvent." I found the theory useful in explaining how investors should react to the unusual bout of M&A (merger and acquisition) activities that took hold of the markets in the first part of 2007.[25] And, as I will discuss in Chapter 4, it offers insight on why certain complex, sophisticated, and hitherto successful investment constructs will prove particularly fragile in the period ahead.

The Bottom Line

My objective in using a rather eclectic and cross-disciplinary analysis in this chapter was a simple one: to help you realize that when you are trying to identify signals within the noise of the marketplace, you need to consider that there are many reasons why our natural inclination will be to resist notions of change. Moreover, once you overcome the recognition delay, you cannot assume that the system will simply reset itself (that is, return to the state it would have been in absent the initial shock). There is a significant chance that the delay itself will give rise to new dynamics.

It is this type of thinking that has led me, and others, to be sensitive not only to the emergence of a new secular destination for the global economy but also to the recognition that the journey warrants careful analysis. This analysis is the subject of Chapters 4 and 5. By understanding the key components of the journey and destination, investors will be in a better position to exploit the benefits of our changing world while also minimizing their risks.

CHAPTER 4

UNDERSTANDING THE NEW DESTINATION

The framework discussed in Chapter 3 makes it possible to better understand the fundamental transformations at play in the global economy. This chapter presents the results of years of analysis undertaken with the help of my colleagues at Harvard Management Company (HMC) and PIMCO. These findings speak to a clash between the world of yesterday and the emerging realties of tomorrow.

These worlds will differ in three important ways:

- First, for those seeking to understand global economic and financial developments, it will no longer be sufficient to get the United States, Europe, and Japan right. It will also be a matter of getting the emerging market economies right. This involves an understanding of their rapidly changing economic and financial conditions and behaviors.
- Second, investors and policy makers (that is, market participants) will have to better understand the increasingly influential role being played by new pools of capital,

several of which are concentrated in the hands of state investment agencies (such as SWFs). Asset valuation judgments will need to include an assessment of what these new investors are likely to buy, what they are likely to sell, and why.

- Third, it will no longer be sufficient to project forward on the basis of economic and financial fundamentals alone. Instead, more often, it will also be necessary to understand the extent to which the technical dimensions of markets that are driven by financial innovation can, and do, influence the fundamentals in what increasingly are two-way interactions. Furthermore, investors must fully recognize the changing nature of the financial infrastructure and product line-up.

Emerging economies are having, and will continue to have, a growing influence on the global economy's rate of growth, the level and direction of trade, the price formation process, and the stability of cross-border capital flows. In fact, they are already the most important contributor to global growth (Figure 4.1), and they have captured a large and growing share of world trade. In supplying low-cost labor to the global production chain, they have helped contain inflation (notwithstanding the surge in commodity prices). And the manner in which they have allocated their international reserve gains has impacted interest rates, although all this is inevitably changing in character and overall impact.

These trends have already proven to be of great consequence. They are an important part of the explanation for historical inconsistencies and aberrations, and yet they have not

Figure 4.1 The Upward Path of Emerging Economies in Their Becoming Major Contributors to Global Growth, Percent Annual Change*

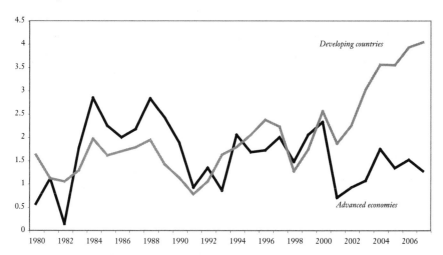

*Based on GDP weights at purchasing power parity (PPP).

Source: International Monetary Fund (IMF).

attracted sufficient analysis in the economics and professional communities thus far. Consequently, many investors have not developed a full understanding of the implications for their investment strategies, expected returns, and portfolio risks.

Similarly, it is only recently that serious academic thinking has been devoted to the impact of the huge technological shock in international finance caused by the proliferation of derivative-based products. This phenomenon has significantly reduced entry barriers to a large number of markets, including housing and many credit areas. The result has been a dramatic shift in the production and consumption of complex products notwithstanding the existence of some basic questions about suitability and sustainability. All this has impacted economic and financial relationships, while complicating policy making. The following sections discuss in some detail these phenomena and set the stage for discussing ways investors can exploit the benefits and navigate the pitfalls.

New Global Engine of Growth

With the U.S. economy facing the prospects of a few years of weak growth as it works through various excesses, there is growing interest in whether the collective of emerging economies can become a sustainable engine of global expansion. The answer to this question is complicated by the uncertainty as to whether the recent upward trends in European and Japanese growth will prove to be long-term phenomena (that is, whether they will be more than just cyclical rebounds).

This issue is critical in the formulation of investment strategies going forward. It boils down to a question that is the source of significant discussion in the marketplace: To what extent can emerging economies distance themselves from a slowing U.S. economy? (Experts refer to this as the "decoupling question.") The answer lies in how we analyze the growth dynamics of these economies—and in particular, of those economies that are systemically important such as Brazil, China, India, Mexico, Russia, and South Africa.

Pragmatic Policy Formulation

I have found that the best insight on this topic comes from the work of Michael Spence, the 2001 Nobel Prize winner in economics. Spearheading the work of the influential and independent Commission on Growth and Development (also known as the "Growth Commission") founded in 2006, Spence has studied in significant detail what makes growth sustainable. Initially he focused appropriately on the experiences of China and, to a lesser extent, India—a focus that is shared widely because of China's and India's systemic impacts and "demonstration effects"—but he has also spent considerable time studying and visiting other countries.

The commission's work found a number of factors surfacing when trying to explain why many emerging economies have not been able to sustain high growth in the past:[1]

- First, and foremost, it is very challenging for country officials to design and execute growth-oriented policies in the context of significant uncertainties about the underlying economic and sociopolitical linkages. These uncertainties assume greater importance if the institutional structures are fragile and the global context is fluid.
- Second, there is no easy way to translate the experiences of the mature market economies to those of the emerging countries. Instead, the emerging countries had to develop sufficient self-confidence and conviction to chart their own way, potholes included. In doing so, they blended more predictable micropredictions with uncertain macro-outcomes. And they will have to continue doing so.

- Third, success in generating high *and* inclusive growth inevitably entails an added set of policy challenges. As a policy maker once remarked to me in the mid-1990s, in the emerging market context, "Managing success can be more difficult than managing a crisis."[2]

Spence's careful reading of actual country experiences and his ability to draw on work done elsewhere produced an important finding: Successful growth policies did not predetermine all the needed steps to attaining sustainability; instead, it is "a decades' long journey" that inevitably requires policy adaptations along the way and has to deal with the realities of still maturing institutions and market infrastructures.

This insight is clear in the analysis of China's very successful growth breakout phase that Spence and I carried out: "At the start there was probably little agreement on anything except that a fundamental restructuring and reform of the economy was necessary. . . . China avoided a mistake that could easily have been done with dramatic results. And that is to simply take their newly acquired knowledge of mature market economies in the rest of the world, and to apply that theory to their own economy without adjustments."[3] Instead, what China did—and what is being done more and more by other developing countries—was to mix theory with lessons from international case studies. This included giving considerable attention to the microrole of market prices and incentives but also being open to midcourse corrections at both the microlevels and macrolevels. Rather than result in slow implementation, this pragmatic approach empha-

sized learning and experimentation and enabled timely adjustments that ended up accelerating the pace of reform.

India's approach was equally adaptive. The authorities
underscored the importance of "respecting the need to bring in
large numbers of people in a democratic system" and thereby
"avoiding an approach based in a static and constant model and
[opting] instead for a dynamic and iterative approach."[4]

Dani Rodrik, a Harvard University professor, reached a similar
conclusion. In a study of a number of successful emerging economies in Africa, Asia, and Latin America, Rodrik found that the
success of the economies was related to the degree to which policy
makers followed eclectic approaches.[5] These successful countries
tailored their policies to their own current circumstances.

This pragmatic mindset and its success are increasingly evident in the developing countries in which I have traveled. In
fact, the success of this pragmatism as it has been highlighted
by the high performance and rapid advancement of China and
India—especially in the speed and extent to which that success
has helped China and India in their efforts to alleviate
poverty—has created in turn a certain amount of peer pressure
among other developing economies. Of course, this is not to
say that all developing countries will also succeed in achieving
breakout growth. They won't. There are many challenges
they must overcome, including that of managing success
domestically and of having the international system accommodate their success in an orderly fashion. But several will,
and as such their success will reinforce the ongoing and fundamental changes in the dynamics of global growth.

Global Growth Hand-Offs

This global hand-off is already being reflected in key economic indicators. In the International Monetary Fund's semi-annual analysis of the international economy in October 2007, the economists there noted that for the first time ever China was the most important contributor to world growth over the year when measured in terms of market prices.[6] In the process, China outpaced the United States, the European Union area, and Japan. *The Economist* described the situation as follows: "The power of this new motor is startling. For several years, emerging Asian economies have accounted for more of global GDP growth than America has. This year China alone will for the first time accomplish the same feat all on its own (at market exchange rates), even if American growth holds up."[7]

For those who worry that Asia's growth is too dependent on exports, *The Economist* noted that "in the first half of 2007 the increase in consumer spending (in actual dollar terms) in China and India together contributed more to global GDP growth than the increase in America did." Moreover, Asia's growth pick-up has been much larger than those in investments, suggesting that the efficiency of investing is increasing.

The changes are even more dramatic when you view the contribution of global growth in terms of purchasing power parity (PPP), a unit of measure that eschews the market exchange rate for a conversion based on what is needed to buy the same amount of goods and services in each country. When measured using purchasing power parity, China and India each contributed more to global growth in 2007 than did the United

States, the European Union, and Japan. And the contribution of China is three times that of the United States. In fact, when combined with India and China, the group of emerging economies accounts for more than half of global output.

Accordingly, and in contrast to past episodes of U.S. economic slowdowns, emerging economies have two distinct secular forces going for them; and these should prove sufficient to partially offset what is likely to be a relatively prolonged period of lower import demand on the part of the United States. First, the internal components of aggregate demand are coming online in a gradual and robust manner, thereby offsetting the prospect of reduced exports to the United States. Second, these economies—and in particular the commodity exporters—are looking at a period of relatively high export unit values.

There is also a third factor that is more cyclical in nature. The majority of emerging economies are in a good position to "turn Keynesian" should they wish to offset the impact of lower U.S. growth. What do I mean by this? The robust nature of many of these countries' balance sheets—historically unusual—gives them the ability to stimulate internal consumption and investment. Indeed, these economies currently have the *ability*, but have not shown much *willingness*, to be populist—and to do so in what Paul McCulley would call "a financially principled way." Compare this to the traditional image of emerging economies that has characterized them as having the willingness to be populist (and usually in a financially irresponsible way) but not the ability.

As I noted in Chapter 1, another startling change in the current phase of emerging markets growth is that it has been accompanied by persistent and substantial surpluses in trade and the current accounts of the balance of payments, as well as by significant pick-up in international reserves. This is quite a shift from past patterns when growth spurts were normally associated with deteriorations in external accounts. Previously, the balance-of-payments constraints—seen in the depletion of international reserves and mounting difficulties in securing foreign borrowing—often forced policy makers to dampen growth through sharp cuts in fiscal spending, higher taxes, and tighter monetary policy. Indeed, at one stage, some economists even spoke of an inevitable and rigid trade-off between growth and the balance of payments.

Interestingly, the global growth hand-offs from industrial to developing countries will be accompanied by a set of other hand-offs *within* developing economies. Most importantly, China will increasingly find that its growth is driven by internal demand rather than by external markets. In the process, policy will gradually shift from supporting the producer to supporting the consumer. If handled in an orderly fashion, this shift will also help to alleviate protectionist pressures coming from outside—especially from the United States where some are calling to label China as a currency manipulator.

A number of other developing countries will experience similar hand-offs, including those that are commodity producers such as those in the Middle East, Russia, and Latin America. There too we will likely witness greater emphasis on the domestic components of aggregate demand. And the gaps in the global production chain that will result will be assumed by other developing countries. As an example, witness the extent to which Vietnam's global impact is starting to look like that of China's a few years ago, albeit on a smaller scale.

Regionalism with an Outward Orientation

So far, we have been concerned about the change in the over-all role of emerging economies in the world as a whole because of what is going on at the country level. But the secular desti-nation is also likely to involve important changes in the set of interactions within the group of emerging economies. This is particularly the case in East Asia where governments are now being more forceful in supporting the cross-border integration of private sector activities.[8]

The Asian private sector has been particularly active in exploiting production synergies. It is clear in the manner in which more advanced countries, such as Japan, have shifted segments of production to lower-wage jurisdictions. More generally, it is evident in the degree to which production is becoming more vertically integrated within the region.

What is new is the extent to which governments are interested in participating in this private sector–driven process. The empha-sis is on supportive activities, as opposed to those that aim to direct the private sector (as has been misguidedly followed in other regions with little beneficial effect). High-profile initiatives implemented in the last five years include those aimed at deepen-ing the financial system (including Asian Bond Funds I and II) and the pooling of official liquidity in the event of individual financing difficulties (the Chiang Mai Initiative). Less visible, but equally important, are programs to harmonize standards and codes, enhance policy coordination, and better disseminate best practices on corporate governance and regulatory activities.

These initiatives hold the potential for enhancing produc-tivity, facilitating efficient cross-border synergies, and opening up new regional opportunities. In the process, they will reinforce the region's global influence as long as the regionalism remains outwardly oriented. The evidence thus far suggests that this will be the case.

The point that I am trying to make is that there is good reason to believe that the following will occur:

- Developing countries will increasingly step up to the plate as significant and sustainable sources of global growth.
- The resulting long-term hand-off in economic growth will gradually reduce the world's sensitivity to variations in U.S. growth performance.
- This will likely occur together with a realignment within the rank of emerging economies that will result in a greater emphasis on domestic components of demand.
- In the process, we will see a greater degree of interactions among emerging economies, especially in Asia.

The image here is a simple one. For a number of years, the global economy has been likened to a plane flying on one engine—fed by the vibrant activities of U.S. consumers who, for some, were viewed as the world's consumers of first and last resort. Well, that engine is now sputtering. But the plane will be able to maintain altitude because a number of smaller engines are coming onstream, and they are doing so in a more coordinated and sustainable fashion. This transition involves bumps, but, despite that, it has the potential to prevent a hard landing for the global economy.

If this dynamic of high economic growth with secular legs continues to materialize over the next few years—and I strongly believe it will—we will also see a further change in the global impact of developing countries that comes from the other three transmission channels—namely, trade, price formation, and capital flow.

The Changing Dynamics of World Trade

The growth strategies adopted by several emerging economies have resulted in a rapid increase in their share of world trade (Figure 4.2). Increasingly, this has been accompanied by the realization of higher value added.

This process has been greatly facilitated by three distinct but interrelated factors:

- The willingness of the United States to sustain consumer demand well beyond income growth.
- The ability of financial markets to monetize assets held by U.S. consumers, including in particular the housing stock (what is sometimes referred to "as using a house as an ATM").
- The willingness of emerging economies to recycle their trade surplus back to the United States through heavy purchases of U.S. Treasury instruments, mortgages, and corporate bonds.

Together, these three factors have resulted in what Larry Summers characterized as a massive global vendor financing relationship,[9] with the United States on one side and Asia and the oil exporters on the other (Figure 4.3). Think about what happens on a daily basis around the United States when a

Figure 4.2 The Steady Progress of the Emerging Economies' Capturing of a Greater Global Market Share, by Percent

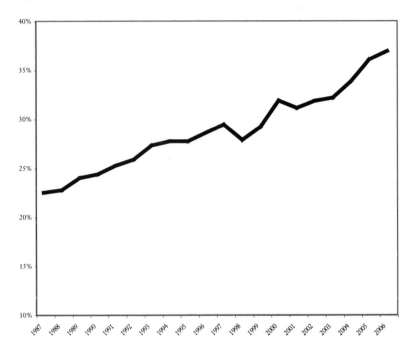

Source: UNCTAD.

buyer walks into a Ford/GM dealership, purchases a car, and finances it by taking out an auto loan from Ford Motor Credit/GMAC funded through the issue of bonds. This is very similar to what has been happening at the aggregate level among the United States, Asia, and the oil producers.

In more simple terms, consider the following links that prevailed in this massive international vendor financing relationship:

Figure 4.3 A Global Vendor Financing Relationship, Current Accounts in Billions of U.S. Dollars

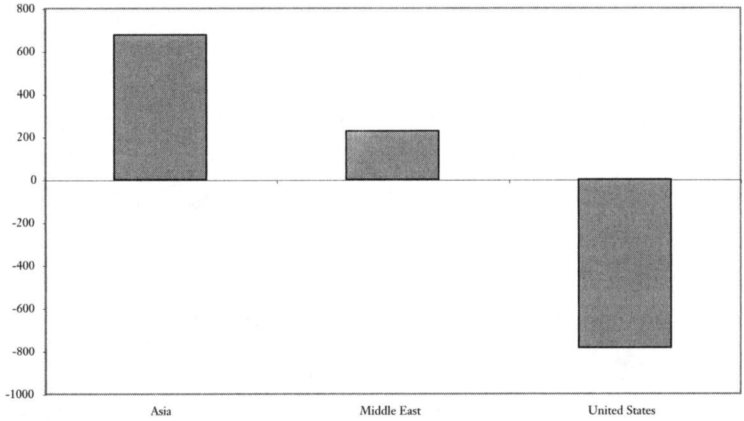

Note that Asia includes developing Asia, newly industrialized economies, and Japan.

Source: International Monetary Fund (IMF).

- U.S. consumers (the "car buyers") purchase goods and services from Asia and energy products from the oil exporting countries ("Ford/GM").
- As these purchases exceed the car buyers' incomes, the U.S. consumers fund portions of their purchases through assuming debt that they initially or ultimately refinance through home equity loans or mortgage refinancing loans (the "auto loans").
- The increased mortgage debts are repackaged by Wall Street and sold to Asian and oil exporting countries that are happy to purchase the mortgage debts because doing

so means that they can deploy their earnings in the most liquid and sophisticated of all financial markets—the United States.

These dynamics have enabled the persistence of the large global imbalances discussed in Chapter 1. The issue of sustainability has gotten lots of ink as well, and it has been the subject of many heated discussions. One camp argues that these imbalances can last a long time, as they reflect deep structural issues. Perhaps the most innovative analysis here comes from the work of Michael Dooley, Peter Garber, and David Folkerts-Landau of the University of California, Santa Clara, and Deutsche Bank.[10] The other camp, including analyses by Nouriel Roubini and Brad Setser of New York University[11] together with that of my PIMCO colleague Chris Dialynas,[12] argues that the imbalances are clearly unsustainable.

Both camps agree that the current underlying dynamics of the United States' large trade deficits being offset by equally large surpluses held by Asia and the oil exporters will need to evolve. But they differ on the timing, speed, and orderly nature of this evolution. One side predicts a slow-motion adjustment that is undertaken in an orderly fashion. The other side foresees a crisis featuring economic disruptions and financial turmoil.

Only time will determine for sure which of the two camps is right. And it may well turn out that the proposed corner solutions will give way to yet other interim outcomes that are subject to multiple iterations. What is clear is that there is an inherent fragility in the global economy. Moreover, regardless of the exact specification of the journey ahead, the growth process of emerging economies, as I've discussed here, will result in very different global dynamics in the future.

Shifting Trade Balances

As emerging economies gradually shift their primary focus from the producer to the consumer, the rate of growth for imports in these countries will increase over that of exports. And in the context of that increase, the composition of the consumer demand will shift to include a larger share of luxuries and related inputs.

This shift is slowly occurring. Expanding Chinese and Indian middle and upper classes have encouraged growth in import demand. Witness also the extent to which these two countries are accounting for an increasing share in the global consumption of energy, basic materials, cars, meat, and so on. For example, approximately two-thirds of the increased demand for energy in the last five years has been due to higher consumption and inventory build-up by Asian economies (excluding Japan).

I am certain that over the next decade the characterization of many emerging economies will shift from being export machines to being consumers, and that will act to balance their impact on world trade. And, at some stage down the road, they will become the importers of choice. Shifts in policies will accelerate the process and reverse the current tendency to favor these countries' producers at the expense of their consumers. Such policy shifts will result in a greater emphasis being placed on stimulating domestic components of aggregate demand. They will also encourage the abandonment of undervalued exchange rates. Specifically, the exchange rates will reach market levels as the structures of the economies evolve. In particular, the absorption of surplus labor from traditional sectors will shift the focus away from incremental job creation to human capital accumulation and knowledge-based activities.

Several factors support this shift, particularly the strengthening of the institutional underpinnings that favor responsible policy changes, as well as the gradual improvement of internal checks and balances. Deeper international economic and financial linkages will also play a role, especially in countries with a diversified economic base. And let us not forget the role of "market vigilantes" whose influence is growing in the context of the liberalization and integration of domestic financial markets.

Part of this change will be reflected in a gradual shift in the relative importance of trading partners such that the increased trade with industrial countries will be accompanied by an even faster growth rate in trade among emerging economies. The pattern is already evident in the findings reported by the IMF: The share going to other emerging economies in total emerging economies' exports grew from around 10 percent at the beginning of this decade to 17 percent in 2006.

Critically, the shifts are also consistent with socioeconomic considerations in emerging economies. Thus the governments will be able to better meet the legitimate aspiration of their people. As I will discuss later, the changes underway can help address some of the inequality issues that are becoming more apparent in the developing economies. They can also reduce the risk of protectionism and place the global economy on a surer footing.

All this is good news for industrial countries from an *income* perspective. The United States in particular will be able to gradually and partially replace its reliance on its overstretched consumers with a new reliance on meeting the growing demand impulses coming from the rest of the world. But this transition has to be well managed, especially as it involves negative *price* effects.

From a Disinflation Tailwind to an Inflation Headwind

The Global Labor Force

Alan Greenspan's 2007 book—an elegant mix of memoirs and case studies—highlights an important point: In implementing its successful efforts to contain inflation within the United States, the Federal Reserve (and other central banks around the world) benefited from the external disinflationary forces generated by both domestic and global productivity gains. These gains helped contain the prices of goods and services around the world, either directly or by putting intense competitive pressures on manufacturers and service providers elsewhere.

These forces will be less supportive going forward.[13] Indeed, their disinflationary impact is already slowly dissipating. Some (but certainly not all)[14] of the key emerging economies are now exhibiting a gradual increase in wages and the partial exhaustion of high-productivity, low-cost labor. As Greenspan notes in his book, the world benefited as "well over a billion workers, many well educated, all low paid [gravitated] to the world competitive marketplace from economies that had been almost wholly or in part centrally planned and insulated from global competition. . . . This movement of workers into the marketplace reduced world wages, inflation, inflation expectations, and interest rates."[15]

The key challenge here is determining the pace of the change.

Commodity Prices

The issue is not just the erosion of the beneficial tailwind coming from the overall effect of emerging economies. It is also that this tailwind is likely to turn into a headwind due to the emerging economies' continued impact on the prices of natural resources.

Commodity prices increased significantly over the last few years. As can be seen in Figures 4.4 and 4.5, this phenomenon has been notable because of the magnitude of the price increases and the broad range of the commodities affected (energy, basic metals, cereals, and so on).

It is now widely accepted that emerging economies have become an important factor behind the surge in commodity prices. Their influence has spread through two distinct channels, and it has fueled a third one. I like to think of this in terms of what I was taught in school about the demand for money. According to basic economics textbooks, there are three distinct components in the demand for money function. The first, "transactionary demand," reflects our use of money as a medium of exchange for everyday purchases. The second, "precautionary demand," is driven by our desire to have some money available in the event of an unanticipated development. (When I was growing up, my father insisted on my having

Figure 4.4 The Sharp Increase in Commodity Prices . . . based on the GSCI Commodity Index

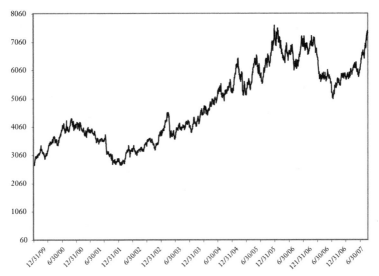

Source: Bloomberg.

some money in my pocket so that I could take a cab home if I needed it.) The third, "speculative demand," provides for the possibility of exploiting a wealth-creating opportunity.

These three components have been in play in the commodity sector. The emerging economies' breakout growth phase has made them a bigger everyday consumer of commodities (see Figures 4.6 and 4.7). Consider the specific case of oil, a commodity that attracts significant attention in view of how often it features in different production and consumption chains. Recent data published by the International Energy Agency (IEA) show that China's consumption of oil has grown

Figure 4.5 . . . And the Many Sectors That Have Been Affected, December 1999 = 100

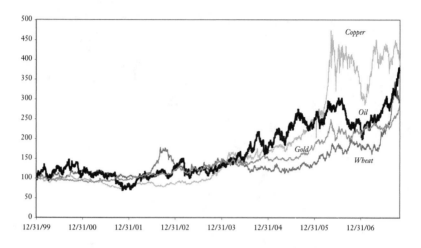

Source: *Bloomberg/GSCI.*

from 1.9 millions of barrels a day (mbd) in 1980 to 4.7 mbd in 2000 and 7.1 mbd in 2006.[16] As a result, its share in world oil demand has increased from 2.9 percent in 1980 to 8.4 percent. India has also experienced rapid growth, and its share of world oil demand has risen from 1.1 percent in 1980 to 3.1 percent in 2006. The IEA expects the rapid growth to continue. It forecasts that, by 2030, China's demand will amount to 16.5 mbd (14.2 percent), and India's will amount to 6.5 mbd (5.6 percent). Because of these increases, the total consumption of oil by developing economies is projected to exceed that of industrial countries for the first time. As a comparison base, in 1980, developing country demand was only one-fourth that of industrial economies.

Figure 4.6 Emerging Markets' Share of Copper Consumption, 2007E

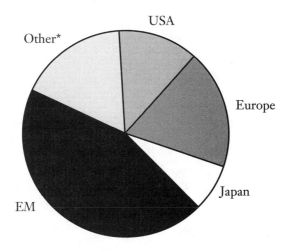

* "Other" may include emerging markets.

Source: Morgan Stanley.

Agricultural commodities are also feeling the impact of higher demand from emerging economies. Indeed, in what is a historically unusual situation, sharp price increases are coinciding (rather than being negatively correlated) with large cereal crops. The increasing wealth in several emerging economies is leading to higher consumption of meat. Suppliers are responding by increasing meat production, which is pushing up the use of grain as animal feed. All this is coinciding with a switch to ethanol, which is further accentuating the pressure on grain prices.

It is not just about demands for immediate consumption. Now that developing countries are also wealthier, they can entertain (and have entertained) the luxury of building inventories to enhance their commodity security. For example, such

Figure 4.7 Emerging Markets' Share of Crude Oil Consumption, 2006

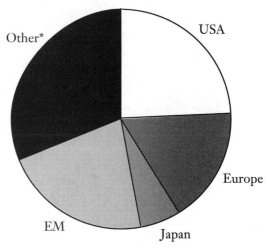

* "Other" may include emerging markets.

Source: International Energy Agency.

considerations have prompted China to engage and invest more in Africa and in Latin America in order to secure better access to natural resources.

With emerging markets providing a "demand floor," financial investors have rushed in to make money on the back of what appears to be dependable fundamentals. As you will see in Chapter 6, this phenomenon has been facilitated by the emergence of new products that expose investors to baskets of commodities without all the headache of sourcing and storing. The result is higher investor financial demand occasioned by strategic, structural, and tactical drivers.

As a result, relative to previous periods, commodity prices have been both high (due to the first two components of demand) and volatile (due in part to the third, as well as to the impact of geopolitical factors and unanticipated supply and delivery hiccups). This pattern will likely continue in the near term, particularly in view of what constitutes a set of supply and demand conditions that are quite price inelastic in the short run.

As emerging economies maintain their high growth rates, they will become even larger users of natural resources. The impact of this extra demand will not be offset fully by the possibility of a reduced consumption in industrial countries, even as the United States enters a phase of declining growth. Why? Because emerging economies are less efficient users of natural resources and will remain so for a while.

I would go so far as to say that notwithstanding enhanced conservation efforts in both industrial and emerging countries, the global economy will experience the same thing as the person who goes to the gas pump after trading in his or her small car for a larger model. It will take more gas to travel the same distance. In addition, the car can now more easily handle longer distances given that emerging economies are growing at a considerably faster pace than industrial countries.

This realization is starting to feature prominently in the important discussions on climate change. The solutions are complicated by the fact that, from a historical perspective, it is the industrial countries that have been the major pollutants—in absolute terms and relative to developing economies.

There are also those that believe that geopolitical issues themselves will act as a sustainable boost to commodity prices. This view speaks to the potential of internal political instability in some commodity exporters. It also refers to efforts to isolate countries that, inadvertently or otherwise, are seen to provide enabling conditions for terrorism.

Now, some of this impact on prices will be offset by the emergence of new sources of natural resources, including fuel alternatives and better technology. But these developments will be neither immediate nor inexpensive. And in some cases, such as oil, the alternative sources reside in regions subject to a high degree of social and political volatility. As such, there is no easy short-term supply-side solution to the demand-side challenge. Pending the eventual introduction of new supplies, the physical demand for commodities will continue to be supplemented by a financial demand. The latter will be driven by the further expansion of financial instruments that enable investors to trade groups of commodities as well as trade individual commodities—an issue that I will return to in Chapter 6.

These combined effects will be most evident in the financial results of oil exporters. Consider the Middle East. According to recent IMF data, earnings from the export of energy products have risen to an annual average of some $700 billion—a fourfold increase compared to what was experienced at the beginning of the decade.[17] As a result, cumulative export earnings for 2004 through 2008 will approach $2 trillion, a truly staggering number. Since the bulk of the energy complex is owned by governments in the region, these export earnings flow straight into public finances. Specifically, the IMF anticipates cumulative budgetary income from oil and gas to amount to $1.5 trillion in the 2004 to 2008 period. Of that amount, some 45 percent is saved (compared to less than 15 percent at the start of the decade), thereby adding to the already large holdings of international reserves.

As high oil prices persist, governments are stepping up expenditure plans, with a particular emphasis on infrastructure. Assuming they can secure a reservation on what have become fully booked flights, this is immediately visible to anyone who visits any of the six economies of the Gulf Cooperation Council (Bahrain, Kuwait, Oman, Qatar, Saudi Arabia, and the United Arab Emirates [UAE]). Building cranes dominate the skyline; construction sites adorn highways built only a few years ago and that are now being expanded; and migrant labor is flowing into the country to supplement the workers there. Yet, despite the increase, the IMF estimates that governments will still be saving around 40 percent of what will remain significantly high earnings from the exports of oil and gas.

Moving Up the Asset Allocation Curve

Having examined what economists call the real side of the new secular destination and its impact on commodity prices and earnings, let us now look at the financial side. Specifically, we can also expect a significant change in the way that emerging economies manage their large and growing reserves. Indeed, the change has already started; and it has important implications for investors.

As I discussed in Chapter 1, several emerging economies experienced a pretty sudden shift in their balance-of-payments situations and international reserves dynamics. As this shift persisted, they went from operating in *debtor* regimes to operating in *creditor* regimes. Similar to people who suddenly inherit significant wealth or win the lottery, many emerging economies did not have the infrastructure to manage their growing international reserves. As such, they understandably adopted a very conservative (read: prudent) approach to wealth management. They essentially placed the funds in U.S. fixed-income instruments, with a very heavy emphasis on U.S. Treasury bills and bonds.

This behavior was an important factor behind the interest rate conundrum: By investing their growing earnings predominantly in U.S. government paper, emerging economies put downward pressures on U.S. interest rates. And the pressures were significant as the investments went well beyond what would be warranted by virtually any investment strategy. No wonder the flows were labeled "noncommercial" and "noneconomic." Research conducted by JPMorgan Chase has shown that these investments were generally insensitive to significant changes that altered the expected rate of return on U.S. Treasuries.

A Four-Phase Process

It is not surprising that emerging economies were not in a position to immediately adopt sophisticated approaches to the investment of their suddenly larger and growing international reserves. Indeed, witnessing the change from PIMCO's emerging markets bond-trading desk—after all, it was a critical development in influencing the value of the investment in emerging market instruments—we came up with a simple four-phase process detailing what countries go through in navigating the transition from a debtor regime to a creditor regime.[18] For purposes of simplifying the discussion here, I will describe the four phases as distinct. In practice, however, they can overlap, the transitions are not automatic, and countries can temporarily opt out.

Phase 1. Benign Neglect

The first phase is one of "benign neglect." Being used to operating as a debtor regime, most countries are slow to recognize the extent of the change occurring in their external accounts. And those who recognize it are not quite sure how to react. Their tendency is to ignore it on the assumption that the change will prove to be both temporary and reversible.

This phase of benign neglect was amplified in the late 1990s and early 2000s by some specific and practical considerations. In the case of many emerging economies, for example, the growing reserves provided an important cushion of self-insurance after a rather traumatic period in which governments faced significant funding challenges. In the case of Asia (and China in particular), the reserve accumulation was also part of a more general strategy aimed at generating productive employment for workers coming off the farm and from state-owned enterprises. And for commodity exporters, it substituted the potential of a stream of financial earnings for the extraction of physical capital in the ground.

As the reserve accumulation persists, benign neglect gives way to a second phase characterized by a traditional policy reaction on the part of emerging economies. The catalyst for the shift is the recognition that the new external account situation, characterized by large capital inflows, is contributing to greater inflationary pressures and/or what is viewed as threatening an excessive appreciation in the exchange rate. The former is correctly seen to be detrimental to national economic welfare, with a particularly adverse impact on the poorer segments of the population; the latter is viewed to potentially undermine future export performance, job creation, and growth.

Phase 2. Sterilization

Accordingly, authorities look for ways to "sterilize" the large capital inflows. In the vast majority of cases, they use market-based instruments. These involve mopping up the externally induced liquidity through the issuance of domestic debt. In some cases, the authorities (including those in Chile in the 1990s and Colombia more recently) have resorted to controls on inflows—sometimes called the "sand in the wheel" approach. However, such approaches have typically been abandoned pretty quickly, as they involve significant distortionary effects and are hard to implement in a sustained manner.

The inflows that are sterilized in this manner are added to the countries' holdings of international reserves. Rightly, these are invested in the highest-quality (that is, risk-free), highly liquid instruments—either directly, through purchases of U.S. government paper, or indirectly by outsourcing the management to the bank of central banks: the Bank for International Settlements (BIS).

While the public sector is the main driver here, the initial impact is amplified by the behavior of the private sector. The natural inclination for the wealthy segments of the private sector, as well as others with relatively easy access to the outside world, is to use the foreign banking system to place savings abroad. This reflects both pull and push factors. The savings are *pulled* out of the emerging economies, attracted by financial systems that have a long history of respecting property rights and providing liquidity in virtually all states of the world. They are *pushed* out by the still recent, albeit increasingly less relevant, local history of financial crises, changes in convertibility conditions, and dramatic exchange rate depreciations.

This second phase usually succeeds in alleviating some of the potentially adverse economic impact of the surge in capital inflows. But the mopping up of liquidity is far from perfect, particularly in the context of incomplete linkages among different segments of the domestic financial market. Moreover, it comes at quite a cost for some countries. Given the differential in risk ratings, the interest payments on the debt issued to sterilize the inflows far exceed that earned on the reserves—what investors call "negative carry."

This negative cost has to be borne by somebody in the emerging economy. It usually impacts the budget—either directly as a cost item or indirectly through lower revenues as a result of lower transfers of central bank profits. And once the budget is impacted, it is the taxpayers who are on the hook or, in the case of too many emerging economies, the otherwise deserving recipients of state funds that are chronically underfunded, such as health care, education, and infrastructure.

This growing cost serves as a catalyst for countries to move to Phase 3. In this phase, the driver is the desire to minimize the negative carry. An obvious step to accomplish this is to go out and buy back the external debt that has been issued in previous years.

Phase 3. Liability and Asset Management

This type of "liability management" has two distinct advantages. First, the operations extinguish debt in foreign currency that trades at higher yields than what was earned on the investment of the reserves, thereby reducing the overall negative carry. Second, it helps the country deal with what has been labeled in the literature as "the original sin problem." Coined by Barry Eichengreen of the University of California, Berkeley, and Ricardo Hausmann of Harvard University,[19] this concept refers to the inherent financial instability of emerging economies that comes with the currency mismatch that has often (although less so today) been associated with a composition of debt issuance that has favored instruments denominated in foreign currency.

The tendency to issue foreign currency debt reflects not only cost considerations but also a basic reality of development: Initial risk factors are perceived to be so elevated in some developing countries that there are few buyers out there willing to assume the combination of risks that come bundled in local currency instruments, including credit, liquidity, and currency components. Accordingly, countries face both price and quantity constraints. As such, they are led to issue debt denominated in "hard" currency (specifically, U.S. dollars, euros, Japanese yen, and British pounds).

The issuance of debt in foreign currency provides access to a larger pool of potential investors. It also results in most bonds being traded under U.K. or New York legal jurisdiction, which is viewed as more predictable than local laws—although the experience with Argentina's December 2001 default gives some cause to pause.[20]

As countries start to run out of debt to buy back, they also focus on "asset management." The objective is to directly increase the returns on the holdings of reserves, thereby again reducing the negative carry. This step is usually associated with a change in mindset: As the reserve holdings increase beyond what is deemed needed for precautionary balance-of-payments purposes, the increment is viewed as de facto constituting "national financial wealth."

This phase is usually associated with institutional changes. Most notably, some countries start setting up sovereign wealth funds (SWFs). The seed capital for the SWF comes from part of the reserve holdings at the central bank that are viewed to be well in excess of what would be deemed necessary for prudential balance-of-payments purposes. As these SWFs extend their footings, both the media and the politicians pick up on their activities.

As an illustration, consider the recent spike in attention given to SWFs. You would think that the phenomenon was totally new—which is not the case. And you would think that the magnitudes are already gigantic, which they are not (currently amounting to around 2 percent of global financial assets under management). Yet the attention is such as to have SWFs included in the group of "the new power brokers"—a term coined by McKinsey & Company in an October 2007 report describing the growing influence of "petrodollars, Asian central banks, hedge funds and private equity."[21]

Interestingly, the focus of the newly wealthy economies goes beyond assets in the advanced economies. There is also considerable interest in investing in other emerging economies. For example, the SWFs of oil producers have also been exploring opportunities in the Middle East and North

Africa, India, Pakistan, and the Far East. As noted in the previous paragraph, Chinese entities have also been pursuing investments in Africa and Latin America, including the October 2007 announcement of a $5 billion investment by the ICBC (Industrial and Commercial Bank of China) to acquire 20 percent ownership of South Africa's Standard Bank.

These three phases provide close to a win-win situation for investors in emerging market assets. Virtually any exposure there benefits from the reduction in country risk (associated with the higher holdings of international reserves), the decline in domestic real and nominal interest rates (assisted by the greater availability of capital), and the possible appreciation in the exchange rate. Moreover, the process opens up investment segments that were previously inaccessible, providing investors with the ability to make even larger returns through first-mover advantages. Finally, investors are able to capture the investment premiums associated with the completion of markets and the application of modern portfolio management techniques. These considerations will be highlighted further in Chapter 6 when I discuss how investors can benefit from this age of economic and financial change.

Investors in industrial countries also benefit. The deployment of SWF assets overseas supports valuations in many market segments. And the willingness, indeed necessity, for SWFs to operate in the context of a long-term investment horizon gives them a value orientation when they invest in the more risky segments in the financial system. This was clearly illustrated in the second half of 2007 when several SWFs stepped in to provide capital to ailing industrial country banks and brokerage companies—a phenomenon that attracted significant attention and controversy, which I will address further below.

Phase 4. Embracing Change

The fourth phase is perhaps the hardest for emerging markets to embark on; it also is the trickiest for investors to navigate well. It involves a basic recognition that the shift in the external payments regime (from debtor to creditor status) has a permanency to it. As such, it warrants basic changes in macroeconomic policies. And usually these changes must be considered at times of great pressure from outside, thereby complicating the ability of governments to sell the changes to their citizens.

Adapting to the change from debtor to creditor status boils down to taking steps to encourage domestic components of demand either alongside or instead of external components of demand. It is most vividly illustrated in the international debate on whether China should "let its currency go"—that is, switch from a system in which the exchange rate is determined by policy within relatively narrow variation bands to one where the rate is the outcome of market forces. It is also being illustrated in calls from certain quarters (including the IMF) for oil exporters to take additional steps to promote domestic demand.

A few years ago, most emerging markets were aspiring to Phase 1! Indeed, they saw this phase as a welcome replacement to continuous concerns about how to finance the balance of payments and concurrent worries about vulnerability to any external shocks. But in the last few years, many of the systemically important economies have raced through Phases 1 and 2, and they are now well on their way through Phase 3. Some—such as China, India, and several oil exporters—are looking closely at Phase 4.

A Closer Look at Phases 3 and 4

There is every reason to believe that, for emerging markets as a whole, this four-phase process will see further consolidation in the years ahead—but with two important qualifications. First, what is true for the group as a whole needs need not be true for every country; and second, the process need not necessarily be an orderly one (an issue that I will address in the next chapter).

Accordingly, investors looking to prosper in the next few years—through both the generation of superior returns and the avoidance of losses—need to understand the nature and implications of Phases 3 and 4. Thus there is the need for some additional analysis that also reinforces other considerations cited earlier in this chapter.

Trust But Verify

The fourth phase requires less space in view of the earlier discussions. Suffice it to say th... the phase is fully consistent with the above-cited secular evolution in the dynamics governing growth, trade, and price formation. Indeed, it becomes in the interest of the country to move to Phase 4 once it feels comfortable that it has the infrastructure in place. Such infrastructure must be able to support a migration away from direct controls (for example, a de facto pegged exchange rate for

China) and toward the use of indirect market instruments (for example, a flexible exchange rate system that relies on, among other things, the smooth operation of a relatively deep inter-bank market).

I think of this shift as involving a transition that many of us face as parents and also as managers at work. It entails a willingness to "give up control," having confidence instead in our ability to, using the late President Ronald Reagan's phrase, "trust but verify."

Accordingly, the infrastructure that is required speaks to different sectors' ability and willingness to trust and verify. For the public sector, this involves a robust supervisory and regulatory regime, the ability to compile the required data on the relevant activities, and the set of instruments to limit the adverse impact of market failures. For the private sector, the emphasis is on the right organization set-ups, the appropriate degree of self-regulation and protocols, and the power of incentives and reported profit-and-loss (P&L) statements to differentiate the good from the bad in a relatively timely and transparent fashion.

Clearly this does not happen overnight. It is a process that is heavily dependent on what development specialists call "second-generation structural reforms." It is particularly acute for countries with more open financial systems and more developed linkages to the rest of the world. And it is something that is being taken more seriously in a growing number of countries—so much so that there is a legitimate debate as to whether international pressure to do more is conducive or counterproductive to local efforts.

Understanding the Shifting Mindset

Returning to Phase 3, a key challenge for investors is to understand what emerging economies, as large accumulators of international reserves, will implement in terms of more sophisticated asset management strategies. Investors need to understand what, going forward, will be bought in large quantities, what will be sold, and when. Policy makers around the world also need to have a view on this as the shift will involve price effects for a range of assets, many of which can impact the real economy.

For emerging economies, the change in mindset views the windfall not as part of prudential holdings but rather as constituting a stock of wealth that needs to be appropriately managed, preserved, and enhanced for future generations. The shift is most obvious for countries where the main foreign exchange earner—the exporting activity—is associated with the depletion of a nonrenewable natural resource such as oil. In this case, the national wealth being held under the ground in the form of a physical asset is transformed into a financial asset.

Because of this, oil exporters were early adopters of what is now called the "sovereign wealth fund approach." This involves creating institutions that are distinct from the central banks and that are charged with managing funds in a manner that takes into account the interest of future generations. Historical leaders in this field include Abu Dhabi (the largest emirate in the UAE), Kuwait, and Norway. They are being joined by Dubai (the second-largest UAE emirate), Oman, Qatar, and Saudi Arabia.

A visit to the Web site of Norway's Norges Bank Investment Management (NBIM)[22] provides many interesting insights as to the considerations that underpin this approach. As the analytical studies illustrate, it is not just an issue of ensuring superior and more durable returns for future generations of Norwegians. The transformation of part of the national wealth from a physical to a financial holding also serves to reduce valuation volatility. As a result, the population experiences an increase in both expected absolute returns and expected risk-adjusted returns.

Singapore, while not having the natural resources of oil exporters, has been visionary in the management of its people and its financial reserves. Reflecting highly effective and responsible government leadership over a number of years, Singapore has generated large budgetary and external current account surpluses.

To help manage the surpluses, the visionary founder of the country Lee Kuan Yew created in 1981 the Government Investment Corporation (GIC). This institution has become legendary for its investment savvy in many asset classes and for the highly effective manner it has managed the country's wealth. As Lee Kuan Yew noted in his book detailing the creation and success of Singapore, the need was to invest "long-term for best returns." And since "investing is a hazardous business," "my cardinal objective was . . . to protect the value of our savings and get a fair return on capital."[23]

I suspect that the broadening of the SWF phenomenon will be deemed a "success" at both the national and international levels if it is underpinned by governance and organizational structures that result in high risk-adjusted investment returns. On the national level, this would preserve and enhance wealth for the current and future generations. On the international level, it would respond decisively to concerns that SWFs could undermine the functioning of global capitalism through politically induced investments and commercially questionable activities. I will return to both these issues in the next chapter.

A successful broadening of the SWF phenomenon would have important implications for the deployment of what Federal Reserve Chairman Ben Bernanke has called the "savings glut." Recall that it will no longer just be an issue of the new flows; after all, the secular destination will be accompanied with a likely fall in the current account surpluses of emerging economies. Rather, the issue also pertains to the stock that has been accumulated mainly on account of the past surpluses.

Bond markets in general, and U.S. government bonds in particular, are staring at the prospect of a lower allocation of sovereign investments. The declining share will reflect a natural diversification in the asset allocations of SWFs. This diversification will be implemented directly and through the use of third-party external fund managers.

By contrast, equity markets (through both public and private vehicles), real estate, and other "real assets"[24] will likely benefit from larger allocations. The extent will depend not only on SWFs' willingness to diversify but also their ability to do so. Indeed, as I will discuss in the next chapter, this natural evolution is already being subjected to resistance in certain industrial countries—some on account of (often ill-defined) notions of national security and others due to monsterlike characterization of motive as it pertains to possible political, military, and mercantilist considerations.

It is worth noting the insights of a keen observer of international finance who sees SWFs involved in a future collision of market participants. In a September 2007 article, Simon Johnson, the IMF's economic counselor, gave an interesting perspective on the development of SWFs. Seeing them as "major state-owned players of the 21st century," he wondered what will happen when they meet "the 19th-century private sector." The latter constitutes hedge funds, which Johnson describes as follows in a historical context: "Hedge funds, while becoming more prominent in this century, are in some sense a throwback to the end of the 19th century, when large pools of private capital moved around the world with unregulated ease—and generally contributed to a long global boom, rapid productivity growth around the world, and a fair number of crises."[25]

Johnson's take is yet another illustration of the underlying theme of this book—that of a collision between the world of yesterday and that of tomorrow. Johnson sees this as involving greater competition within what McKinsey called the "new power brokers in international finance." Be that as it may, it is a confirmation of the growing systemic influence of SWFs in the world of today and tomorrow.

Internal Financial Markets

This transformation in asset and liability management in emerging economies will come at a time of rapid change in domestic financial markets. Indeed, as I will argue in Chapter 6, this change will offer investors a wider range of potentially profitable opportunities going forward.

History suggests that the current mix in emerging economies of internal macroeconomic stability and high financial cushions acts as a strong catalyst for the development of internal financial markets. The result is both a deepening and broadening of markets. Existing segments become more liquid and robust, thereby developing a larger menu of instruments; and new segments emerge that involve the linkage of hitherto disjointed activities and the application of financial techniques to new areas.

The speed with which this can happen is particularly striking. Consider the case of China: It has experienced an explosion in the provision of financial services to the population. To illustrate the point, I like using the case of an asset management firm—the China Universal Asset Management Company—that was established in January 2005 by a Chinese national who had recently graduated from the Harvard Business School.[26]

The firm's client base consists of nationals living in China. By the end of 2006, the firm was already managing RMB 10.4 billion in clients' assets. This tripled in the next six months to RMB 30.7 billion. It more than doubled in the next four months to RMB 81.6 billion as of the end of October 2007.

Like many other numbers in the emerging world, the growth in assets under management is staggering. Yet they pale in comparison to things that underpin the assets. At the end of 2006, the firm had around 190,000 clients. By the end of October 2007, this had grown to almost 2.5 million! Within this total, 1.8 million consisted of investors with less than RMB 200,000 in assets at the firm.

These impressive numbers are just one indication of the process of financial deepening that is taking hold in many emerging economies. And they explain why the big western banking and brokerage institutions are so eager to expand in the region. They also speak to why private equity firms are lining up for what is likely to be a stepped-up process of corporatization as companies emerge from dormant family and state holdings.

The Changing Technical Landscape

The recent proliferation of derivative products has facilitated a remarkable reduction in the barriers to entry to many markets. As a result, new participants have engaged in activities that were hitherto not accessible to them. Derivative products have also enabled a far greater degree of linkage across markets than at any other time.

As such, some see derivative products as representing an important advance in the development of financial markets. But others see them as sowing the seeds for major market calamities. Yet all agree that their influence is to significantly lower barriers to entry to various markets, thereby enabling new participants to engage in activities that were hitherto not accessible and, in some cases, are now inadequately understood and poorly supported.

The growth in derivatives has been spectacular up to the summer of 2007. As an illustration, consider the data that have been carefully compiled by the Bank for International Settlements (BIS) that cover currencies, commodities, credit, equities, and interest rate and loan markets. As of the end of June 2007, the market for derivatives stood at $516 trillion.[27] This is more than twice its size just three years earlier (end of June 2004) and about 10 times its size in 1995. Credit default swaps, which are instruments that provide for the buying and selling of credit protection on underlying risk exposures, have shown the fastest rate of growth.

Many investors now spend more time trading derivative products than they do trading the traditional ones that provided the underpinnings for the derivatives. For the person in the street, the most visible illustration of the derivative revolution has been in the explosion of mortgage products. Indeed, at one stage, borrowers were encouraged to customize virtually all elements of their mortgages—from the profile of interest and principal payments to the amount that they can borrow to not only pay for the home but also cover all types of other costs. Some of you will no doubt recall all the "exotic mortgages" that were heavily marketed in the United States on the radio, on television, and via direct-mail and Internet channels. They included interest-only mortgages (IOs) and negative amortization mortgages (NegAms).

The proliferation of derivative products did more that just radically reduce the barriers to entry to a host of markets; it also contributed to a change in the way certain types of business transactions were being conducted. This was most visible in the explosion of "securitization." After booming on Wall Street, securitization attracted more general attention when things were taken to excess and started going wrong—first in the subprime sector and spreading thereafter to many segments of the financial markets. Indeed, in many ways the subprime debacle (and related turmoil) constituted the first (but not the last) modern episode of a global securitization crisis.

The Good, the Bad, and the Ugly of Securitization

The easiest way to think about how securitization works is to focus on two main steps: first, the bundling of many individual loans into a "reference pool" (see Figure 4.8a); and second, the subsequent bundling of this pool into different "tranches of risk" (see Figure 4.8b).

These two basic steps in securitization can and have been supplemented by additional structuring. For example, the new risk tranches can, themselves, be bundled and tranched again and again. Indeed, the number of permutations and combinations is very large, thus enabling issuers to tap a significantly large investor base.

Figure 4.8 The Dynamics of Securitization

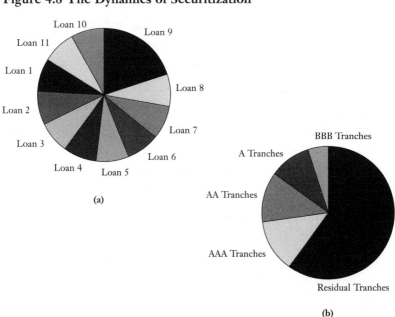

143

In theory, there is virtually no limit to the customization that is possible. This has been reflected in the proliferation of structured products with such fancy acronyms as ABCP, CDOs, CDOs squared, CLOs, and CPDOs—to name a few. And as this proliferation has become more complex, the products have experienced an erosion of their market liquidity, growth in their technical complexity, and a further distancing from the underlying components of basic (as opposed to structured) risk. They have also posed important challenges for risk managers and regulators, while simultaneously putting pressure on operations, technology, and settlement systems. Put another way, in order to be sustained in an orderly fashion, the proliferation of structured products requires retooling and upgrades at virtually every level of the financial system, including a revamping of the pipes through which transactions flow. This inevitably takes time and requires managerial focus.

Despite these observations, the system has not been given sufficient time to adapt. To understand why, you have to remember that the type of securitization that takes place in today's Wall Street need lots of intermediaries. Some assist in the design face; others in the origination, securitization, and warehousing of the collateral; and yet others in the marketing and placement; and then there is the investment manager. And let us not forget the rating agencies that de facto decide, on behalf of far too many people, the degree of riskiness and suitability of each tranche.

At every stage, a fee is charged. Thus, for a large part of the system, securitization is perceived to offer a huge revenue potential. It is not only a function of the number of intermediaries and the specific expertise they bring to the table (actual or perceived); it is also often linked to the size of the transaction. Indeed, it's the perfect incentive alignment for all the intermediaries. Every institution in this *agency* chain is thus prone to excesses. It is therefore not surprising why too many people, including the *principals*, ended up in 2007 with far too much risk exposure at the wrong price, on the wrong terms, and at the wrong time.

Changes in Business Models Because of Securitization

Not surprisingly, the phenomenon has also altered business approaches on Wall Street. This has been most visible in the shift of banks to the "originate and distribute model." As Professor Darrell Duffie of Stanford University notes in his study of the phenomenon: "The picture emerges: banks often sell loans that are designed specifically for an intermediation profit rather than a long-run investment profit."[28]

This shift has been part of a generalized erosion in due diligence activities undertaken by investors as a group—either directly or through the use of third parties. It has also diluted the attention investors as a group generally give to liquidity disruptions and, therefore, to the proper assessment of risk.

With so many people busy intermediating, few have been paying sufficient attention to who still has "skin in the game" (that is, a meaningful financial stake). And those who have had a meaningful stake in this construct—the ultimate investors—have been, as never before, spread all over the world. And far too many of them have been relying on rating agencies that have been entering overly optimistic parameters into models that rely on untested scenarios and/or data from the world of yesterday. This and other elements of the financial system infrastructure were inadequately tested to support the explosion in securitization that has been taking place. And it is a vivid example of one of the general themes of this book—namely, allowable activities too often exceed the ability of the system to sustain them.

As a result, the first hiccup—occasioned by the difficulties that some subprime mortgage holders faced in meeting their contractual obligations in 2007—resulted in dislocations that far exceeded the intermediaries' ability to absorb them.[29] Visualize a line of dominoes toppling over, one by one. Consistent with our discussion of multiple equilibria, the toppling gathered momentum and developed into a major financial dislocation, impacting a broad set of structured products and having a systemic effect on economies and financial systems throughout the world. Wall Street's problem became Main Street's.

The impact has gone far beyond the first wave of investment losses. It has included widespread writedowns in large portfolios, the resignations of CEOs, and the failures of hedge funds. It has threatened the integrity of the money market segment, and it has caused a contraction in the commercial paper (CP) market. In the process, the negative externalities have shifted from Wall Street to Main Street. House foreclosures have risen, credit card facilities have declined, and job layoffs have increased.

The alarm bells that finally started to be heard in the summer of 2007 jolted central banks and governments to take emergency responses. They also illustrated the extent to which many investors, institutions, and balance sheets were fundamentally ill equipped to deal with the massive jump in the production and consumption of structured products.

Securitization Is Here to Stay

But here is an interesting twist: Despite the debacle that started in the summer of 2007, securitization still has a future.

Indeed, as I said in reply to a question posed to me after a presentation I had made to one of the Harvard student clubs, What would I advise my daughter to do today if she were to ask me about the most promising areas and/or skills in the financial sector? "Structured finance" is how I responded.

To some, this may seem strange. After all, structured finance will undoubtedly bear the brunt of the job cuts on Wall Street after the 2007 subprime disaster; and rightly so. It will also attract the attention of regulators and politicians. But this setback will ultimately prove cyclical. The secular drivers of the phenomenon are strong if properly implemented and supported.

Securitization offers many advantages that are highly valued by the marketplace, and these will not go away any time soon. Indeed, the basic question is whether powerful securitization techniques will be used in a more responsible and, therefore, sustainable manner. Fundamentally, these techniques offer a much larger degree of potential diversification and customization. As a result, they broaden the potential set of buyers and sellers, thereby enhancing liquidity and hedging activities, reducing transaction costs, and breaking down geographical and product boundaries.

The advantages of securitization read like the typical marketing material for financial globalization. After all, the combination—of greater liquidity, diversification, customization, and so on—is illustrative of the more general process of integration of financial markets. And like other components of this process, it is subject to excesses, including overproduction and overconsumption; but this need not necessarily derail the phenomenon over the medium term. Indeed, it may even render it more sustainable over the long term.

The Bottom Line

So where does all this leave us? The analysis suggests that the markets are heading toward a secular destination involving consequential changes for investors:

- First, the engine of economic growth worldwide will no longer be so highly dependent on the United States; instead, emerging markets will increasingly constitute a consequential and independent driver for growth.
- Second, the nature of this new growth driver will evolve away from a high reliance on exports and toward domestic components of demand (namely, internal consumption).
- Third, this evolution has the potential to facilitate the much-needed and long-delayed adjustment in a U.S. economy that has been overly dependent on debt-financed consumption. In the process, the global economy will regain greater balance and reduce its financial vulnerability caused by an overly skewed distribution of global trade imbalances.
- Fourth, global inflation trends will be negatively impacted by continued pressures on natural resources. Moreover, they will be influenced by the gradual dissipation of the disinflationary impact previously associated with large chunks of efficient and cost-effective labor entering the global economy. This will complicate the policy challenge facing central banks, which are already operating in an unusually fluid world.
- Fifth, the global allocation of capital and related moves in asset prices will increasingly be influenced by the activities

of SWFs. These SWFs are likely to gradually shift away from fixed-income investments and go toward higher-risk instruments and those that are deemed to offer stronger protection against inflation.

• Finally, these economic and financial changes will be accompanied by further technical developments centered on a highly nonlinear path for structured finance and other activities that depend on the continued proliferation of derivative products.

For investors, these changes alter the configuration of risk and returns. They call for changes in institutional and strategic approaches, and they realign the patterns of comparative advantages. They also modify the effectiveness of national and multilateral policy responses.

Given the nature and depth of these structural changes, market participants need to adjust if they wish to remain successful in this new age. Specifically, they have to develop an appropriate action plan that speaks to the characteristics of the new secular destination—thus the focus of Chapter 6. But this is only a *necessary condition*; it is not *sufficient* to ensure success. Market participants also need to be able to navigate the journey—a topic that I address in the next chapter.

CHAPTER 5

PROSPECTS FOR THE JOURNEY

Interestingly and counterintuitively, I am much more certain about what the new economic destination will look like than I am of the nature of the journey that will get us there. Sound strange? Not if you consider how ill prepared the infrastructure of the international financial system was (and, to a large degree, still is) for the transformations we are experiencing and will face in the near future.

As is typical of disruptive innovation, structural transformations have enabled—and will continue to do so—new activities that cannot as yet be adequately supported. As a result, it is inevitable that there will be a series of collisions between the world of yesterday and that of tomorrow.

The world of tomorrow will see a proliferation of new activities and instruments in finance, as well as a growing influence of new actors on the global stage. Meanwhile, the world of yesterday is embedded in the infrastructure and plumbing systems that seek to support these new activities, and we have already seen that they have limited and declining success in rendering that necessary support. Yesterday's supporting structures and institutions are also reflected in the growing displacement pressure on hitherto dominant actors at the national and international levels, as well the decline in the market share of traditional instruments and products.

Collisions between these two worlds inevitably cause friction. If they occur sequentially or are met with timely circuit breakers, only isolated phases of market turmoil will result. If, however, they occur simultaneously, investors face the real prospect of having to deal with a major and prolonged slowdown in world economic growth, defaults, an intensification of trade wars, and greater restrictions on the free flow of financial capital across national borders.

This chapter details specific transition-related issues that investors should be aware of as they navigate the coming journey. The focus is on the potential causes of *policy mistakes* and *market accidents* that confront investors with the possibility of periodic sudden stops in liquidity, episodes of ill-defined balance sheets, institutional casualties, and emergency policy responses.

Adjusting to Change

In the recent past, the world has seen the types of effects that inevitably result from the move from old to new. So we already know that we need to anticipate that different parts of the system will find it difficult to adjust quickly to the new realities. These difficulties will be experienced at individual firm and country levels, as well as at multilateral levels, and blunting these difficulties will require fundamental changes in mindsets and infrastructures.

Sports fans will be familiar with the dynamics. Recall what happened when the "West Coast offense" was first introduced in American football. This new approach to moving the ball forward contributed to a realignment of power within the league. Why? Because existing defenses could not adjust quickly enough. The defenses' failures also dented the effectiveness of these teams' offenses, which were kept off the field and/or forced to play catch-up. With time, defenses adjusted to the West Coast offense. As a result, it became less potent, and today it is less prominent in the game plan of the top teams in the league.

That situation is the same as what is happening today in the global economy and what is likely to occur in the years ahead. Different groups vary in their ability to recognize and adjust to the ongoing structural transformations; and some are hindered by rapidly outmoded and, in some cases, obsolete operating models. The reasons for this are many, and they relate to the cocktail of economic, financial, and behavioral considerations discussed earlier in Chapter 3. Combined with more mundane "plumbing issues"—that is, the extent and speed with which the institutional infrastructure can accommodate the emergence of new strategies and behaviors—the struggles with the transformations will periodically result in unpleasant clogging that requires both clean-up operations and major retooling efforts.

These points are best illustrated by looking in turn at the experiences and challenges facing private sector organizations, national governments, and multilateral institutions. For the purposes of this discussion, I will describe each one as a stand-alone. In practice, however, they do and will continue to interact.

Indeed, investors will get their arms fully around the challenges they face only if they also understand what difficulties lay ahead for national and multilateral policy makers. After all, the three parties are engaged in the equivalent of a complicated game of multidimensional chess. The game inevitably involves interdependency among players with diverse objectives, tools, and constraints.

Private Sector: Faster but Far from Even or Smooth

As you would expect given their larger degrees of freedom (as well as the discipline imposed by frequent and increasingly public measures of profit and loss), private sector participants have been the quickest to feel the need to adjust to the ongoing transformations. This is apparent in many metrics in the corporate and financial world.

Witness the growing importance for U.S. corporations of the earnings and profits coming from their foreign operations. Earnings on foreign sales now account for a fifth of all U.S. earnings, almost double the level of just 10 years ago. In the case of the companies in the S&P 500, the contribution of foreign operations to earnings growth was 6 percent in 2007. In the context of a relatively consistent earnings multiple, this *in itself* translates into a rise of about 6 percent in the value of the U.S. equity market. Not bad for an economy that is traditionally viewed as being "closed."

As I noted in the previous chapter, the private sector was very quick to embrace the production of structured products and to create delivery systems. The manner in which this was done inevitably led to an overproduction and overconsumption of structured products, consistent with what we have seen throughout the history of major technological innovations. As an example, consider the following observation from *The Economist* in an article on the last round of changes in the telecom industry: "The pattern is always the same: a new technology emerges on the scene, and nobody can be quite sure how it will be employed, or the appropriate etiquette for its use. So users have to make the rules as they go along."[1]

In relying more and more on earnings from international activities, companies exploit the hand-off in growth from industrial countries (and the United States in particular) to developing countries. Not a day goes by without some news of an international expansion for U.S. companies. This corporate internationalization process is proving to be a two-way road. The last few years have witnessed a significant expansion in the concept of a "developing country multinational." This expansion is elegantly detailed in Antoine van Agtmael's book *The Emerging Markets Century*.[2] A pioneer in the field, van Agtmael is credited for having coined the term "emerging markets." His latest research shows that companies in the emerging markets regions are starting to spread their wings. They are capturing a growing share of world markets, rapidly improving operational efficiency, and steadily climbing up the value-added curve.

As this phenomenon gathers momentum, emerging markets start to develop brands that attract growing recognition. This serves to further solidify the process under which the countries develop secular roots that can help withstand cyclical volatility.

For example, companies in China are at this threshold; companies in India are well into the process; and companies in South Korea have made significant progress.

It is therefore not surprising that these companies are also expanding their global aspirations. The last couple of years have witnessed an evolution in cross-border M&A activities that would have been unthinkable previously: A growing number of high-profile acquisitions have occurred that have involved companies from emerging economies taking over counterparts in the industrial countries. This is happening across sectors, including cement, financials, food, natural resources, telecoms, textiles, and tourism.

In doing so, these companies have also expanded their pattern of successful growth within the emerging world. As an example, consider the case of the Middle East: An Egyptian telecom company (Oroscom) is now a household name around the region, as is a Brazilian frozen food company (Sadia). The Egyptian financial firm EFG-Hermes continues to profitably expand its regional footing and is attracting the interest of foreign institutions. Meanwhile, Mexican companies like CEMEX and AmericaMovil have become major players in the Americas and beyond. Chinese firms increasingly go to Africa and Latin America, investing in and operating natural resource ventures.

This combination of expansion in both industrial and developing countries is powerful. It facilitates both horizontal and vertical integration (including through the outright transfer of entire production operations), thereby enabling such companies to become more common entries in various global surveys of corporate dominance and strength.

On the investment front, endowments were early adopters of the internationalization theme. As an example, consider the allocation of capital that Harvard Management Company (HMC) historically made to non-U.S. public markets.[3] In 1980, U.S. equities represented 100 percent of the allocation to public equities. The share fell to 69 percent in 1981 and to 48 percent in 2000. In 2008, the share is 35 percent. As a proportion of the *total* holdings of Harvard's endowment, the importance of U.S. public equities fell from 65 percent in 1980 to 12 percent in 2008.

As we will see below, a similar pattern is occurring in other asset classes, including natural resources, private equity, and real estate.[4] Increasingly, HMC's portfolio managers are looking overseas to find attractive investment opportunities. This is true not only for "tradable" sectors like timber and natural resources; it is also the case for commercial and residential real estate. Moreover, private equity is establishing a bigger footing overseas in the context of great macroeconomic stability, a deepening of markets, and less uncertain legal and business environments.

The explosion in the manufacturing and use of structured products is even more notable than the change in the global corporate landscape. In fact, the growth has been so sharp that it has totally eclipsed the volume in the underlying products. In the process, this has altered the liquidity dynamics of markets.

In a March 2007 column for the *Financial Times* (FT), I likened this process to the emergence of new "liquidity factories" on Wall Street.[5] As a result, "market drivers of liquidity currently exceed influences coming from traditional monetary policy instruments," both in the expansionary phase and in the contractionary phase. With the leverage in the system being driven primarily by a multiplier that is *endogenous* (or internal) to the market, the monetary authorities face a very difficult and complex policy landscape when it comes to influencing the internal liquidity multipliers and the corresponding cross-border flow of capital—an issue that I will return to below.

When viewed as an amalgam, the private sector *as a whole* appears to have embarked on a path that would enable it to better exploit the new destination. However, like many things in life, what is true at the general level tends to hide important differences in its make-up. Indeed, within the private sector, there are notable differences in adjustment propensity and speed. At the minimum, this multiplicity poses interesting internal corporate management challenges and offers the prospects of major institutional realignments within and among market segments, including a high probability of outright failures. It can also evolve into something larger as the multiplicity sows the seeds of potential systemwide disturbances and market accidents.

Willingness versus Ability

Perhaps the biggest tension within the private sector is that which lies between companies' desire to participate in the new activities enabled by the secular transformations and their ability to do so. This tension is related in particular to the difficulties that are inherent in retooling the support functions that are so critical to maintaining company focus, discipline, and risk mitigation.

The clearest illustration of this phenomenon—and the one that has already led to significant bumps in the journey—

comes from the financial system. Simply put, financial companies' inability to reconcile properly willingness and ability has led to what, with hindsight, has turned out to be a massive overreliance on structured products, thereby requiring a messy clean-up process. As the FT's Martin Wolf stated in his September 5, 2007, article, "It took foolish borrowers, foolish investors and clever intermediaries, who persuaded the former to borrow what they could not afford and the latter to invest in what they did not understand."[6]

Witness the due diligence undertaken in a sector that was visibly exhibiting the advanced indications of a bubble—housing in such hot markets as California, Florida, and Nevada. As far as I know, very few professional investment managers followed the advice that Bill Gross gave a few years ago to PIMCO's mortgage team led by Scott Simon. Scott and his colleagues looked closely at the way the housing market actually functioned at the microlevel. Their research included participating in "ride alongs" with local real estate and mortgage agents. Their findings, which were summarized in periodic "Housing Project" write-ups posted on the PIMCO Web site (www.pimco.com), spoke clearly to the excesses taking place. Combined with the firm's top-down analysis, it informed three distinct elements of the investment strategy as outlined in an interview Scott gave in December 2006 before the sector embarked on its contagion-filled downturn:

- *First, how the dynamics of the overall sector were likely to evolve, including the relationship between price changes and inventory:* "One of the things we've realized from this study is that real price gains increase turnover considerably. The flip side is that if you go from insanely high appreciation to nothing, you get a really big drop-off in volumes."

- *Second, the extent to which indications from the rating agencies about credit robustness need to be supplemented:* "In the asset-backed sector, we've clearly changed the way that we invest because of our concerns about the housing market. For example, on negative amortizing ARMs (adjustable rate mortgages), S&P and Moody's require 10 percent credit support for AAA-rated, standard structures. We build in 45 percent credit support."

- *Third, the importance of avoiding the complacency that inherently accompanies instruments that carry the top, AAA, rating:* "In subprime loans, we tend not to buy the AAA-rated piece of the loan. We carve the AAA-rated piece up and take the first cash flows off the AAA piece, which are self-liquidating if the deal performs normally for about four months. The biggest complaint you could make about our approach to those kinds of loans is that we've been too conservative. But given our view, that's a criticism that we will gladly bear."

PIMCO was correct in its willingness to underwrite the perception that its approach may be "too conservative." For once the housing finance dislocations started in earnest, their impact was quickly amplified by limitations in the supporting infrastructure, which fed a series of adverse feedback loops. The industry's modeling of mortgage-based structured products proved inadequate, further burdening the already stretched ability to value a range of complex instruments and composites. With the industry's valuation matrix in disarray, it became very difficult for buyers and sellers to find each other. The resulting disruption in liquidity spilled over to other markets.

There was simply too much of a gap between the levels where each side of the market was willing to transact. It literally was similar to two people speaking different languages, with neither understanding what the other was saying. As a result, the price discovery process broke down. The number of transactions slowed to a trickle, while balance sheet valuations assumed an excessive degree of arbitrariness and troubling opaqueness. This breakdown aggravated and was aggravated by other factors. Visibility and transparency were issues in the context of lots of market chatter about losses by financial institutions that they had yet to fully acknowledge and make public. This further intensified the hesitancy governing the flow of capital.

Kevin Warsh, governor at the Federal Reserve Board, elegantly detailed the phases of a market turmoil (retrenchment, reliquification, and revaluation) in his speech to the New York Association of Business Economics in late 2007: "As the strains in financial markets intensified, many of the largest financial institutions became jealously protective of their liquidity and balance sheet capacity. Amid heightened volatility and diminished market functioning, they became more concerned about the risk exposures of their counterparties and other potential contingent liabilities."[7]

Uncertainties about the related losses that were yet to be made public made traditional buyers retreat to the sidelines, intensifying the market-for-lemons tendencies discussed in Chapter 3. There, they joined those that had recently accumulated significant wealth but were yet to engage forcefully in the markets, preferring instead to focus on the areas of greatest familiarity. And as they all waited for clarity, legitimate questions were raised about the adequacy of the balance sheets of intermediaries. These questions were illustrated by the extent to which long-established financial institutions experienced a widening in the credit spreads on the issued debt. These spreads point to the market's assessment of the robustness of the institutions' creditworthiness (that is, the extent of default risk). In November 2007, the average for financial institutions, as compiled by researchers at Merrill Lynch, reached a record level of 149 basis points (bps) over U.S. Treasuries.[8] And this was before the January 2008 announcement of another large round of sizable losses and writedowns that ate significantly into capital and required these institutions to scramble to raise new funding.

While the November credit spread levels matched those reached in 2002 in the midst of the chaos fueled by the collapse of Enron and WorldCom, there was an important difference: The average spread on the debt issued by financial institutions was wider (that is, pointing to greater default risk) than that for the corporate sector to which the banks lend. Specifically, the average spread for the corporate sector stood at 134 bps. This unusual pricing of the capital structure of the economy became even starker in January 2008.

This comparison is even more striking when you look at the specific players involved. In November 2007, the 10-year debt issued by the financial giant Citigroup carried a credit spread of 190 bps while Merrill Lynch came in at 224 bps. Meanwhile, the electricity company serving Boston and its surrounding areas—NSTAR, which was rated by Moody's two notches below, yes below, Citigroup and which makes use of bank credit lines—issued 10-year debt at 140 bps.

The dynamics were expressed in the well-written August 2007 paper delivered by Ben Bernanke, chairman of the Federal Reserve, to the Jackson Hole, Wyoming, economics symposium organized by the Federal Reserve Bank of Kansas City. This annual conference provides a relatively intimate venue for central bankers to deliberate with other members of the economic and financial community. In his speech to the gathering of experts, Bernanke noted the extent to which market activities were being impacted by participants' growing inability to assess "opaque" products with "complex payoffs." This, along with the higher cost of capital, "seems to have made investors hesitant to take advantage of possible buying opportunities."[9]

Equally interesting is how the situation impacted the segments of the financial system usually taken for granted. For a considerable time, the scariest prospect for central bankers and regulators was playing out—a dysfunctional interbank market together with an essentially frozen commercial paper (CP) market and a growing loss of confidence in the money market segment. This is a nightmare not only for policy makers but also for leveraged private sector vehicles (including hedge funds and private equity firms) and for anyone else that needs liquidity or has been running large maturity mismatches (that is, borrowing short in order to fund longer maturity investments such as the now infamous SIVs). They face sudden stops in the availability of funding that may well have nothing to do with their own circumstances.

Increasingly, banks were reluctant to assume greater exposures; they were even uncertain about the magnitude of the contingent claims that they had already had—overall, relative to their capital base, and in relation to their risk limits. The situation was further complicated by the fact that some of these contingent liabilities were associated with off-balance-sheet activities, including the setting up of conduits. And most of the time, these conduits lay outside the normal purview of the traditional oversight bodies, effectively raising a question about the long-standing view that banks obtain privileged access to the Fed's financing windows (and other official safety nets) in exchange for operating in a tougher and more explicit regulatory environment.

Remember that the banking system is the nerve center of the economic and financial system. I liken it to the oil in the car that we drive. We do not spend much time thinking about it. Yet any breakdown will paralyze the car regardless of its impressive engine, fancy interior, ultramodern technology, or highly rated safety features. The car simply will not function; and it will constitute a hazard for its occupants and for other vehicles if it is left in the middle of the road.

A Retooling Challenge

It takes time to work through these types of issues as the challenge is not simply unclogging various blockages. There is a need to retool the plumbing system at its fundamental level. New pipes are needed, the network must be altered, and the quality upgraded. Meanwhile, the incentive for prematurely restarting the flow is enormous.

For the vast majority of private sector companies, this speaks to a retooling challenge that involves the trio of people, processes, and systems. The repairs must be undertaken in full flight and under the eager eyes of analysts and competitors. There is no practical way for management to press the "pause" button on the markets, undertake the repairs, and then resume by pressing "play." Indeed, management often finds itself in the uncomfortable position of having to oppose those who are still blindly impressed by how derivatives provide for the tranching and bundling of risks and, as ridiculous as this sounds, those who feel totally confident in essentially relying on a "just-in-time" risk management approach.

As each company tries to retool, it quickly realizes that implementation is further complicated by the fact that many others are trying to do the same thing at the same time. As an illustration, witness the dearth of back-office personnel with derivative expertise and the concurrent large increase in the cost of filling such a job. Witness also the sharp rise in compensation for top-quality compliance and risk officers. With management pressing the issue and the front office expanding its footprint, it will not be surprising if many companies wind up compromising on quality and thereby significantly increasing their operational risks going forward.

Rating agencies are in a similar dilemma. Indeed, their challenges may be even more severe given that, through their designation as Nationally Recognized Statistical Ratings Organizations (NRSROs), the major agencies enjoy what has essentially become a "regulatory monopoly." As such, they are expected to keep an eye on the public good in pursuing their individual activities. The rating methodologies, while possibly defensible in isolation, are essentially based on yesterday's considerations. As such, they have become increasingly outmoded. Agencies' statements about the "proper use" of their ratings will do little to alter the current dynamics. Moreover, recent studies have shown that the set of ratings undertaken in the last couple of years are proving less robust, especially when compared to previous ones.

Agencies appear to face a lose-lose situation. They are operating under enormous scrutiny because of their regulatory monopoly status, yet they cannot stop their activities in order to retool their methods. In continuing to pursue "business as usual," they risk creating even greater complaints down the road, triggering a major revisit of their corporate influence and the manner in which they are allowed to operate—which then impacts profitability. Meanwhile, concerns mount about the independence and robustness of their ratings. All this leads to investors *as a group* looking for ways to reduce their reliance on ratings, at least for a period of time.

The tension between pressing ahead and pausing to repair is inherent to the duality of financial globalization and cross-border/product integration. As noted earlier, this overall process has both stabilizing and destabilizing forces. The "net" is one of greater stability and welfare enhancements—over time and on average. But as any portfolio manager will tell you, during periods of disruptions (which inevitably involve greater basis risk), it is the "gross" that can get you in trouble and not just the "net."

The Headwinds of Disintermediation

The retooling challenge is accentuated by a trend in banking toward disintermediation that would be happening even if the financial system were not navigating the transformations I've been discussing here. Increasingly, activities have migrated away from their traditional institutional home. Indeed, a number of factors, both positive and negative, are eroding the monopoly that has been enjoyed by those servicing institutions at the center of the global system (often called "the sell side").[10]

In the old days, investors were highly reliant on these institutions for a range of outsourced activities. The most important was price discovery. There were inherent technological limitations on the availability and timeliness of electronic screens that detailed the bid-offer for a large range of instruments in different market segments. Even when prices were available, investors tended to rely on the sell side for analysis and evaluation. Investors would call analysts at the major investment banks for specialized views on credit and for technical modeling. The system also relied on banks for establishing the link between sellers and buyers, particularly in the case of new issuance. In effect, the sell side had a "natural monopoly" similar to what utility companies used to enjoy in many countries.

This monopoly is now subject to an accelerating process of long-term erosion. Similar to what is happening in many other areas, technology is undermining the role of the sell-side institutions as intermediaries in price discovery and analysis. Issuers and investors have understood the benefits of direct contacts. Entry barriers to investment banking activities have eased, with the reality and prospects of new entrants' putting downward pressures on fees. The secular impact of these factors has been amplified by some of the recent scandals on Wall Street. Questions about the role of the sell side in the run-ups to the spectacular collapse of Enron and WorldCom earlier this decade served to fuel long-standing concerns about conflicts of interest and biased research. Partly because of this, an ever growing number of investors have built in-house expertise in an effort to relegate the role and status of sell-side research.

The resulting erosion of monopoly power has accentuated the forces of disruptive technology discussed earlier. By putting pressure on revenues and profits, it has also encouraged sell-side firms to extend their activities to new areas. The objective is to move up the value-added curve. The reality is that in doing so, many firms must abandon their comfort—and expertise—zones, which means that they risk ending up in areas where they possess neither a comparative advantage nor a tradition of excellence; moreover, their understanding is less than complete.

Where does all this leave us? It suggests that the potential for *market accidents* will be a recurrent feature as we move along this journey. Similar to what we saw in the summer of 2007, this will inevitably translate into episodes of market turmoil, sudden stops in liquidity, and institutional casualties. *Investors need to recognize this prospect and react accordingly.*

There is a question as to whether the repeated episodes of market disruptions will be felt as bumps in the road or evolve into something more sinister. The answer lies not only in the private sector's success in retooling itself; it also depends on the extent to which the official sector facilitates their repairs, both by doing good and refraining from doing harm.

National Governments: Slower and Potentially Disruptive Reactions

Like the private sector, governments face the challenge of understanding ongoing structural changes and revamping a set of policy instruments that were originally designed to serve the world of yesterday and, as such, are now less potent. The situation is further complicated by the involvement of politicians. These actors are attracted by the natural resistance of voters to any erosion in historical entitlements and immediate comfort, as well as the sudden appearance of questionable developments in the financial sector that adversely impact Main Street—a sector that naturally attracts a certain amount of attention (and envy) in light of generous compensation packages.

The need for policy to catch up to market realities will not be impacted just by domestic considerations. There is also growing recognition that you can't solve the problem even with effective internal measures because of cross-border interdependence.

In isolation, each of the factors discussed below offer some probability, albeit manageable, of a *policy mistake* in this journey. In combination, they could serve to trigger a set of events that would seriously hinder investors' abilities to navigate their way to the new realities.

Addressing Endogenous Liquidity

One of the challenges that the Fed and other central banks continue to face is how to deal with "endogenous liquidity." Specifically, central banks have lost a significant part of their ability to fine-tune liquidity conditions now that market drivers of liquidity exceed the influences of traditional monetary policy instruments—on the way up and on the way down.

This phenomenon was highlighted over 2006 and in the first half of 2007, as we frequently discussed in the meetings of HMC's Portfolio Committee. The Federal Open Market

Committee (FOMC) in the United States had hiked interest rates to 5¼ percent; the European Central Bank had embarked on a well-publicized tightening of monetary policy reinforced by talk of steadfast vigilance against inflation; and emerging economies were also raising interest rates. Yet the talk in the market was continuously of massive liquidity sloshing around in the system and lifting all boats, including some with highly questionable fundamentals, erratic integrity, and limited understanding and modeling.

In assessing this, my HMC colleagues and I quickly came to the conclusion that the issue was not the stance of monetary policy around the world; instead, it pertained to the role of the new liquidity factories. And it was most visible in the exploding popularity of "alternatives" among both those who manage them and those who invest in them.

To illustrate, consider what happened when a pension fund decided to attempt to bolster its return by increasing its allocation to private equity at the cost of that to public equities. The dollar it took out of the public markets it gave to a private equity firm. In most cases, the firm enhanced the purchasing power of this dollar by borrowing an additional $3 to $5 in the debt markets, and it ventured into public markets looking for a company to "take private." The sellers of the company ended up with the combination of original and borrowed funds.

Critically, the liquidity multiplier process was internal (endogenous) to the market. Balance sheets expanded without the benefit of a reduction in interest rates; indeed, the expansion occurred *despite* hikes in rates around the world. That is to say, monetary policy adjustments proved ineffective in gradually mopping up liquidity.

Now remember, this endogenous liquidity is more than just difficult to understand fully; it is also fickle. It can, and often has, reversed abruptly simply because of a shift in the market's risk appetite (or what John Maynard Keynes called "animal spirits"). It thus places monetary authorities in an extremely difficult position. On the way up, they are accused of being enablers of a phenomenon that will end in tears. Yet, if they hike too aggressively, they risk suddenly transforming the endogenous multiplier from being overly accommodating to being massively restrictive.[11]

The difficult dilemma does not stop there. It actually intensifies when the endogenous liquidity shifts to its restrictive cycle—as it inevitably does. When this happens, monetary authorities face loud and conflicting calls from the professional community: Some urge them to cut rates aggressively in order to protect the real economy from the vagaries of Wall Street's liquidity factories; others urge restraint, arguing that a rate cut will simply bail out those who overextended themselves, thereby weakening market discipline and increasing moral hazard. And then there is the uncomfortable reality that whatever they do, the instruments in their policy arsenal are simply too blunt; they lack effectiveness and involve collateral damage.

One way of illustrating this phenomenon is to consider the underlying compositional issues. When endogenous liquidity fluctuates, as it inevitably does, the authorities observe the "average" but end up falling victim to the extremes of the distribution. Again using a liquid-based analogy, when reducing the depth of a river from six to five feet in order to safeguard lives, it is not enough for the authorities to know whether the average height of the population is over five feet; they also need to know how many people are below five feet. *Distribution counts as much as the average.*

This is the precise situation that the Federal Reserve (and other central banks) found itself in during the summer of 2007. And it played out dramatically on the financial channel CNBC. I suspect that any investor who watched Jim Cramer that Friday is unlikely to forget any time soon his emotional outburst. As Erin Burnett, the CNBC anchor, calmly tried to get his take on the day's sharp market sell-off, Cramer went on a verbal rampage. With his sleeves rolled up and his hands banging on the table, Cramer accused Fed Chairman Ben Bernanke of being an "academic" and "not getting it."[12] He yelled, "Bernanke needs to focus on this." He went on to state that the chairman "has no idea how bad it is out there; no idea." Burnett, in her typically calm and reassuring manner, tried to moderate Cramer's outburst. She told him: "Hold on. I know you are passionate but . . ." Well, Cramer would have none of it. He felt particularly strongly, having received many calls from market participants telling him that the situation was really awful. Accordingly, his outburst gathered momentum and extended to other Fed officials. Cramer told his television audience, which was watching with a mix of intense interest and bewilderment: "They are nuts. They know nothing. The Fed is asleep."

Cramer's satisfaction came when the Federal Reserve surprised the markets by delivering on what he had advocated strongly: easing access to the discount window and also cutting both the discount rates and fed funds rates by larger-than-expected amounts. This contrasted to the reaction of others that CNBC subsequently interviewed. Several of these felt that the Fed had "overreacted." These commentators shared one concern—that the Fed's actions would further fuel irresponsible and dangerous behavior. Some also felt that the easing of monetary policy would accentuate inflationary pressures.

The challenge of how to deal with consequential and volatile endogenous liquidity relates to another policy issue that I will discuss in detail in Chapter 7: how to refine the traditional instruments of monetary control and ensure more meaningful and sophisticated supervision on a range of activities, with volatile leverage, that have been enabled by the ongoing structural transformations and yet are outside meaningful oversight.

The Challenge of Stagflation

The continued prospect of wide fluctuations in endogenous liquidity is not the only challenge the major central banks and, in particular, the U.S. Federal Reserve is facing. They also face the likelihood of what we referred to earlier as an *adverse change in global price dynamics*—namely, the replacement of a disinflationary tailwind with an inflationary headwind on account of the natural evolution of labor and wage conditions in emerging economies. This adverse change is alongside less favorable productivity trends in the United States and the long-term commodity price trends traced to the notable expansion in global demand. These considerations increase the risk of stagflation—a situation characterized by disappointingly low economic growth and high inflation.

This is a particularly tricky issue for the Federal Reserve. The Fed differs from several of its peers, including the European Central Bank (ECB) and the Bank of England, in that the Fed has a "dual mandate." Governor Frederic Mishkin of the Board of Governors of the Federal Reserve reminds us that the legislation governing the institution calls on it "to promote the two *co-equal* [my emphasis] objectives of maximum employment and stable prices."[13]

An environment of global disinflation is a wonderful thing for meeting this dual mandate. It is like running downhill: Gravity helps you cover a specific distance in less time and by exerting less effort. It is a very different matter when you are running on flat ground and then you have to run uphill. The same amount of effort will not get you as far; you need to find something more.

The unfavorable change in the global price dynamics comes at a time when the United States also faces the prospects of subpar economic growth. As I suggested earlier, this is an inevitable consequence of the need for the U.S. economy to work out some of the excesses of the recent past. These excesses include the large trade deficit, bubblelike conditions in certain asset markets (including segments of the housing market), and overstretched consumers who can no longer use appreciating house values to refinance mounting indebtedness. These excesses also involve market interest rates and relative dollar strength that have been maintained by a temporary phenomenon: that of newly wealthy, emerging market central banks investing for now the vast majority of their windfall gain in reserves into U.S. fixed-income products. Indeed, the question is not whether the United States will experience a period of relatively slow growth. It is whether this and the subsequent evolution will look more like a V, U, W, or L.

Due to these inevitable changes, the Federal Reserve will have to spend a lot more time trying to get the balance right—between containing the more pronounced inflationary pressures and countering the slowdown in demand and economic growth. The former calls for a more "hawkish" monetary policy (that is, an inclination to hike interest rates), while the latter requires a more "dovish" policy (that is, an inclination to cut rates). Under normal conditions, this trickier balance would increase the risk of a "policy mistake." Under the type of economic and financial fluidity I have described in this book, the risk of such a mistake becomes significant and potentially costly.

Dealing with Surges in Capital Flows

The global phenomena of endogenous flows present a specific challenge to several emerging economies: how to deal with huge surges in capital inflows. Similar to what organic growth can do for companies, capital inflows hold the potential to lubricate the efficient and orderly growth of an emerging economy. They do so by relaxing financing constraints, completing markets, and enhancing financial integration. Moreover, the flows are often accompanied by a transfer of expertise, technology, and other institutional benefits.

Capital inflows also bring challenges. For example, they can overwhelm the domestic financial system, resulting in macroeconomic overheating as well as imprudent lending and borrowing activities at the microlevel. Studies of banking crises show that many have occurred after periods of high liquidity. Simply put, notwithstanding the presence of sophisticated firms, the financial systems in emerging economies also include institutions that are not as yet able to deal with major increases in capital inflows. As such, some of them make bad decisions, often with significantly negative results for them and for the system as a whole.

A temporary, albeit large, surge in capital inflow can also weaken the international competitiveness of the domestic economy by fueling inflation and/or pushing the exchange rate to an overly appreciated level from a medium-term perspective—that is, a level that is inappropriate when the inflows eventually slow or reverse.

This risk goes under the label of the "Dutch disease," so named for the deindustrialization that the Netherlands suffered when huge energy (gas) reserves were discovered in the North Sea in the 1960s. The surge in foreign exchange receipts led to an appreciation of the real exchange rate and undermined the health and outlook of the nonenergy sectors.

The unfortunate irony is that countries may end up actually worse off after a period of sudden large capital inflows. At first, this sounds counterintuitive. After all, these inflows are beneficial inflows. Surely, at worst, the countries will simply be no better off. How can they be worse off?

To illustrate the underlying issues that can make this scenario occur, consider again the phenomenon of lottery winners. On the surface, there is no way that lottery winners can be worse off since they can simply give away all the winnings. Yet, there are many cases in which, within a few years of unexpectedly winning the lottery, some of the winners end up in bankruptcy. The reason is that the act of winning changes the behavior of individuals. And such changes can be either constructive or destructive.

The "psychology of money" draws on the fact that people react differently to sudden, large, and unanticipated changes in wealth. (This phenomenon served as the premise behind the 1983 film *Trading Places* starring Dan Aykroyd and Eddie Murphy and is among the favorites of many investors that I know.) Remember, the seed of many past banking crises in both advanced and developing economies were sowed during periods of large capital inflows and abundant domestic liquidity—an observation that is confirmed by the financial dislocation in the United States that started in the summer of 2007.

A recent IMF study has shown that the risks of developing countries' winding up worse off after experiencing large sudden capital inflows are particularly elevated for countries that run large current account deficits.[14] The reason is that the surge in capital inflows enables a set of activities that are inconsistent with the countries' fundamentals. As such, the economies' underlying vulnerabilities increase. These risks are especially acute for those countries with weak banking systems and inadequate supervision and regulation.

Politicians' Interest

Not surprisingly, there is an additional group to adjust and that is the one consisting of politicians within the official policy sector (that is, the executive, legislative, and judicial branches, as well as some related regulatory and supervisory bodies). Almost by definition—indeed by design—the political system amplifies the voices of the minority segments facing disruptions, thereby ensuring a process of checks and balances within societies.

Interestingly, and challenging for some long-term investors, the requirements of capitalism do not always line up with those of democracy, particularly in the short term. In fact, politics can sometimes amplify the potential conflicts that arise when capitalism's economic and institutional anchors begin to erode. As such, interventions that are made in response to legitimate political issues may result in what economists and finance professionals would regard as "policy mistakes." To demonstrate this risk factor going forward, consider the following considerations pertaining to the structural transformations discussed earlier in Chapter 4.

Protectionist Threats

The hand-off in global growth is fueling the threat of protectionist trade legislation, especially in the United States but also in other industrial countries. The threat is aimed at developing countries that have been successful in gaining significant global market share. It is most pronounced in the case of China, as protectionist forces have found allies among some economists who feel that Beijing should be labeled a "currency manipulator" due to its refusal to strongly revalue its currency.

At the same time, industrial country politicians are increasingly more vocal in calling on emerging economies to become "more transparent" in the manner in which they invest their large holdings of international reserves. Indeed, the standards being advocated far exceed what would be considered customary for financial firms in the industrial countries.

Consider the views of Ted Truman, a former U.S. official who is now at the Peterson Institute for International Economics (IIE) and who recently testified to Congress on the subject of sovereign wealth funds (SWFs). In an October 2007 paper on the management of China's international reserves, Truman wrote: "China is being held, will be held, and should be held to the highest standard of accountability and transparency in this area. The Chinese authorities may not like this fact, but as a citizen and former official of the country that was long characterized as the elephant in the international financial system, my advice is to get used to it."[15]

This type of pressure has already resulted in some emerging economies' abandoning their bids for industrial country assets. In 2005, the Chinese oil company CNOC (China National Offshore Oil Company, with majority government ownership) made an $18 billion bid for Unocal (known to many of us through the "76" gas stations). The bid caused a political outcry that included the preparation of bills in both chambers of the U.S. Congress to block the transaction. The result was that CNOC withdrew its bid.

A few months later, Dubai World Ports (majority owned by the government of Dubai) made a bid for U.S. port facilities located mainly along the East Coast (including in Baltimore, New Jersey, New York, and Philadelphia). The bid was reviewed by the Committee on Foreign Investment in the United States (CFIUS), which brings together various (12 at last count) government agencies. This committee is charged with safeguarding national security interests. Despite getting the green light from CFIUS, the proposed transaction triggered an enormous reaction that included a one-sentence letter from a member of Congress to the president of the United States: "Dear Mr. President: In regards to selling American ports to the United Arab Emirates, not just NO—but HELL NO!"[16]

Now, the Dubai bid had passed the formal screening required by U.S. law that is aimed at protecting national security interests. As such, the White House was ready to counter congressional attempts to block the bid from being accepted. Moreover, it was generally agreed that Dubai Ports was an able and experienced operator of ports around the world and that it consistently subjected itself to a high standard of security and safety measures. However, the Dubai officials decided to withdraw the bid, fearing that a public fight would adversely impact future activities.

The reactions of the politicians in these cases were motivated by a mix of concerns about national security, state capitalism, and nationalism. And ultimately, their concerns were sufficient to derail cross-border flows of capital. Moreover, in the case of Dubai Ports, they effectively negated the specific domestic mechanisms put in place to review, using expert advice, the validity of the concerns.

However, crossing over from political to economic and financial considerations, cases of erecting obstacles to the cross-border flows of capital have amounted to capital account protectionism aimed at blocking foreign ownership. This type of activity constitutes an economic policy mistake. It disrupts the smooth adjustment of the global economy, and it also risks fueling more delays in the liberalization of trade in goods and services. Moreover, in episodes of major market turmoil, such obstacles can also undermine the ability and willingness of fresh capital held by SWFs—which constitutes the most desirable capital because of its long-term investment horizon and relative permanency—to reduce the risk that a technical dislocation will contaminate economic fundamentals.

I made this point on October 19, 2007, in a conference in Washington, D.C., when I was participating in a panel that was discussing reserve management by China and other emerging economies.[17] Little did I know that the next few months would see a parade of executives from Europe and the United States traveling to Asia and the Middle East to raise capital for their struggling companies. *The Economist* reported that "on January 15 the governments of Singapore, Kuwait and South Korea provided much of a $21 billion lifeline to Citigroup and Merrill Lynch."[18] This was part of an estimated $69 billion that had been provided in a short period by SWFs to recapitalize "the rich world's biggest investment banks"; and it was almost half the value of the stimulus package that was making its way painfully through the administration and Congress at that time. Not surprisingly, the magazine characterized the process as one in which "Wall Street, the flagship of capitalism, has been bailed out by state-backed investors from emerging economies."

Other media sources also portrayed the image of Wall Street being given a lifeline by the SWFs. The evening news program on NBC led with the news that U.S. banks had "gone overseas" for capital. The next morning, the front page of the *Financial Times* was dominated by the headline that "US Banks Get $21bn Foreign Bail-Out." That same morning, the *Wall Street Journal* ran the following headline across three of its five front-page columns: "World Rides to Wall Street's Rescue." Yet, in welcoming the much-needed injection of capital by long-term investors, there remained a concern about what *The Economist* called "mischievous behavior." And the undertone was apparent in the title that the magazine chose for its cover ("Invasion of the sovereign wealth funds") and the accompanying image (that of *military* helicopters delivering bars of gold).

Concerns about the motives of the SWFs were evident in many political venues in the United States. Consider the following exchange that occurred in the Nevada debate in January 2008 that brought together the Democratic Party presidential candidates. The moderator, Brian Williams, remarked that the image of U.S. banks' going to foreigners "hat in hand" looking for funding "strikes a lot of Americans as just plain wrong." He then asked, "What can be done? And does it strike you as fundamentally wrong, that much foreign ownership of these American flagship brands?" Hillary Clinton responded as follows: "Brian, I'm very concerned about this. . . . We need to have a lot more control over what they [the SWFs] do, and how they do it." Later in the debate, she lumped the SWF issue together with the debacle in the subprime market, noting that "I'd like to see us move much more aggressively, both to deal with the immediate problem with the mortgages and to deal with these hedge funds."[19] This type of political reaction is not limited to the United States. As an example, *The Economist* cited the case of French President Nicolas Sarkozy who "has promised to protect innocent French managers from the 'extremely aggressive' sovereign funds (even though none has shown much interest in his country)."[20]

The nature of the political debate, including the recent spike in SWF bashing, is particularly hard to understand when viewed from the perspective of emerging economies. They see themselves being lectured by those that overspent on consumption and wish to be financed cheaply. They see restrictions being advocated by some that previously had championed the cross-border flow of goods and capital.

They are puzzled at the obstacles that are being put forward to slow a natural asset diversification process that benefits the global economy and that responds to the legitimate aspirations of their population. Indeed, the SWF's injection of capital into key U.S. banks (including Citigroup, Morgan Stanley, and UBS) has helped stabilize a financial sector destabilized by large subprime losses. Just imagine how much worse the situation would have been without these sizeable injections of pure capital. SWFs are also puzzled that the "standards" and "transparency" requirements that others advocate for them go far beyond anything that has been envisaged for the highly leveraged hedge fund and private equity communities in industrial countries.

This is not to say that the SWFs should not take steps to improve their governance, investment processes, and risk management. As I discuss in Chapter 6, these steps are required if emerging economies are to benefit from the secular destination. Rather, to be meaningful, the adoption of such steps are best based on rational and realistic assessments rather than exaggerated external pressures that go against the long-term interest of the global economy.[21]

Regulatory and Supervisory Issues

Politicians have also been questioning why a host of complex financial products have migrated away from an appropriate level of regulation, supervision, and taxation, and their questions have focused on three recent developments:

- First, the debacle in the U.S. subprime sector, including the noisy and heart-wrenching images of foreclosures on homes bought by the less-well-off segments of the population, as well as the ousting of renters in properties that can no longer be sustained by their owners
- Second, the huge losses announced by major banks that, despite their access to government safety nets and their reputation for sophistication and professionalism, have demonstrated important lapses in risk management and control
- Third, the threat that this has posed for sensitive issues that are as generalized as the holdings of money market funds and as specific as the working capital of Florida's Jefferson County school board[22]—all of which have been threatened by the collapse of structured investment vehicles (SIVs).

Political interest has been further piqued by the timing—including the coincidence—of the announcements of the large compensation packages earned by private equity firms (with Blackstone in the lead). These announcements have been amplified in the news, and that amplification has been a natural consequence of the "alternative" investment firms' looking to raise permanent capital through issuing initial public offerings (IPOs), which requires the public release of hitherto private information.

As the smoke slowly clears, it will become increasingly evident to politicians that the subprime crisis has raised difficult issues about fraudulent lending activities, weak consumer protection, inadequate risk management, poor regulation and supervision, and lax lending practices. These factors have aggravated a situation in which too many households were enticed by "exotic" mortgage loans (one of the symptoms of the structured product phenomenon discussed earlier) that they could afford over time only if house values continued to appreciate at a pace that was both historically unusual and inconsistent with basic parameters of affordability.

With real estate foreclosures' also voiding the leases of tenants that have remained current on their rent, politicians have been hearing complaints from a pool of people that goes well beyond those directly impacted by inappropriate financing. Indeed, pressure has been building to provide tenants greater protection in cases in which they are current in their rent payments and the landlord has defaulted on the property's mortgage.

While politicians have been pushing for expanded congressional inquiries as part of a heightened blame game, regulators have already taken steps to tighten lax lending practices. The regulators' steps have reinforced the self-regulatory (albeit overdue) actions that the market has taken which have included the bankruptcy of a number of specialized institutions such as mortgage originators and the contraction of the activities of bond insurers.

This scenario speaks to the components that are essential to the viability of self-regulating market systems. Yet it has come at a rather delicate time for the U.S. economy. These actions have served essentially to tighten credit conditions at a time when the housing market is already weak, other segments of the credit markets are disrupted, and the consumer faces headwinds on account of higher energy prices. So these actions while justified at the microlevel could end up, in terms of timing, constituting a macroeconomic policy mistake.

Similar considerations apply to the stepped-up scrutiny of the alternative investment management industry and of bond insurers. It is understandable and legitimate for politicians to ask why parts of this highly remunerated area has benefited from seemingly preferential tax treatment. It is also legitimate to ask how bond insurers migrated to complex activities that have now disrupted a host of markets (including municipal finance). But, again, it is important to consider the extent to which timing could have unintended consequences.

Who Is Rating the Rating Agencies?

Inevitably, the political spotlight will also shine on the rating agencies. In addition to benefiting from operating under a de facto regulatory monopoly regime, the major agencies have acted as gatekeepers for accessing the balance sheets of a large number of investors. Those investors have included public pension funds. Therefore these agencies operate in circumstances that involve a contingent liability on public finances in the event of a credit debacle. Moreover, questions have been raised about potential conflict of interests that may have arisen from the combination of these agencies' commercial and rating activities. After all, the two major rating agencies (Moody's and Standard & Poor's) have secured an increasing part of their revenues and profits from the business of rating structured products.

The basic question that will be asked is whether rating agencies can be trusted when buyers and sellers are either unable or unwilling to carry out in-depth due diligence. These agencies should expect their activities and expertise to be subjected to considerable political scrutiny. Pending greater clarification of where the stepped-up scrutiny will lead, there is a possibility that the related uncertainties may inhibit the flow of capital into rating-sensitive activities and portfolios.

Multilateral Institutions: Fewest Degrees of Freedom

The discussion in Chapter 2 highlighted a key multilateral predicament occasioned by the ongoing structural transformations: On the one hand, there is need for better coordination at the multilateral level to facilitate the realignment of national economies and the smooth functioning of the international financial system, including the orderly correction of the payments imbalances. On the other hand, there is a distinct lack of effective multilateral mechanisms that command the necessary expertise and legitimacy to inform the much-needed coordination activities.

Interestingly the issue is not one of identifying what different countries in the world need to do to facilitate a smooth adjustment that is in the interest of all. Indeed, a strong consensus exists as to what constitutes the correct policy response at the level of countries and regions. This consensus has been reinforced by the analysis of the IMF in the context of its "multilateral surveillance," the six-monthly communiqués of the G-7 and the International Monetary and Finance Committee, and the work of numerous researchers and think tanks. Rather, the problem is one of implementation, and specifically that of dealing with the same theoretical considerations that are associated with any other typical coordination problem.

The global solution calls essentially for countries to implement specific measures in a *coordinated and simultaneous* fashion in the context of a *"shared responsibility."* The specific steps are as follows: The United States is to reduce consumption to allow for a halt and reversal in the mounting external and internal imbalances; Europe and Japan are to implement structural reforms that will allow their economies to increase growth capacity and productivity; and Asia and the oil exporters are to stimulate domestic components of aggregate demand. The result of this policy cocktail is to be the maintenance of a high global growth rate concurrent with the reduction in global imbalances and a lowered risk of financial system instability.

Sounds easy, right? Well, here is the rub: In the absence of strong coordination mechanisms that ensure simultaneous policy implementation, no rational, free-choosing country would necessarily proceed on its national policy agenda. This is called a "prisoner's dilemma." In order to act, each individual country needs strong assurances that others will also implement their policy agendas. Why? Because any country that goes it alone ends up in a worse state. In other words, a national policy action may not be actionable unless it is implemented simultaneously with the other national policy measures set out for other countries.

Given these considerations, it is not surprising that we have seen very few effective policy actions on the global trade payments imbalances notwithstanding agreement on the required policy actions and broad recognition that (1) the imbalances are unsustainable and (2) the longer the delay in addressing them, the greater the risk of a disorderly and costly unwinding.

This situation is like the predicament of an orchestra that has been given a new score to perform but lacks a conductor. There is no good alternative: The attempt of individual musicians to proceed and start playing on their own will most likely end up in a rather raucous and ineffective composition that will have the audience asking for their money back; and the alternative of not playing and waiting for a conductor who is slow to appear also results in audience impatience and dissatisfaction.

So why have multilateral institutions that are desperately in search of a new role in the global economy been unable to respond to a widely recognized multilateral policy coordination problem? The answer to this question also speaks to the broader issue of their failure to perform other functions that could help the world accommodate more smoothly the ongoing secular transformations. In the meantime, they are compounding the risk that we will end up with a "policy mistake," one that has the potential to complicate, rather than facilitate, the journey to the new secular destination.

The Legacy Burden

Some of the positive structural attributes of multilateral institutions, including their broad membership and historical standing, also limit their flexibility to adjust and respond in a timely fashion to large and unanticipated global transformations. Chapter 2 identified some of these key structural weaknesses. Most pertain to the difficulties of altering historical entitlements that were given to various countries at *particular moments in their history*. These entitlements were hardwired through the specification of voting powers, the assignment of key managerial positions, and the allocation of board representation. In addition and unfortunately, the multilateral institutions' refusal to update these entitlements sends the worse message about respect and inclusiveness for those countries that have earned the right to have a voice in international financial policy formulation.

Multilateral institutions will usually recognize the need for change. Indeed, this is the case of the IMF under the leadership of its managing director, Dominique Strauss-Kahn. Yet they also face great difficulty in making those needed changes.

The key reason for this dichotomy is that effective multilateralism requires the delegation of policy sovereignty from the national to the international levels. And this is hard to do at the best of times, let alone when nationalism is on a rebound as it is today. Moreover, most politicians are domestically oriented, and, as such, they may lack a thorough understanding of the overall international architecture—which means that the technocrats in the central banks and the ministries of finance are deprived of the type of backing they need to be able to deal effectively with these issues.

The sovereignty transfer becomes even harder when there are doubts about the expertise, legitimacy, and objectivity of international organizations. And that challenge is compounded by the fact that certain members of the existing arrangements enjoy considerable historical entitlements that they are loath to give up. The result is either inaction or, perhaps worse, some muddling compromise that further erodes the credibility of the institutions.

In today's world, this phenomenon is also playing out in what used to be the key mechanism for global policy coordination—the economic grouping of industrial countries known as the "Group of Seven" (G-7).[23] Gone are the days when the G-7 could agree on policy coordination mechanisms that meaningfully impacted the course of the global economy. Instead, their communiqués increasingly call on *other* (non-G-7) countries to take certain policy actions.

The evolution of the communiqués is, of course, a reflection of secular developments—namely, that a new set of countries now has an important effect on such key variables as global growth, trade, price formation, and financial flows. You would expect a well-functioning global coordination body to welcome countries that now have an important systemic role. Yet the G-7 has been very reluctant to do so. Instead, it has relied on the cover-ups of "special invitations," "breakfast meetings," and so on. No wonder that some countries, such as China, are showing less interest in attending these events.

History suggests that a good panic is the best way for institutions to overcome the hesitancy of individual constituencies to create effective multilateral mechanisms. Indeed, it took the panic of 1907 in the United States to establish the Federal Reserve System.[24] Similarly, the emerging markets crises of the 1980s and 1990s acted as catalysts for revamping some of the IMF's lending facilities and increasing its quotas. But for investors looking to navigate the journey, the prospect of a catalytic crisis does nothing to reassure them. They will need to judge whether the reform measures that are theoretically in the hands of the owners of the IMF as a group (and that are detailed in Chapter 7) stand much chance of being implemented. If not, the risk of a policy mistake increases further.

The Bottom Line

The analysis of this chapter suggests that the international economy has embarked on a major course of global change with an outmoded infrastructure. This consideration accentuated the challenges of the adjustments associated with Chapter 3's discussion of behavioral aspects. Moreover, there are distinct differences among and within the three groups of market participants when it comes to ability and willingness to adjust.

There are therefore many reasons to expect that the journey will be inevitably bumpy. The risk is best captured in the concept of potentially compounding market accidents and policy mistakes. Accordingly, following the next two chapters' discussion of how to benefit from the secular destination, I will spend some time talking about how best investors can also navigate the journey.

CHAPTER 6

BENEFITING FROM GLOBAL ECONOMIC AND FINANCIAL CHANGE: AN ACTION PLAN FOR INVESTORS

There is an old joke about a car pulling up to a man sitting at a crossroad. The driver asks: "Does it matter which road I take to the city?" The man responds, "It doesn't matter to me!"

I have detailed the anomalies of recent years—the likely causes, and the consequences for the journey and upcoming destination. I have talked about ongoing structural transformations. I have referred to realignments in economic fundamentals, wealth dynamics, and market technicals. All this is interesting stuff; but it is highly relevant for market participants only if they can do something about it.

To this end, the analysis in this chapter speaks to steps that investors should take to ensure that they benefit from these changes, present and future.

Since investors do not operate in a vacuum, the next chapter also considers the to-do lists that face others that, along with investors, have been inelegantly bundled under the label of "market participants" (that is, national governments and international institutions). Together, Chapters 6 and 7 speak to what is necessary to ensure that they each react appropriately, and do so in a self-reinforcing manner.

For investors, the basic challenge boils down to the ability to capture attractive risk-adjusted returns; for national policy makers, it is the ability to respond in a manner that sustains economic growth and reduces the probability of periodic financial dislocations; and for multilateral institutions, it is the potential to contribute to an efficient reconciliation of national policies at the international level, thereby ensuring consistency and mutual reinforcement among national policies.

For purposes of this discussion, I will address each action plan on a stand-alone basis. In practice, however, the interrelationships among these groups are such that each of them also needs to be aware of how the others are doing. This is particularly so for investors who are effectively at the receiving end of the actions taken (or not taken) by policy makers. Chapter 8 then considers the best way to navigate the risks—that is, minimizing the (now fatter) "left tail" of the distribution—that will be particularly acute as the journey continues. Combined, these three chapters detail steps that may be taken by investors and others to improve their welfare as the markets of yesterday collide with those of tomorrow.

Investors will do well in the years ahead if they remain anchored by the secular themes detailed earlier in this book. Having specified their expected return target and their risk tolerance, they must adequately design and execute the three basic steps of portfolio management: choosing the right asset allocation, finding the best implementation vehicles, and conducting the appropriate risk management. Specifically, investors need to design and implement a portfolio management approach that accomplishes the following:

1. Targets a new secular destination
2. Utilizes the right instruments

And they must do so in a manner that also enhances their ability to navigate what is likely to be a rather bumpy journey.

These are not easy tasks, but they may well be highly rewarding.

For simplicity's sake, the following discussion looks at each of these steps and presents the process as strictly sequential. In practice, investors will find that an iterative approach is required—that is, an approach that embodies a certain degree of high-frequency monitoring and portfolio responsiveness.

Asset Allocation

Think of the asset allocation question in the following way: How would you best allocate your capital among different asset classes if you knew you were going to be forced to go away for three years and would thus be unable to change the allocations?

In practice, of course, most elements of an asset allocation can be changed in the interim—either through direct sales and purchases or indirectly through a combination of hedging and risk augmentation trades. Yet it is important to start the analysis from the presumption that changes cannot take place in order to achieve a clear analytical anchoring of the neutral asset mix that, ideally, draws heavily on the correct secular events. It also provides for better clarity and visibility as to the long-term return objective (that is, at least over a market cycle) and the amount of pain that you can tolerate in the extreme eventuality that you're faced with zero degrees of operational freedom when it comes to midcourse corrections.

Disciplined asset allocation also helps investors avoid some of the traps that too many have fallen victim to over the years. These traps have been explained in the multidisciplinary review in Chapter 3. They include the tendency to view individual investments in isolation (that is, through a "narrow framing") even though they inevitably are implemented as part of a bigger portfolio (that is, through a "broad framing"). They also include the tendency of some investors to exhibit time-inconsistent preferences, to be seduced by herd mentality, and to overreact at the wrong time and in the wrong way.

Many sophisticated and successful investors have found that a disciplined approach to asset allocation provides *structure* that performs an important anchoring function. Such anchoring facilitates constructive outcomes *and* makes destructive outcomes less likely. Of course, the pursuit of structure is not a risk-free activity; and excessive structure can lead to the sort of rigidity that is often associated with a slow-moving and inefficient bureaucracy. Accordingly, while the asset allocation exercise typically takes a three-year view for most investors (with your typical endowment and foundation adopting a longer period), it is not necessarily frozen for that time. Specifically, it should be reviewed on an annual basis, with the up-front recognition that such a review may or may not result in changes. And it certainly deserves review should there be reasons to revisit the secular themes that anchor neutral asset allocation.

With this in mind, and based on a set of subjective assumptions that are open to change, Table 6.1 presents illustrative point estimates for an asset allocation (excluding cash) for a U.S.-based investor, with corresponding variation ranges. The underlying assumptions pertain to a range of asset classes, and they cover more than the traditional aspects of expected returns, volatility, and correlations; they also account for the secular outlook.

Think of the approach as a way to answer the question of how best to mix and match the various risk factors that are embedded in the conventional specifications of asset allocations (what market practitioners call "beta"); they will need to be supplemented by complementary efforts aimed at adding value through active investment management ("alpha").

Based on the midpoint estimates, this example targets a reasonable "steady-state" nominal annual return of 8 to 10 percent over a three-year period and at constant exchange rates. By drawing heavily on the book's analysis of structural transformations, it assumes the ability to sustain short-term (that is, one-year) deviations of 8 to 12 percent on both sides of the expected mean target return. Those with greater risk appetite can target higher-than-expected returns along with the likelihood of larger volatility in the pattern of these returns.

To the extent that the secular themes play out in a rapid fashion, the investment return potential goes up; and it falls should the world fail to sustain the anticipated pace and dis-

Table 6.1: An Illustrative Neutral Asset Mix for Long-Term Investors, Percentages as of 2007

	Midpoint	*Range*
Equities		
United States	15	12–18
Other advanced economies	15	12–18
Emerging economies	12	6–18
Private	7	6–8
Bonds		
United States	5	4–6
International*	9	6–12
Real Assets		
Real estate	6	3–9
Commodities	11	7–15
Inflation protected bonds	5	4–6
Infrastructure	5	3–7
Special opportunities	8	2–14
Expected long-term nominal return (baseline, annual average)	8–10 percent	
Expected long-term real return (baseline, annual average)	5–7 percent	
Expected standard deviation (baseline)	8–12 percent	

*Includes emerging market bonds issued by sovereign and corporate entities.

tribution of economic growth and capital flows. Similarly, specific entry points will have an impact, with post-dislocation investments offering the greatest potential.

The following sections detail some of the main considerations for each asset class. They also raise some important qualifications, particularly with respect to handling exposure to "alternatives."

Equities

Most investors tend to be well allocated to public equities, if not overallocated. This phenomenon is driven by the view that, over the long term, equities "outperform"—a view that is forcefully advocated by Jeremy Siegel of the Wharton School of Business in Philadelphia. In a provocative introduction to his book *Stocks for the Long Run*, Siegel cites a proposal put forward in 1929 to invest in stocks right at the end of the 1920s bull market and just ahead of "the next 34 months [that] saw the most devastating decline in share values in U.S. history." He notes that, by July 1932, "when the carnage was finally over, . . . the market value of the world's greatest corporations had declined an incredible 89 percent."[1] He then asks the reader an interesting question: What would have happened to your wealth had you started investing a regular amount each month? And the surprise answer is that you would have made more money than investing in "risk-free" Treasury bills in less than four years. And if you had held the position for 30 years, your wealth would have grown by an average of 13 percent per year.

Siegel is among several analysts who have used history to demonstrate the long-term effectiveness of equity exposures. Underlying these analyses is the view that the market offers an attractive "equity risk premium" that long-term holders can realize—that is, consistent positive returns over time in excess of the returns on short-term risk-free bonds. Simply put, this premium compensates investors for holding a potentially (and historically) volatile asset class.

As usual, what seems simple and straightforward hardly ever proves to be the case. There have been endless debates about how to measure this premium and what it actually captures. There have been heated discussions about measurement periods and related investor behavior—particularly whether the "typical" investor can hardwire sufficiently his or her response to avoid selling after a major and reversible market correction—that is, selling at the worst time. And when all else fails in answering the legitimate analytical questions, proponents have appealed to the powerful notion that equities are the best bet on capitalism, a system that has delivered riches for many generations.

I won't detail or judge the outcome of these debates. Indeed, I suspect that they will continue for quite a while. Instead, let us postulate the issue as follows: If our secular destination of more balanced growth materializes, investors will wish to be exposed to a *globally diversified* set of stocks.

The words "globally diversified" are key in contrasting what makes good long-term sense with what most investors do today. Specifically, and while this is changing slowly, most investors—individuals and, to a lesser extent, institutions—still show a very high degree of "home bias" in their capital allocations. This is particularly true in the United States where domestic stocks dominate overall equity exposures as a result of either historical inertia or the view that international stocks excessively expose investors to a host of additional risks (for example, exchange rate fluctuations, differences in accounting and governance structures, rule-of-law concerns, convertibility, and capital control risks). Some also justify holding on to a heavy domestic exposure on the view that U.S. companies are deriving a growing proportion of their earnings and profits from foreign operations—as such, domestic allocations already include international exposures.

The persistence of home bias is explained by the insights of the behavioral finance work discussed in Chapter 3. After all, home bias is consistent with the attractiveness of the familiar—whether this comes from name recognition or geographical proximity.

While international investing does involve a different set of risks, the cumulative impact of risk has been declining in recent years when compared in relative terms to domestic investing. This is one of the main outcomes of the globalization and integration phenomenon that has been powerfully in play. In some cases, it has been facilitated by government action, progress toward international standards and codes of conduct, and gradual harmonization of regulatory and supervisory regimes.

International exposure is also justified by the secular growth hand-off that will result in less reliance on the dynamism of the U.S. economy and more on the expansion in economic activities throughout the rest of the world (and particularly emerging economies). For the reasons discussed earlier in this book, we will likely witness a period of subpar U.S. growth and significantly more buoyant expansion elsewhere. As such, the benefits of internationalization are significant, even when you take into account the growing interdependence of the global financial system. To this end, investors may wish to think about equity exposures in the 30 to 54 percent range with, at most, only up to a third to a half of this in the United States.

Currency Considerations

Positioning in this way provides investors with a way to hedge some of the U.S. dollar exposure that comes with holding U.S. equities. For the reasons discussed earlier in this book, the U.S. currency has embarked on a long-term path of depreciation. While this will inevitably involve periods of cyclical retracements, it is well anchored by a combination of factors that will continue to put pressure on the dollar in the period ahead that include the large U.S. trade deficit, diversification of investor portfolios in which the dollar starts from a position of overwhelming dominance (that is, faces only downside), and the change in growth and productivity differentials away from the United States and in favor of the rest of the world.

The repricing of the U.S. dollar will be accompanied by an interesting change in the behavior of other currencies. So far, the most important counterpart to the general weakness of the dollar (which economists traditionally measure using a basket of currencies that are weighted according to their importance in U.S. trade) has been the appreciation of the euro. In fact, for the last five years, the euro has appreciated against the dollar at more than twice the rate of the basket as a whole. This striking divergence in the behavior of currencies against the dollar is not explained just by what currency moves *ought to have happened*. It also reflects how currencies have been *allowed to move*.[2]

For the last few years, Europe has allowed its currency to move freely while other countries—and China in particular—have been reluctant to do so. As a result, the euro has carried the bulk of the burden in the global process of accommodating the required depreciation of the dollar. This pattern is likely to change going forward. For the reasons discussed earlier, it will increasingly be in the interest of China (and, more generally, that of Asia and other emerging economies) to allow greater flexibility in the management of their exchange rates. As such, they will likely replace the euro as the rapidly appreciating currencies. Indeed, they are likely to gain against not just the dollar but also the euro. In the process, they will gradually emerge as a powerful force in international finance and gain a larger share in the allocation of investor capital.

Implementation Vehicles

Much has been written about the best way to invest in equities. Some feel strongly that investors, especially individuals, should limit themselves to index funds.[3] This approach to investing serves to contain fees in a world in which too many of the higher-priced, actively managed funds tend to underperform the market. Others recommend that investors use various techniques and services that seek to identify the exceptional funds.

Typically, investors end up doing a bit of both. The most common pattern is to use passive instruments for the most efficient markets (for example, U.S. equity exposures) and more actively managed ones for the less efficient markets (for example, exposures to emerging economies). The specific choices are typically guided by internal due diligence and various consultancy and research services, while retail investors can also gain insights from the research conducted and published by investor intelligence services such as Lipper and Morningstar. Such an approach is certainly understandable.

Having said that, it is important to be sensitive to four issues in designing and implementing such an approach:

1. Passive exposures typically track indexes that are backward looking—that is, they reflect the world of yesterday rather than the world of tomorrow. Moreover, as demonstrated by the debate raging among professionals on the benefits of "fundamental indexing" versus the more traditional capitalization-weighted approach, many indexes may be subject to construction biases that could have meaningful valuation effects over time.[4]

2. Certain mutual funds allow investors to supplement a passive positioning in the equity market with overlay strategies that target supplemental returns in a manner that is complementary and lowly correlated. This speaks to a notion that I will discuss further below—that of separating beta from alpha (or distinguishing between returns that come from an exposure to the markets and those that result from the investment skills of the manager).

3. The arguments for passive and index-enhancing funds do not mean that there are no appropriate actively managed funds. Rather, the issue centers on the identification, assessment, and monitoring of managers.

4. In choosing active managers, it is better to make an error of omission than an error of inclusion. Simply put, do not opt for an active manager over passive exposure unless you have good reasons to do so. Indeed, we have witnessed in the recent past a dramatic increase in performance dispersion of active managers across virtually all asset classes.

Real Assets

It is not just that the average investor does not allocate enough to international equities in a broadly diversified portfolio; he or she is probably also underexposed to "real assets"—that is, instruments that tend to preserve their value during periods of higher inflation. Similar to the situation of investors with insufficient equity exposure outside the United States, under-exposure to real assets could be consequential given the characterization of the new secular realities.

Institutional investors are increasingly signaling their willingness to increase investments in real assets. Consider the case of the largest state pension fund in the United States, the California Public Employees' Retirement System (CalPERS). In December 2007, the board of directors approved a proposal to allocate about $28 billion (or just over 10 percent of the fund) to what the state treasurer referred to as "a hedge against inflation."[5] The purest exposure in this area comes in the form of inflation-protected bonds issued by governments around the world. Introduced in the United States in the mid-1990s (where they are known as "TIPS"), the value of these bonds (that is, the combination of distributions and capital value) fluctuates with the rate of inflation.[6] Put another way, investors are guaranteed a real yield (that is, a payment above the inflation rate) at the moment of purchase.

Other asset classes that traditionally fall into this category include commodities, infrastructure, and real estate. Historically, their nominal value has tended to keep up with inflation, as has their income in some cases. These asset classes are, what traders call, "higher beta" than TIPS in that the inflation protection is not guaranteed and the adjustment can overshoot considerably in either direction.

Despite their more volatile nature, commodities, infrastructure, and real estate have constituted growing components of more sophisticated global portfolios, albeit starting from a rather low base. Part of this reflects their strong historical performance, and part reflects the role they play in diversifying the overall portfolio. Historically, the three have demonstrated relatively low correlation with the more traditional asset class mix (that is, those incorporated in the old "60 percent equities and 40 percent bonds" standard allocation).

Investors can gain access to real assets in a number of ways. Some are as easy as buying TIPS directly from the U.S. Treasury; others involve baskets of instruments such as real estate investment trusts (REITs) and commodity index exposures. Those with greater ability to undertake the necessary due diligence can also invest in actively managed products offered by a growing list of investment management firms. Unfortunately, those that are coming late to this group of assets will not find the experience as fulfilling as did the early adopters. This is not to say that real assets should not constitute a meaningful part of a diversified portfolio; they should. It is simply to recognize that their impact will be less potent, be it in terms of expected return or diversification benefit.

Like so many things in life, the characteristics of a particular investment phenomenon that attract people end up changing as it becomes more widely adopted. In economics, this phenomenon carries the label of "Goodhart's law."[7] Named after the U.K. economist Charles Goodhart, the law states that any recognizable statistical relationships will fail as they result in behavior adaptation. Goodhart's law was derived in the context of the attempts by central banks to follow monetary policy rules that targeted a specific monetary aggregate. Researchers found that the targeting of a specific monetary aggregate changed the behavior for which the aggregate was chosen.

There is a risk that the historical properties that have made some of the less traditional asset classes so attractive in terms of their risk-adjusted returns may dissipate as more investors migrate to them. Harvard Management Company (HMC) has come across this phenomenon in the context of its path-breaking investments in timber.

Harvard Management Company's timber team, led by Andy Wiltshire, was among the first in the institutional investment world to understand and act boldly on the attractiveness of such investments. Up until the mid- to late 1990s, timber assets were typically held as part of the large portfolios of industrial conglomerates, and they tended to be managed inefficiently when judged against their potential. Part of this was due to an inadequate combination of forestry and financial expertise; and part pertained to constraints imposed by factors involving other assets on the conglomerates' balance sheets.

Surrounded by supportive functions—in the areas of analytics, operations, and technology—Andy and his team set out to accumulate timber assets and manage them in a highly effective way. The hypothesis, which resulted in handsome payoffs for the university's endowment over time, was a simple one: By combining in-depth forestry expertise and modern portfolio management techniques, the value of the activity was enhanced significantly.

The investments spoke very well to the structural advantages of HMC's "privileged capital." Specifically, Andy and his team could move quickly in making substantial commitments of capital to a long-term and rather illiquid activity that offered attractive expected returns and played the role of effective diversifier for the endowment as a whole. They could commit the endowment up front to a long holding period. And they were backed by an AAA balance sheet.

The beneficial impact on Harvard's endowment was accentuated by the subsequent, virtual herdlike, migration of other institutional investors to timber. Indeed, the migration's dramatic impact on valuations prompted Andy and his team to sell a large part of HMC's timber holdings in the United States and look for opportunities in new locations in Africa, central and eastern Europe, Latin America, and the Pacific.

The spike in popularity of U.S. timber as an asset class changed the characteristics that had made it so attractive for HMC a number of years earlier. Initial valuations are now significantly higher for new investments. The nature of the new holders has increased the previously low (if not virtually zero) correlation of timber to other asset classes. And the multiplicity of investors has made it more difficult to accumulate the optimal plot size of forests.

This pattern will most likely repeat itself in other components of the real asset basket, such as infrastructure and the "special situations" discussed below. It is a virtually inevitable outcome for a financial industry that is subject to intense competitive behavior and imitation. However, although the outcome is to reduce the potency of capital allocations, the reductions will not be so great that such investments become either inconsequential or undesirable.

Nominal Bonds

The perceived role of lower-risk, "plain vanilla" types of bonds (that is, government and corporate bonds) has declined in recent years. This change has been partly due to the unusual market conditions that have prevailed in which virtually all risk assets have gone up in price with the abundance of market liquidity up to the summer of 2007; and it has been partly due to a move among the most sophisticated investors toward more targeted risk management strategies.

In the long-term outlook described in Chapter 4, bonds face additional headwinds in maintaining their current role in global investment portfolios. After all, as an asset class, bonds would underperform others given the major secular themes detailed in this book—robust global growth in the context of a country rotation; higher inflationary pressures; portfolio adjustments among sovereign wealth funds (SWFs) that serve to reduce their relative (and, much less likely, absolute) holdings of fixed-income instruments; and the continued growth in structured products.

While that view is understandable, it is essentially too partial an analysis in the context of a broader optimization of asset allocation. Specifically, it is subject to three important qualifications:

- The first pertains to the drivers of prudent and effective portfolio construction. From a bottom-up perspective, this involves mixing different asset classes that perform diverse functions; and from a top-down perspective, it speaks to having a combination of asset classes that is consistent with the investor's return objective and risk tolerance.
- The second qualification speaks to the important distinction that I have been making here between the journey and the destination: What may be appropriate at the destination may not be suitable for all investors during the

journey. Yet the destination is of little use if the journey cannot be handled. This point was vividly illustrated in the way in which government bonds strongly performed during the market turmoil that started in the summer of 2007.

- Finally, and drawing from the insights of behavioral finance, a bond allocation provides much-needed (albeit partial) elements of automaticity and structure to investors' risk mitigation strategies that would otherwise fall victim to problems of time inconsistencies, inappropriate discounting, and good old procrastination.[8]

These qualifications change the manner in which the bond allocations (and indeed, most other asset allocations) are best viewed. Rather than just ask whether bonds will be a top-performing asset class (as measured by total returns), investors should consider whether holding bonds enhances the expectation of the *risk-adjusted* return for their *total* portfolio. In addition, given the inevitable inconsistencies between the destination and the journey, investors must be confident of their ability to sustain their position during both the good and bad times.

I think of this framework as being very similar to the one that emerged from my family's repeated visits to a wonderfully casual Italian restaurant in Cambridge, Massachusetts. Initially, my wife, daughter, and I would each focus on the dish that appealed to each of us most on a stand-alone basis. After a couple of visits, we realized that we were basically all ordering individual servings of essentially similar pizzas. So we decided to switch to an approach that combined an order of a large pizza with a pasta dish and a side of vegetables. This combination actually gave us greater satisfaction than the initial approach. In the process, we replaced an approach driven *only* by what we each regarded as constituting our top pick by broader "portfolio considerations."

When viewed in this way, bonds end up playing a valuable role for investors. This is especially the case for those that cannot, either for expertise or access reasons, use the more sophisticated hedging instruments (such as the overlay and tail insurance programs discussed in Chapter 8).

For the average long-term investor, the size of the bond allocation would normally be in the 10 to 18 percent range depending on his or her risk aversion and other components of the portfolio. Assuming a given set of financial circumstances, this range is sensitive to a few important factors. For individual investors, it increases with age as capital preservation assumes a greater role in the context of shorter investment horizons; it is also sensitive to prosperity levels as living costs are not necessarily just a function of wealth and income. For institutional investors, it goes up alongside the immediacy and the fixed nature of related liability and payouts. And for both, it also increases with the degree of risk aversion.

Having decided on the allocation, investors must also ensure the appropriate focus. For this purpose, a prudently run fund that is benchmarked against either the Lehman Aggregate or the Lehman Universal indexes—two widely used market indexes—would fit the bill for most investors. Investors with greater flexibility and access to sophisticated monitoring systems could also look at a combination that targets a passive approach to running the underlying bond exposure (the beta component) and an active instrument that delivers value added on top (the alpha component).

Those who know me well will be surprised that I have not included a special category for emerging market bonds. Having spent so many years trading them, you would expect me to highlight their role in a diversified portfolio construction. Moreover, emerging markets have done well. And they continue to offer the prospects of relatively robust returns given the secular outlook. What has changed is the way one thinks of emerging market bonds. In the old days, emerging market bonds fit badly in the traditional portfolio construct. As an illustration of this, I started a September 2004 publication with the observation that, for some, the phrase "emerging market bonds" was an oxymoron: "Emerging markets" used to denote high risk while bonds denoted "safety."[9]

In those days, emerging market bonds constituted what, from an analytical angle, may be viewed as an opportunistic asset class. Investors added these bonds to their asset allocations in order to enhance the yield of the portfolio and, more importantly, expose it to the scope for capital appreciation as the countries climbed the credit quality ladder—and climb they did.

The situation has changed. Reflecting the maturation of the asset class, many of the bonds have become "rate" rather than "credit" plays. As such, they fit comfortably as permanent members of a more general bond allocation (such as that discussed earlier) as opposed to requiring a special characterization. They also offer investors with a way to exploit a greater array of relative value and structural alpha—which is a function of capital market segmentation and regulatory and risk biases.[10]

The credit maturation of the asset class is not the only thing contributing to this change. The role and standing of emerging market bonds have also been enhanced by two additional factors. First, the size of the "dedicated" (as opposed to the "tactical") investor base has expanded significantly, reducing one of the technical components of volatility. Second, new sectors have opened up within the segment, including most notably local currency and corporate bonds. The result is a much broader range of investment opportunities.

Alternatives

Many investors think of alternatives as an asset class that has a certain amount of mystique. And for good reason. It is the fastest-growing category among institutional investors, and it is one that retail investors tend to look at with envy and wonder how they can get part of the action. It includes hedge funds, private equity, and special situations.

Hedge Funds

When viewed as a distinct asset class, hedge funds offer the potential of delivering absolute returns. They attract most attention in periods—such as 2000 and 2001—when equity markets lose money and investors are looking for ways to register positive returns, or at least minimize the negative returns.

The most visible are those known as "macro" and "multistrategy" funds. The former, made famous by legends in the hedge fund world like Julian Robertson and George Soros, tend to take large bets based on big macrocalls—the most illustrious being Soros's hugely successful bet against the pound sterling, the U.K.

currency, in September 1992. Multistrategy funds, which include the success stories of The Baupost Group (founded and run by Seth Klarman) and Citadel Investment Group (Ken Griffin), seek to provide investors with access to many strategies that have low correlations and high expected returns.

Beyond these two general cases, it is difficult to argue that hedge funds constitute a meaningful asset class; rather, they consist of an enlarged set of investment tools—most notably to enable investors to

- Leverage, that is, borrow money to invest in excess of 100 percent of the capital
- Short, that is, borrow instruments that are not part of the core holdings in order to bet on a fall in price
- Make liberal use of derivatives, that is, use instruments that are distinct from but linked to an underlying cash instrument and whose use requires only a partial deployment of cash
- Be innovative in the manner they look for opportunities, particularly across boundaries that separate traditional asset class classifications.

Because of this, hedge funds may be used in virtually any asset class. This can be done directly in the case of hedge funds managing both the beta and alpha components or indirectly by overlaying the hedge fund's alpha capabilities on top of a beta allocation. In principle, the latter case offers investors greater opportunities to optimize their investment implementation strategy because the hedge funds they are considering may be thought of as distinct from any particular asset class.

They go by the label of "relative value," "market neutral," and "long-short." They also enable investors to obtain exposure to the volatility of markets. Theoretically, all this allows investors to implement alpha overlays, on top of their beta exposures, the benefit of which lies in the potential to realize additional returns that are lowly correlated to the underlying asset class positioning.

Now, let me tell you a badly kept secret concerning the hedge fund industry: Many overlay strategies are hardly ever market neutral (that is, with no underlying asset class, or beta exposures). Instead, they use some beta exposures to augment efforts at realizing consistent returns from alpha positioning. The reality of this "dirty alpha" has been illustrated by the growth in the hedge fund replication industry—both research and new vehicles.[11] It confronts investors with an interesting operational dilemma: Either take comfort from the possibility that the hedge fund managers are able to "market time" the beta exposures in a profitable way, or worry about the fact that it is virtually impossible to know exactly what the underlying market exposure really is as the beta of a typical hedge fund in this space would demonstrate a certain degree of volatility over time.

Private Equity Funds

Private equity funds (including venture capital funds) are best thought of as implementers of a four-step investment model that usually plays out over a number of years:

- The fund managers seek underexploited companies operating either in the public or private domain.

- Through a mix of some cash and debt, the funds take control of the companies to enhance their operational efficiency and profitability.
- The revamped companies are sold—either in their entirety or in parts—thereby allowing the debt to be repaid and the funds to make a significant return.
- The funds return the now-augmented cash (after fees) to the investors.

Sounds simple enough, right? Well, yes and no. First, if it were really that simple, then potentially profitable opportunities would have been arbitraged away quickly. Second, the construct requires cooperative creditors willing to extend debt at reasonable terms and also willing to refinance this debt in the event that the company's restructuring takes time. Third, and most critically, the private equity funds must possess the expertise to unlock value in the companies that are purchased.

In the last few years, research has shed light on the actual experience of what has been considered a rather mysterious area. The results speak to the importance of careful investor due diligence. The most notable factor that repeatedly emerges from the research is the importance of manager selection. Consider the findings of Josh Lerner, a professor at the Harvard Business School. Lerner's work illustrates the wide dispersion in performance of private equity funds, particularly when it comes to those that are in the top quartile and those in the bottom quartile.

For the period he studied, the average difference amounted to almost 15 percentage points—that is, the representative top-quartile fund returned an extra 15 percentage points of return per year as compared to the representative fund in the bottom quartile. This is a large absolute number; and it compares to around 3 percentage points for equity mutual funds and 1 percentage point for bonds funds. Other studies support this finding, including those that cover more up-to-date periods.[12] In fact, Kaplan and Schoar's more recent work points to an even larger dispersion. And those that have looked at the average fund have often found that, after fees, it has done no better than the S&P notwithstanding the extra leverage (and, therefore, extra risk). A 2007 study done for the European Union parliament that used data from some 6,000 private equity deals points to average historical returns that were just 3 percent ahead of the S&P 500 Index before fees and some 3 percent behind per year after fees.[13]

The point of all this is a simple one: Having a general exposure to private equity is neither a necessary nor sufficient condition for obtaining superior investment results; you need to be in the right funds at the right time. The studies also suggest that it is difficult for new investors to get into the right funds. Why? Because the individual performance differences among funds are rather sticky.

Empirical analyses point to a positive relationship between performance and the sequence number of the fund (the higher the Roman numeral, the longer the track record of the fund manager); moreover, first-time funds *as a group* tend to notably underperform.[14] This is problematic for new investors because they generally have limited access to well-established successful funds.

The quantitative findings on manager performance are supported by research that looks at the private equity phenomenon from the point of view of the investors. Here again researchers have found a significant difference in performance. Endowments, which were first movers in this space, have captured consistently higher returns from the private equity asset class than have been the case for other, more recent entrants. And the picture is particularly unfavorable for the intermediaries that try to deliver the private equity asset class to "the masses." One study ranks the annual gains captured by different types of investors in the private equity space.[15] Endowments come at the top end, generating average annual *gains* of some 20 percent. At the other end, we find advisors and banks with average annual *losses* of 1 to 3 percent.

So large disparities persist at both the individual investor and private equity funds levels. They thus confirm the challenges that new entrants have in finding the right funds to generate superior investment results. Interestingly, these rather robust findings have not slowed the migration of capital to private equity. And recent surveys suggest that the migration is still expanding.

In 2007, researchers at Citigroup Global Markets surveyed about 50 chief investment officers that oversee a total of $1 trillion in assets.[16] They found that 85 percent of them were tending to raise their allocations to alternatives over the following three years, with private equity funds capturing a large bulk of the flows. And while both hedge funds and private equity funds have been projected to receive considerable capital, the former is expected to grow at half the growth rate of the latter.

This projected growth comes at a time when a growing number of investors have recognized the likely decline in future investment returns, including those on the part of the private equity industry itself. We may well look back at the last few years as constituting the golden age for private equity managers: Debt financing was abundant and cheap; investors were fighting to gain access to managers; and financial alchemy was rampant. All this suggests a greater amount of realism is warranted for investors seeking to enter this segment for the first time.

Special Situations

Think of special situations as investment opportunities that are attractive but do not fit comfortably into the categories I have covered so far, nor should they be expected to. They usually relate to two types of activities: new longer-term activities that are supported by a secular hypothesis but are yet to gain broad-based acceptance; and shorter-term activities that materialize due to sharp dislocations (especially of the market-for-lemons type) that involve significant overshoots.

Let us start with the first type. Certain institutional investors that have typically been trailblazers in this field are currently looking at increasing their involvement in such areas as water, agriculture, and carbon credits. These are believed to be long-term plays that will evolve over a number of years. They involve activities that are shifting gradually from having no focus on them to having bright spotlights pointed at them.

If the trailblazers are right, these opportunities will develop over time into stand-alone asset class categories. As such, and similar to what HMC experienced for timber, the investment returns that can be generated will be turbocharged by the growing involvement of other investors over time, thereby enhancing the first-mover advantage.

The second type of special opportunity involves activities that are fundamentally robust but have suffered from a sudden and sharp loss of investor confidence and sponsorship. In 2007 and early 2008, this involved the creation of distressed-debt funds to buy securities that had been excessively beaten up by contagion from the subprime mortgage debacle. It also entailed funds being set up to buy high-quality (agency) mortgages, bank capital and the bank loans languishing on the balance sheets of financial intermediaries that had overcommitted during the good times and had insufficient capital to sustain them.

Qualifications to Consider

Alternatives do, and should, play a role in portfolios. But they are often misunderstood. And they are certainly not simple to manage, especially if you lack the infrastructure, time, and expertise of sophisticated institutional investors. As such, they need to be approached with a certain amount of care and caution.

The first feature of alternatives worth noting up front is that not all members of the asset class fit neatly into a category or do so in a permanent fashion. This is the case for most hedge funds, which, as noted above, do not analytically constitute an asset class—they should be seen either as enhanced investment management vehicles (that is, possessing a larger set of tools for positioning portfolios) or as overlays (that is, a strategy that supplements a cash allocation to a more traditional asset class). It is also the case for some of the special opportunities that will make only a temporary appearance.

The second feature to note is that these instruments usually require a long-term commitment of capital (known as a "lock-up"). The resulting stability of capital enables investment managers to target attractive opportunities that play out over time. Indeed, this is critical for private equity, as time speaks directly to the investment approach. It is also the case for a growing number of hedge funds that are now investing in illiquid assets through what are known as "side pockets."

Accordingly, investors should accompany their allocations to illiquids with robust and prudent cash management planning. Such planning should take account of how capital calls and distributions back to investors vary with the stage of the economic cycle. Specifically, economic downturns tend to encourage managers to accelerate the capital calls (in order to use the funds to buy the cheapened assets) and to slow down the distributions back to investors (as they loathe selling existing asset holdings at depressed prices). These actions can put pressure on cash management at a time when it is also likely to be difficult to arrange bridge financing.

The third feature relates to cost: Alternatives are expensive. They usually adopt the "2 and 20 structure" (or "2/20 structure")—that is, investors pay a 2 percent management fee and 20 percent of the returns in excess of some threshold (which, for some hedge funds, is set at the ridiculously low level of zero as opposed to, at least, the rate of return on Treasury bills). This compares to more traditional actively managed vehicles that generally charge in the 0.5 to 1.5 percent range.

In its original design, the 2/20 structure aimed at establishing an optimal set of incentives for hedge funds that are aligned with those of the investors. Experience suggests that this design works but only for the subset of truly gifted hedge fund managers. In other cases, the structure can expose investors to a series of disappointing investment results, asymmetrical manager responses, and a higher downside of total loss.

With the 2/20 structure, the investor starts in the negative return category. He or she is committed to pay a 2 percent management fee regardless of how well or badly the hedge funds do. And if the 20 percent incentive fee is over zero, the investor also gives up 20 percent of the return that he or she could have gotten by investing in a risk-free instrument such as a Treasury bill. Depending on what happens in the event of losses, the structure can also encourage excessive risk taking and style drift among managers—the private sector's equivalents of moral hazard and adverse selection. (Note that, in reaction to the massive losses experienced in recent years by major banks on Wall Street and elsewhere, similar concerns are now being expressed with respect to these institutions' compensation systems.)[17]

The fourth feature pertains to the inherently fragile structure of hedge funds and, to a lesser extent, private equity vehicles. In a *Newsweek* column, I compared them to thoroughbred horses: Even those that have done extremely well in the past can suddenly stumble if the terrain changes, and with disastrous consequences.[18] After all, most of these vehicles operate with a combination of leverage, maturity mismatches, and basis risk in their hedges. And while this combination works well during the good times, it can prove to be a huge burden when the going gets tough.

Fifth, one reason hedge funds and private equities are considered "alternatives" is that their institutional identities are still evolving. Managers make it to the top because they are good portfolio managers. As their expertise is recognized and rewarded, the assets under their management grow. This poses a number of challenges to these managers. They have to invest a larger asset pool. They have to broaden their client interactions and enhance their reporting. They have to manage more staff members and therefore face a broader array of talent management issues. Not all great investors have been able to cope well with these challenges.

Those that follow hedge funds carefully, including early investors, express their concerns in the following way: What makes a hedge fund very successful also increases the temptation for its managers to transition from an *investment return* mindset to one of *asset accumulation*. Specifically, managers may be seduced by the possibility of earning a predictable 2 percent management fee on a large asset base, thereby forgetting that the basic rationale for the high 2/20 fee structure is performance.

This temptation is accentuated by the growing desire among hedge funds and private equity firms to raise more permanent capital. There are many ways to do so, ranging from securing term financing to issuing IPOs. Increasingly, alternatives that can are opting for the latter option, especially those that face a generational transition in the next few years and are yet to develop deep institutional roots and culture.

The greater the number of firms succeeding in securing permanent capital, the more intense is the pressure on others to follow suit. After all, an IPO does more that just raise capital and enable founders and other senior members of the firm to monetize part of their accumulated equity stakes. It also provides them with a market-based valuation metric, as well as a currency that can be used to incentivize junior staff. Both these factors are viewed as constituting a comparative advantage in an intensely competitive environment for talent.

Permanent capital does have considerable attractions. Indeed, as argued elsewhere in this book, it is one of the reasons why university endowments have been able to take long-term views and to do so well in terms of delivering superior investment returns. Yet the process is far from risk free when pursued by hedge funds and private equity firms. It subjects them to a whole set of new distractions. It creates an inherent conflict between the owners of the firms (the general partners, or GPs) and the investors (the limited partners, or LPs). And it requires a level of business management and expertise that can often be lacking in alternatives.

Firms that are considering the possibility of issuing an IPO to raise permanent capital are also more likely to fall into the trap of becoming asset accumulators as opposed to remaining highly focused on investment management. In part, this is due to how the stock market values different income streams. Specifically, in analyzing the range of multiples for an IPO, analysts will likely place less value on a volatile and possibly decaying stream of income (that is, the income associated with the 20 percent performance fee) as compared to a more stable stream (that is, the income associated with the 2 percent management fee).

Finally, over the next 10 years we will likely experience a rapidly blurring of the boundaries between alternatives and traditional investment vehicles. The process has already started. It is visible in the marketing of "130/30 funds," which enable the traditional investors to leverage the longs in the portfolio to 130 percent of capital while simultaneously shorting the equivalent of 30 percent of capital. It is also illustrated by the longer-term availability of indexed products that come with actively managed overlays. Indeed, by the increased use of a wider set of portfolio management tools, the financial industry will likely encourage the shift by investors to an approach that differentiates the delivery of underlying returns (beta) from true value added (alpha).

All these considerations accentuate the critical importance of good manager selection, thereby reinforcing the points made earlier. They also suggest that investors would be well advised to target a diversified set of alternative managers rather than trust their capital to a very small set of managers. Finally, they speak to why sophisticated institutional investors, such as HMC, go through the headache of establishing and maintaining internal portfolio management teams to complement the selective use of external managers (which is the so-called hybrid model).

An HMC Diversion

This final observation sets the stage for an issue that links nicely to operational challenges facing newer SWFs and that occupied a significant amount of my time at the Harvard Management Company (HMC).

When I accepted the HMC job in October 2005, we spent considerable time discussing how to best rebuild the investment capabilities of the institution. Almost a year earlier, a group of highly talented HMC staff members (including the previous CEO) had announced that they would spin off to form a new hedge fund. This constituted the sixth direct spin-off of an internal portfolio management team in HMC's history. Four of the previous five spin-offs had left Harvard to establish hedge funds in areas such as commodities, credit, and equities; and the fifth had spun off to establish a private equity fund.

The sixth spin-off had been particularly large. It involved over 30 people, including the company's CEO, chief risk officer, chief operating officer, and chief technology officer. It centered on investing activities that commanded significant risk capital and had produced stellar results for the endowment. Its immediate impact, as well as the cumulative effect of the prior five spin-offs, rendered wide open the question of HMC's institutional design going forward.

There were people who felt that HMC should shift away from the hybrid model and instead go in a direction that would rely very heavily, if not exclusively, on external managers. Some argued that HMC's repeated loss of personnel pointed to the fragility of the hybrid model. Others argued that while, relative to market realities, HMC underpaid its internal portfolio managers, the sums involved were still problematic in an academic context notwithstanding the fact that they were totally performance based. After all, you may have to explain to a Nobel Prize–winning Harvard professor that he or she earns less than a thirty/forty-something portfolio manager at HMC. And a small group argued that it was simply too difficult to convince highly talented portfolio managers to come to HMC after all the turmoil and media coverage of the departures and the compensation controversies.

The easy answer would have been for HMC to shift to an external management model. By outsourcing the management of the university's funds, we would be required simply to sit back and have external managers present their expertise in what industry observers label "beauty contests." By abandoning the hybrid model in favor of overwhelming reliance on external managers, we would also "solve" future compensation controversies—not by lowering the cost of managing the endowment but rather by obfuscating it.

It generally costs at least twice as much to manage a dollar outside HMC as it costs to do it internally by relying on its own portfolio management expertise. But this significant difference is obfuscated by the reporting practices of the industry. In the case of external managers, the costs are essentially netted from the returns that are delivered to HMC. However, in the case of the internal management platforms, the costs are disclosed as compensation and thus attract considerable attention in the media.

The deeper we went into it, the clearer it became that the *easy* thing to do was not the *right* thing to do. Cost was not the only issue. There were other reasons (of both the positive and negative varieties) that led us to embark on a successful 18-month effort to establish an internal portfolio management platform consisting of five fully functioning teams populated by highly talented professionals with strong track records and experience.

At the most basic level, we realized that shifting to heavy, if not exclusive, dependence on external managers would partly negate the potent return potential associated with Harvard's structural advantages. These advantages emanate from its privileged capital attributes—namely, the permanency of the funds, the predictable nature of annual distributions to the university, the hardwiring of a long-term investment orientation, and the backing of a triple-A balance sheet.

Harvard Management Company's capital attributes are the analytical equivalence of a permanent and patient capital pool. These attributes cannot be outsourced easily or fully to external managers, especially in today's world. Consider the investment dollar that goes from being managed internally at HMC to being managed by an external investor. And assume for now that the level of expertise is the same in both cases. The capital context changes significantly. Few external managers end up adopting a truly long-term investment orientation, and the few that do so with enormous success are generally closed to new investors and significant new capital.

Despite many external managers' stated intentions, they end up heavily influenced by short-term considerations. At the macrolevel, this is highlighted in repeated observations of "herd behavior." The behavior is apparent from the analysis of the periodic high correlation among hedge fund beta (position sensitivity) exposures to key market indicators. It is also apparent in the effort that is being made to come up with cheaper replicating vehicles, be they index funds or hedge fund replication methodologies.

There are many reasons that account for this outcome. Some involve human considerations, including those elucidated 70 years ago by John Maynard Keynes in Chapter 12 of the *General Theory*. Indeed, Keynes's insights have stimulated quite a bit of work that shows how herd behavior that "is inefficient from a social standpoint . . . can be rational from the perspective of managers who are concerned about their reputations in the labor market."[19] Others relate to business strategies, including the need to safeguard against client redemptions. And yet others are heavily influenced, if not driven by a common practice in the financial industry and media: that of comparing hedge fund returns on a high-frequency—monthly or quarterly—basis.

There are other considerations. In exiting the HMC door to an external manager in the hedge fund space, Harvard's investment dollar goes from being backed by a triple-A balance sheet to, most of the time, what would be a triple-B balance sheet. Given the higher funding costs for a triple-B investment vehicle, this immediately eats away at Harvard's investment returns. It also increases the probability *and* severity of losses induced by a sudden stop in market liquidity.

Such losses were seen in July 2007 when one of HMC's spin-offs, Sowood Capital Management, failed. This did not reflect inherently bad trades on the part of Sowood. Rather, the hedge fund was unable to secure sufficient liquidity to keep the trades on during the market and liquidity turmoil of that summer. It is commonly agreed that these trades could have been sustained at HMC given the institution's privileged capital attributes.

There is also the issue of transparency. Some external managers, particularly in the hedge fund space, jealously guard the confidentiality of their positioning. They worry that disclosure would undermine their competitive edge. While this is generally understandable, the practice of limiting the disclosure of information to investors has gotten well beyond what is sensible and defensible. Indeed, in some cases, it raises important questions for the fulfillment of the fiduciary responsibilities of investors. It can also seriously pull the legs out from under an effective risk management practice.

Finally, the internal portfolio management platform provides HMC with significant positive externalities. Most importantly, it allows the institution to design and implement effectively sophisticated risk mitigation strategies that rely on a broad array of market tools and approaches. The positive externalities were evident in the way in which HMC successfully navigated phases of market turmoil, using a combination of asset allocation adjustments, overlay strategies, and tail insurance programs. As I will discuss in Chapter 8, this consideration assumes added importance given the expectation for the bumpy journey to the new secular destination.

These are the basic reasons that led HMC to rebuild an internal portfolio management platform. They speak to positive reasons for doing so—reasons that safeguard and exploit the institution's capital attributes and its structural edge. However, while this drove the process, we were also aware of a "negative" consideration: Given the size of Harvard's endowment ($25.9 billion in June 2005 and $34.9 billion in June 2007),[20] it was unlikely that Harvard would be able to find sufficient capacity among the best-in-breed external managers. Indeed, it is a well-accepted fact that finding the right capacity among managers is hard; and where significant capacity is on offer, it is usually because the manager is not particularly skilled or lacks a meaningful track record.

Having decided to rebuild an internal portfolio management platform, we faced the challenge of convincing great investors to come and work at HMC for less than what they would earn elsewhere, and to do so without the possibility of the significant upside that comes with an equity options program. They could also be subject to the possibility of being among the five individuals (along with the CEO) whose compensations would be disclosed in the context of an annual exercise that attracts substantial media interest.[21]

I used to tell those interviewing for portfolio management jobs that the public disclosure of compensation potentially confronted them with a lose-lose situation: If they made it to the list of top earners at HMC, people would read specifics about their compensation in the press; and if they did not make it on the list, people would know that they were not one of the top investment performers at HMC!

Despite all this, HMC had little difficulty in hiring talented professionals with prior standing in the industry. They came to Harvard for three main reasons. First, they believed in the mission of the institution, which is to support research, student aid, and teaching at a top-ranked university that has significant global reach and provides a public good. Second, they were attracted by the possibility of a virtually pure investment job that has no marketing requirements, a single client, and privileged capital characteristics. Third, the breadth of the experience and contacts provided them with important options, which, in the past, had been illustrated by the ability of the six spin-offs to raise significant capital from a wide variety of investors.[22]

Time will tell whether HMC's internal portfolio management platform will prove sustainable. In the meantime, it is important to stress that having a strong internal portfolio management platform does not equate to doing all the investments internally. There are many activities that are outside the skill set of the small group of talented professionals that work at HMC. These activities are best tapped using external managers that specialize in them. Indeed, it is this combination—of inside and outside portfolio management expertise—that makes the hybrid model so powerful.

In this context, HMC made an important hire by bringing Mark Taborsky in the summer of 2006 from the Stanford endowment to HMC. In just a year, Mark and his team revamped HMC's external manager relationships, albeit with some constraints on account of existing lock-ups. This was done to ensure that HMC was investing with the best external managers and to align this risk capital allocation with the secular investment themes of the institution. In the process, Mark's team worked with colleagues in analytics and operations to enhance the monitoring of the stable of external managers.

A Forward-Looking Qualifier

So far, I have focused on asset class classifications in building a diversified portfolio that can capture the upside of the projected secular destination while simultaneously taking into account what is likely to be a bumpy journey. This is the approach that dominates the industry, and, as such, it is the easiest to implement. But it is also an approach that will come under pressure in the years ahead and that will require some bright minds to come up with enhancements.

Anyone who traffics frequently in this world will tell you that the specification of appropriate asset allocations inevitably involves a mix of science and art. Those that get into the details of these exercises will tell you that the balance has shifted significantly in the last few years away from science and toward art (also known as "judgment" and "gut feel" or, if you wish to be less charitable, "guesstimates"). This is due to several factors: Traditional boundaries between asset classes are blurring; correlations are increasing; and when not linked by fundamentals, asset classes get connected by technical factors, including the "common ownership" of investors.

So why has the industry persisted in using an approach that has become less robust over time? It has done so for negative rather than positive reasons. Specifically, we have yet to come up with a better alternative.

The most promising ongoing work in this area goes one step earlier in the return generation chain. Rather than look at asset classes, this approach starts with the risk factors that give rise to investment returns over time. Put another way, it looks at why investors are paid for allocating their capital in a certain way.

The ideal situation is to come up with a small set (three to five) of distinct (and ideally orthogonal) risk factors that command a risk premium. The next step is to assess the stability of the factors and how they can be best captured through the use of tradable instruments. This provides for a portfolio optimization process whereby the factors are combined in a manner that speaks directly to the investors' return objective and risk tolerance. The end product is a more robust and time-consistent combination of asset classes that map clearly to the underlying factors.

Having been involved in some initial work on this approach at HMC that drew heavily on expertise at the university (particularly, John Campbell and Jakub Jurek) and subsequent work at PIMCO (led by Jamil Baz and Vineer Bhansali), I can tell you that it is hard. Conceptualizing the approach is one thing; coming up with answers is a completely different thing! Yet it's a very worthwhile effort as even partial progress is valuable.

Success here involves coming up with a new method that bypasses many of the limitations of the traditional approach. This would shift the balance back toward more robust science, and it would allow investors to better capture risk premiums in a more efficient and sustainable manner. Partial success is coming up with a methodology that enables an investor to better check the consistency of his or her current approach, including whether the selected asset classes provide an efficient mix of risk premiums.

CHAPTER 7

AN ACTION PLAN FOR NATIONAL POLICY MAKERS AND GLOBAL INSTITUTIONS

T he types of sound investor positioning and execution discussed in the previous chapter are certainly *necessary* to ensure sound risk-adjusted returns going forward, but they are not *sufficient*. Investors must also understand and incorporate the likely behavior of others that influence markets and asset prices through their actions, words, and intentions (including the possibility that others will make mistakes). This is particularly so for national and multilateral policy makers whose key challenge is to find a way to efficiently accommodate the ongoing secular structural transformations.

As I discussed earlier, these transformations have a way of weakening the effectiveness of traditional policy approaches and instruments, and they tend to erode the information content of traditional economic and financial indicators. Moreover, while their net impact is unambiguously favorable for the global economy, not all components benefit equally.

There are winners and losers, both in an absolute and in a relative sense—across countries and within individual countries.

To help identify the components of an action plan for national governments, the following sections detail the primary focal points. Of course, any suggestions must take into account the particular circumstances of each country. As such, the details will vary from country to country. Nevertheless, the general discussion serves an important function in identifying the areas that, at the very least, need serious deliberations and thus require investor monitoring.

There is a natural temptation to focus on the areas that constitute potential downsides for national economies around the world. After all, they attract the most immediate attention, often in a loud fashion. Yet remember the wise words of the policy maker back in the mid-1990s who alerted me that managing success can be as difficult as managing a crisis. This is particularly true for emerging markets that lack institutional robustness, policy experience, and timely policy-relevant information. Accordingly, this chapter looks at both types of policy challenges—those that face segments of the population that are potentially worse off and those that are potentially better off.

Understanding the New Financial Landscape

As Bill Gross noted in one of his *Investment Outlooks*, "The modern financial complex has morphed into something unrecognizable to many astute market veterans and academics."[1] In addition, and while regulators and politicians will be playing catch-up, there is no reason to expect a reversal of this complexity in the years ahead. Therefore, governments will need to develop a better understanding of the new realities of the financial system and respond accordingly.

In order to gain this insight, financial authorities need to be better plugged into day-to-day market developments. The Federal Reserve Bank of New York is the leader in this regard, maintaining close (formal and informal) contacts with markets. The ability of other countries to do the same—and that of the United Kingdom in particular—has been inadvertently hindered by the move to separate bank supervisory activities from the institutions that are conducting monetary policy.

The separation was originally motivated by concerns that monetary policy actions could be contaminated by considerations that pertain to bank supervision and regulations. Yet, with the growth of "endogenous liquidity" and the related phenomenon of a "shadow banking system," this separation now serves to inhibit rather than facilitate the conduct of good monetary policy. As such, I suspect that the trend will be reversed over time, or at least it will be complemented by much better coordination and information exchange among those conducting monetary policy and those safeguarding financial stability.

The financial authorities will also have to improve their ability to conduct appropriate oversight on activities that have migrated outside sophisticated jurisdictions. In the case of national supervisory and regulatory bodies, this involves gaining a better handle on off-balance-sheet activities and other forms of financial alchemy and regulatory arbitrage. It will also entail retooling the bodies overseeing areas that have assumed either quasi- or full capital market characteristics yet are still subject to backward-looking regulatory and supervisory approaches (for example, the insurance and mortgage areas). Finally, either through moral suasion or more direct methods, the fiduciaries of various investment vehicles will have to develop stronger expertise and more robust oversight modalities. This is particularly the case for vehicles that may involve some type of contingent liability for public finances (such as pension funds).

Dealing with Capital Inflows

How to respond to the change in the external payments regime—that is, from being a debtor to becoming a creditor—constitutes one of the biggest challenges of managing success. This is particularly true when it comes to managing surges in capital inflows.

As I discussed earlier, sustained capital inflows can benefit economies in a number of ways. They help better channel resources to underfunded activities, thereby facilitating productivity growth, output expansion, and employment gains. Having said that, I have also argued that in addition to pressuring the bank supervision framework, the inflows confront policy makers with a new set of complex economic questions—including how to counter the adverse impact on inflation, how to ensure an orderly evolution of the real exchange rate, and how to avoid an ultimately costly erosion in discipline in the financial sector.

There are no easy answers to how best to manage this new regime. Indeed, repeated attempts to use a targeted approach—

typically some type of capital controls—have proven to have limited long-term effectiveness and have entailed collateral damage. Instead, the key lies in pursuing appropriate macroeconomic policies—particularly a prudent fiscal stance that is well coordinated with the stance of monetary and exchange rate policies. Such macropolicies can be effective in navigating through the surge in capital inflows, especially if accompanied by steps to ensure that public and private institutions are managed for long-term success and handling counterpart funds well.

This rather lame policy conclusion may well disappoint those who are looking for some magic solution to the management of large capital inflows. Unfortunately, there is no such solution that I am aware of. Indeed, a comprehensive study that recently analyzed over 100 episodes of surges in capital inflows in advanced and emerging economies since 1987 was unable to add much to the debate.[2] Consistent with previous research in the area, this study raised questions about the effectiveness of capital controls and the long-term sustainability of intervention. It also reinforced a boring but important point: The best way to minimize the potentially disruptive impact of heavy capital inflows is to maintain the right degree of fiscal responsibility. This can help counter excessive aggregate demand pressures and limit the real appreciation of the currency, thereby enhancing the possibility of a soft landing.

This rather boring point is particularly important for investors looking to expand their activities in emerging economies (and consistent with our secular themes). They are well advised to keep an eye on how the countries' fiscal stance is evolving in the context of the large capital inflows. This includes not only the overall fiscal numbers but also the composition of expenditures (particularly the balance between consumption and investment, particularly in infrastructure).

Evidence of fiscal responsibility signals a certain amount of sophistication on the part of the policy makers in "managing success," as does the ability to adapt supervision and regulation. By contrast, indications of highly procyclical budgets—and, in particular, large expenditure growth coinciding with heavy capital inflows—would tend to increase the probability of eventual financial market instability and large exchange rate fluctuations, especially if accompanied by lax financial system supervision.

Managing National Wealth

At a conference in Washington, D.C., Ted Truman formulated a policy question in the following way: "Once they are there, what does a country do with them?"[3] His remark referred to the large international reserve holdings accumulated by China and other emerging economies. It applies equally to the large liabilities that have been accumulated in recent years by countries such as the United States—an issue that I address in the next section.

In the new secular destination, emerging economies must be able to manage their large and growing financial wealth in a commercially oriented manner that is consistent with their longer-term economic and social aspirations. And they must do so subject to strict governance and operational control standards.

This is not just a national obligation toward current and future generations; it is also required in order to minimize the growing risk of protectionist measures that inhibit the flow of capital across geographic and product boundaries. Indeed, it is the only effective way to counter a debate on sovereign wealth funds (SWFs) that is being heavily influenced by incomplete analysis, ill-defined concepts of national security and reciprocity, and monsterlike characterizations of motives pertaining to political, military, and mercantilist issues.[4]

The focus of the institutional effort should be on governance, investment process, and risk management.[5] The importance of such a focus is driven by more than just the benefits of better informing a public policy debate. With time, SWFs will shift from being important sources of temporary and permanent capital for alternative fund managers to being more important competitors. As such, SWF scrutiny will likely increase and broaden.

The *governance structure* should separate the political ownership of the SWF from operational issues, and it should subject it to the required level of checks and balances. This involves a clear delineation of authority and autonomy, enhanced reporting, and a solid control framework (that includes internal compliance). It should be supported by clear investment objectives (absolute return targets as well as criteria pertaining to institutional and peer bogeys); modalities governing the list of restricted investments and activities; the specification of the risk parameters applicable to the pool of assets being managed by the SWF as a whole; and the appropriate delegation of day-to-day investment management to the management and staff of the institution.

Governments will have objectives that go beyond investment returns. In this regard, they are similar to universities that wish to use part of their wealth to seed particular internal activities or fund campus expansion. Indeed, the point is not whether such objectives should be pursued. The point is that they are best pursued outside the purview of SWFs and thus subjected to the appropriate oversight and transparency. In the absence of such segmentation, there is a material risk that these objectives will operationally (and otherwise) contaminate the activities, effectiveness, and standing of the SWFs.

This consideration is similar to one of the points that has emerged from the extensive literature on the effectiveness of aid given by industrial countries. A meaningful part of such aid was motivated by political and military considerations rather than social ones. Thus the deployment mechanisms for the social considerations, including appropriate targeting and monitoring, were severely hindered when they were also used for the political and military considerations.

The *investment process* should be clear as to how the "neutral asset mix" is determined, consistent with the national return objective and risk tolerance. The process should seek to maximize the use of the structural advantages of the SWFs (their "edge"), particularly their status as managing "privileged and patient capital"—that is, capital that is not subject to short-term redemption, has predictable distributions (if any), and is encouraged to pursue long-term opportunities. In doing so, it should be clear about how it will choose the appropriate investment vehicles, including the mix between the capital managed by internal portfolio managers and that allocated to third-party (external) managers.

The *risk management process* should be governed by the macro risk parameters and anchored by a clear identification of risk-mitigating instruments. It involves the constant updating of risk scenarios and a methodology (include scenario analyses) to shed light on potential market disruptions that long-term investors may face.

Some of the long-established SWFs—such as those in Abu Dhabi, Kuwait, Norway, and Singapore—are already there or very close. Some of the newer ones are trying to get there, such as in the case of those formed recently by China, South Korea, and Russia. Yet, as discussed earlier, there is a general misunderstanding in certain industrial country quarters of the actual and systemic role of these SWFs—a misunderstanding that is fueling the risk of protectionism. In the process, industrial countries risk imposing (de facto or de jure) capital controls that are not only distortive but also should be redundant given existing mechanisms and regulatory agencies aimed at safeguarding the national interest.[6]

Interestingly, the mere threat by industrial countries of introducing such controls could result in an outcome that is detrimental to their own interests. After all, the threat could inhibit the process of asset diversification that the SWFs are, and should be, embarking on. The result of this would be a greater probability that the type of capital markets aberrations that were detailed earlier in this book would reemerge, including a new round of relative risk mispricing in U.S. markets. This would encourage a line-up of activities that could raise the likelihood of subsequent episodes of liquidity sudden stops and market turmoil.

The threat could also lead SWFs to an excessive reliance on third-party investment managers in industrial countries, some of which are subject to a higher degree of nontransparency (for example, hedge funds) and may not be able to efficiently deal with the size of the assets involved. The result could well be a higher systemic risk of market disruptions and institutional dislocations.

These considerations suggest that a greater degree of rationality should anchor SWF discussions in industrial countries than is presently the case. However, while this is desirable, it runs counter to some domestic political considerations (as do, for example, well-established arguments for trade liberalization). Indeed, if for this reason alone, the SWFs should consider how best to disseminate to the public more information about their investment philosophy and process, as well as their institutional governance.

Similar considerations while I was at Harvard—that is, those involving a lack of understanding on the part of the public of how HMC manages the university's endowment and why—played a role in our decision to launch an HMC Web site to supplement the information contained in the annual release of the "John Harvard Letter" and the university's financial statement. The Web site tries to strike the appropriate balance between providing information on investment activities and preserving the competitive positioning of the endowment. As such, the focus is on governance, investment process, investment performance, institutional structure, and relations with the university. It does not detail HMC's individual investment strategies and its holdings. As such, it does not place HMC at a competitive disadvantage.

Dealing with High National Debt

The new secular destination is one in which the United States will be gradually working off its financial excesses. Specifically, the country's large current account deficit will be adjusting in the context of the anticipated domestic growth differentials and exchange rate realignments. This will stop an aggravation in the already high level of liabilities, but it will not provide an immediate solution.

The liabilities are concentrated in the household and government sectors within the United States, with the counterpart being large foreign holdings of U.S. assets (particularly fixed-income instruments). Indeed, the new secular destination will require something that goes well beyond the past approach of relying (1) on price appreciation in the housing sector to keep the household sector afloat and (2) on the depth and liquidity of the U.S. financial markets, as well as the reserve currency status of the dollar, to maintain the buying interest of the rest of the world.

Within the United States, we should expect to see a significant shift toward better liability management by households—directly and on their behalf by entities that have recently been overly generous with loan extensions. With regard to the former (and more orderly) alternative, households will be offered further means to manage liabilities through the use of expanded products, including various forms of insurance. In the case of the latter (less orderly) option, lending standards will likely be tightened and will include better assessments of income suitabilities and collateral values. Both carry the risk of accentuating the likely slowdown in the U.S. economy, in absolute terms (that is, a period of subpar growth) and relative to other countries and global averages.

As the balance-of-payments situation in the United States improves, the government will be faced with a larger set of trade-offs in managing its liabilities. Specifically, choices will have to be made between the three basic objectives of debt management: maintaining a predictable and stable issuance policy; ensuring adequate liquidity for individual debt issues; and establishing a balanced yield curve (that is, with appropriate issuance throughout the major benchmark maturities).

In this manner, the debt management policy performs a much-needed public-good function by providing important anchors for financial markets at large. This effect is most evident in the availability of robust benchmarks against which other instruments can be priced—for example, for instruments that vary relative to U.S. government paper in terms of credit and liquidity risk and that play an important role in greasing the wheels of industry and commerce.

In past episodes when such choices have arisen, the U.S. government has consulted appropriately with domestic market participants. One channel for this is the Treasury Borrowing Advisory Committee (TBAC) on which I had the privilege to serve.

The Web site of the U.S. Treasury explains that this is "an advisory committee governed by federal statute that meets quarterly with the Treasury Department. The Borrowing Committee's membership is comprised of senior representatives from investment funds and banks. The Borrowing Committee presents their observations to the Treasury Department on the overall strength of the U.S. economy as well as providing recommendations on a variety of technical debt management issues."[7] The committee meets on a quarterly basis, and the minutes of the discussions and the background material are posted on the U.S. Treasury's Web site.

Increasingly, such consultations may well have to go beyond domestic holders of U.S. government debt. It is likely and desirable that foreign holders will also need to be consulted in some regular manner. Accordingly, given potential political sensitivities on Capitol Hill and beyond, it is important for the government to initiate and maintain a briefing process that explains why such consultations are in the national interest of the United States.

Conducting Monetary Policy

One of the trickiest elements of the national action plan is how best to conduct monetary policy in a world in which "endogenous liquidity" and asset prices can (and do) impact real economic activity. There is simply no easy answer. What is clear is that the current approach—typified most clearly by the Federal Reserve's actions—will need to evolve in the years ahead.

Some of you may think that my view is being driven by the heated debate out there about "moral hazard." Indeed, a lot has been said and written about the dilemma that the monetary authorities face when reacting to market disruptions that can undermine the real economy. Should they allow market discipline to chasten those that have made bad investment decisions, regardless of the extent of collateral damage; or should they bail out these investors for the sake of protecting the rest of the system?

I will spend more time on this interesting debate in Chapter 8. For now, suffice it to say that it is unlikely to be resolved fully any time soon. Even if you get sufficient agreement on the middle ground—that is, that moral hazard considerations do not translate into "no intervention" but rather "highly limited and focused intervention"—you are unlikely to get agreement on policy instruments that allow that outcome. Specifically, as a former senior G-7 policy maker remarked at a recent gathering over lunch, the basic problem is not a conceptual one; it is an operational one. We are yet to find refined enough instruments that allow policy makers to distinguish adequately between "the good guys and the bad guys."

Consistent with this view, the outlook for the conduct of monetary policy is not really about how the moral hazard issue will be addressed. Rather, it relates to other considerations that will likely result in a change in what has become an excessive dependence on the federal funds rate as *the* instrument of monetary policy.

The impact of this instrument has been eroded by the important transformations that have taken place in the global economic and financial systems. As such, it no longer offers the degree of effectiveness needed to moderate sharp expansions and reductions in endogenous liquidity. With asset prices playing a larger role in impacting domestic demand (through the combination of securitization, credit variation, and the wealth effect), the impact of any given change in the federal funds rate has lessened when it comes to meeting the dual mandate of encouraging economic growth while maintaining low rates of inflation.

Fortunately this policy challenge is coming at a good time. The Federal Reserve is embarking on a comprehensive analysis of its approach. The current focus at this point is said to be on the potential role of inflation targeting and on the appropriate level of transparency and public communication. It is likely that this focus will expand to include a review of the appropriate tools of monetary policy. Within this, we should expect the continued use of the fed funds rate to be accompanied by a revamping of the discount window, the expanded use of open market operations (through changes in maturity terms and collateral terms), and better regulatory and supervisory coordination.

The problem facing the Federal Reserve is amplified when we look at emerging economies. Some, like China, are still in the process of shifting from direct instruments of monetary control to indirect instruments that operate through market channels. In the process, they have to develop the needed infrastructure and be willing to give up on a notion of control. Others, such as Brazil and Russia, have shifted but will need to continue to gain credibility on both the domestic and international front. Yet others, such as Mexico and South Africa, are reaping the benefits of the significant institutional progress they have made in recent years.

In continuing to develop their domestic monetary policy framework, most countries, and particularly for those with small open economies, will also have to find ways to take into account the impact of international issues. Recall in this regard the graph in Figure 2.3 showing how the exchange rate of the New Zealand dollar appreciated strongly notwithstanding the fact that the country ran a sizable current account deficit and the minister of finance questioned the "rationality" of those looking to gain local currency exposure! Iceland experienced a similar situation when it registered capital inflows that exceeded the country's GDP.

In these cases, the cross-border flows are responding to more than just the conduct of policies in each of the countries. They are also responding to how these policies compare across a very large set of countries. Moreover, any single country can—and many have—experience significant changes in domestic financial conditions on account *solely* of things happening outside its borders. This accentuates the importance for any individual central bank of understanding how the country fits in a global financial system that is increasingly integrated and interdependent.

These observations speak to a broader point that is yet to be fully internalized by both industrial and emerging economies. As their systemic importance grows, several emerging countries will be forced into a transition that sees them having to spend more time thinking about global considerations when setting domestic policy agendas. At times, they may need to subordinate short-term domestic interests for longer-term global welfare. Indeed, it is not just a question of whether "the world is flat," to use the phrase coined by Tom Friedman in his enjoyable book that carries this title; for these countries, the world now seems upside down.[8]

As yet, and despite their growing economic and financial heft, these countries have not been forced to confront this. In large part this is because of the refusal of industrial countries to welcome them properly into existing multilateral policy coordination mechanisms—an issue that I will return to shortly.

Investors are well advised to keep these topics front and center on their radar screens. They speak directly to the ability of markets to minimize very wide technical fluctuations occasioned by the current asymmetry between the role of endogenous liquidity and official monetary actions, as well as the relative openness of economies to developments elsewhere in the world.

Income Inequality and Social Policy

Given the nature of the ongoing structural transformations, the new secular destination will involve winners and losers around the world and within individual countries. Most of the losers will suffer a relative loss (that is, relative to their initial conditions, they will not gain as much as others); but some may also face the prospect of an absolute loss.

More generally, the upcoming changes will likely reinforce—and will certainly not reverse—what is a growing analytical consensus on how incomes have evolved in recent years. Three elements are increasingly evident from research that is slowly overcoming long-standing data limitations in this area:

- First, the majority of countries around the world have experienced significant growth in per capita income in recent years (when the evaluation is conducted at the level of the population *as a whole*).
- Second, this growth has facilitated a significant reduction in the number of people living under the poverty line, led by impressive gains in China and India.

- Third, when the analysis shifts to looking at income groups *within countries*, many economies have experienced an increase in income inequality. This appears to be particularly the case for middle- and high-income countries.

So the vast majority of people are better off in the world with the important qualification that, within most countries, those that are already well off are gaining at a better rate than the poor. This poses an interesting issue for governments: Should they focus on the absolute or on the relative?

There is no easy answer if the question is posed in terms of a trade-off between the two. Significant growth in a country's absolute income has been shown to provide the best opportunity for decisively reducing the incidence of poverty and for protecting the most vulnerable segments of the population. Yet, if this is accompanied by a notable increase in income inequality (because the rich are benefiting at a greater rate), the sustainability of the process will increasingly come under pressure.

Evidence of this is starting to multiply. In industrial countries, it takes the form of increased protectionist pressure and selective political repugnance at some of the fortunes that are being made. In emerging economies, it takes the form of isolated protests by vulnerable groups, such as the protests that have taken place recently in Brazil, China, India, and Mexico. It also feeds resurgent populist movements. And all this comes at a time of significant increases in the prices of consumer staples, including bread and rice.

Recent research suggests that it is both unhelpful and unnecessary to pose the question as one involving a trade-off between absolute and relative prosperity. Specifically, by looking at the contributors to the recent rise in inequality, researchers are also shedding light on policy actions that can better align absolute and relative considerations. And their conclusions are intuitively appealing.

A lot has been written about the drivers of recent income trends.[9] Fortunately, this is an area in which research has been cumulative, and it has been well served by concurrent efforts to strengthen the raw data used for empirical analyses. As a result, the most recent studies have been able to shed important light on the main contributors to the growing inequality in the context of the generalized global increase in incomes.

Consider the work undertaken by economists at the IMF and published in October 2007. Using recently upgraded data, they found that the major contributor to inequality around the world has been technological progress. Indeed, this factor alone "explains most of the . . . increase . . . from the early 1980s."[10] Why? Because technology "increases the premium on skills and automates relatively low skill inputs,"[11] thereby benefiting those who are already better off and displacing those that are already worse off.

Interestingly, globalization as a whole is found to have an offsetting impact on inequality. On the one hand, the trade channel reduces inequality as it enhances the demand for labor in developing countries and facilitates for some the shift out of an overcrowded agricultural sector. On the other hand, the financial channel increases inequality as it speaks directly to those in developing countries that start with sufficient wealth and income to participate in the process of financial integration.

Given these findings, governments have yet another reason to increase spending on the social sectors, particularly education and health. While the details will inevitably vary from country to country, it is unambiguous that this can serve to broaden the segments of the population that can benefit from technological progress by enhancing skill acquisition, expanding training, and making access to education and health care easier and more effective. This would also allow the benefits of globalization to accrue to larger segments of the population, therefore countering some of the resistance that is now being felt in a growing number of countries around the world. In the process, governments would make further progress in meeting an important social welfare objective that has merit on a stand-alone basis.

An Action Plan for Multilateral Institutions

I argued in Chapter 5 that multilateral institutions face the most difficult adjustment challenges. Given their quasi-universal membership, their government ownership structure embodies the widest set of actual and potential conflicts in a changing world. Those who are empowered by the structural transformations coexist with those who have something to lose. Moreover, given the ... .ture of the ongoing transformations, those who face potential losses start with a high level of historical entitlements that have been hardwired into the structure of the institutions—through skewed voting rights, unbalanced representation in the executive boards, monopolies over key positions in management and staff, and so on. And while these entitlements—or as the French elegantly say, *"les droits de seigneur"* (or the lord's entitlements)—made some sense in the world of yesteryears, they openly conflict with the realities of today's world and the prospects for tomorrow.

The question is not *whether* and *how* the multilateral institutions should adjust. Virtually everyone iterates to a similar conclusion on this, including the leaders of the IMF and the World Bank (Messrs. Dominique Strauss-Kahn and Bob Zoellick). The question is, can they do it? The need for adjustments is most extreme in the case of the IMF, an institution that has gone from being seen as the lynchpin in the complex of multilateral institutions to being questioned almost on a daily basis about its relevance, effectiveness, and standing.

The Public Debate

Much of the public debate on the role of the IMF has been on what it no longer does. Recall Chapter 2's reference to the statements made by various public and private sector officials. Gone are the days when the IMF would run to the rescue of countries, providing them emergency assistance in exchange for agreement on comprehensive adjustment and reform measures (the technical term being "conditionality"). Gone is the time when markets would follow extremely carefully every signal coming out of the IMF and position portfolios accordingly.

The major reason for this change is that the vast majority of emerging economies no longer need IMF financial support. Indeed, with high and increasing international reserves, they have not only stopped borrowing from the fund but most have also repaid past loans ahead of schedules. Indeed, if it were not for Turkey, the IMF would essentially be out of the business of lending to most categories of developing countries.

I argued earlier that this change has had dramatic implications for the institution. It robs the IMF from its major source of revenue used to fund its operating budget: the difference between the cost of its funding and what it charges to its borrowers. It reduces the influence of the institution since countries no longer have to engage it in delicate policy discussions that, in the past, included quarterly performance targets and other policy conditionality. It renders obsolete a whole institutional structure that assumes that the IMF's lending business remains relevant.

Now here is the rub: As long as the IMF debate focuses on these legacy issues without updating the overall analytical framework, the outcome will be a rather blunt and ineffective slimming down of the organization. Indeed, absent the reemergence of emerging market crises (which is my book's baseline scenario), its future will be dominated by repeated actions to cut internal expenditures, attempts to counter the inevitable deterioration of internal staff morale, and disappointing use of one of the most qualified (and rapidly eroding) group of economists residing under any single institutional roof.

This would not be a major issue were it not for the arguments detailed in this book that speak to the importance of having a strong and credible multilateral mechanism at the center of the international economic and financial system. Such a mechanism can help address the list of cross-border challenges embodied in phenomena such as the large global payments imbalances, various cross-country hand-offs, inconclusive debates about exchange rate misalignments, unfair characterizations of the motives of the SWFs, and persistent trade protectionist pressures. These challenges can be addressed only through a common understanding of the issues, a degree of cross-border policy coordination, and a minimum level of assurances that national policy makers will consider international factors when taking certain policy actions.

I have argued in this book that there is a lot at stake for the global economy. Indeed, it is not whether the international system will ultimately adjust to the ongoing structural transformations and the new secular realities. It will. It is whether it will do so in a way consistent with the maintenance of high global growth, the continued containment of inflation, and the minimizing of the risk that disruptive financial turmoil will occur and reoccur.

As I noted in Chapter 2, institutions like the IMF start with the best set of structural attributes to play a constructive role, at least in theory. For the IMF to now be able to step up to the plate, it must shift the public debate away from what it no longer does and direct it toward its other three important functions. It can do so in the following ways:

- First, it can access its internal expertise and its ability to look into the experiences of many countries, and in so doing, it can perform the role of "knowledgeable trusted advisor" for countries that are facing new policy challenges on account of the ongoing structural transformations.
- Second, the IMF can supplement its policy interactions with countries by providing them focused and highly specialized technical assistance that draws from its own internal resources as well as those of member countries.
- Third, the IMF can help impart the much-needed multilateral dimension to those national policy actions that can be effective only if implemented in an internationally consistent manner.

To have any chance of convincing a skeptical world, the IMF needs to enhance its own expertise and operating modalities. It then has to position and market its services as part of the response to the new secular global realities. Finally, it needs to do so in the context of strong leadership.

The Reform Agenda

There is little disagreement on the needed enhancement of the IMF. Indeed, a common set of issues has emerged from the work done by the institution itself (as illustrated by the *Managing Director's Medium-Term Reform Strategy*),[12] the reports of committees (such as that of the recent Crockett and McDonough committees),[13] and the views of observers and practitioners (as demonstrated by the volume prepared at the Peterson Institute for International Economics).[14] These include the need to accomplish the following:

- Retool the internal staff expertise to ensure that the traditional focus on economic issues is adequately complemented by a good understanding of the manner in which increasingly complex financial markets behave and influence the real economy.
- Alter internal modalities so that the IMF's country missions respond to the actual challenges facing member countries as opposed to imposing a discussion agenda that is driven by more narrow and inevitably dogmatic headquarter-based views.
- Strengthen the analytical standing of the institution so that it is able to engage credibly in sensitive national pol-

icy issues that require reconciliation at the global level, such as the surveillance of exchange rate policies.

- Develop a more robust internal income model that diversifies the sources of revenues and links them to the range of activities of the institution.
- Adequately budget and price where appropriate the services that the IMF is providing, and do so within the context of a more transparent system of cross-taxation and subsidization.
- Remove feudal practices that reserve key management and staff positions for certain industrial country nationalities.
- Allocate voting power and board representation on the basis of today's realities rather than those of the outmoded past.

This is quite an agenda, in terms of both the number of items and the manner in which they speak to altering historic entitlements. Moreover, certain changes require amendments to the IMF's articles of agreement, and obtaining those amendments is a multiyear process that involves approvals by individual member countries at the level of their national political institutions (that is, executive and legislative branches).

The Vision Thing

Understandably, the temptation is to pursue the agenda in a sequential manner. Indeed, that is the approach that was being adopted in 2007 when I was writing this book. Unfortunately, such an approach is unlikely to result in meaningful reform progress.

Each item is inevitably subject to negotiations and compromises among member countries. Unless the negotiators believe in a "grand bargain," or what I called elsewhere "a critical mass,"[15] they will pursue individual positions that have little chance of striking the correct macrolevel trade-offs. Indeed, this is already apparent in the manner in which the discussions have evolved over modifications to the quotas that determine, among other things, voting power.

The result is an outcome that leaves everyone with a sense of underaccomplishment and unsatisfactory compromise and a recognition that some further changes will be needed. Indeed, this episode has reminded me of an observation by the late physicist Richard P. Feynman in his insightful assessment of what had gone wrong with the space shuttle: "Reality must take precedence over public relations, for Nature cannot be fooled."[16]

Michael Spence and I have suggested a way in which this grand bargain can be pursued with a higher probability of success: Do so in the context of a unifying theme that speaks directly to the common challenge facing the global economy. Not surprisingly given the earlier discussion in this book, we have proposed that this theme be defined in terms of "facilitating the ongoing breakout phase in the economic development of emerging economies."[17]

We have argued that such a theme should do more than just reflect global realities; it should also offer strategic advantages for realizing a shift in focus from entitlement-driven, bilateral discussions toward more multilateral deliberations—including providing greater assurances to individual countries that their policy actions will be accompanied by reinforcing measures on the part of others. By contrast, the more hesitant and disjointed strategy being pursued up to now has risked undermining the health of the international economy.

The Leadership Issue

This leads us to the final component of an action plan for the IMF—that of strong and credible leadership. The challenge here goes well beyond what a CEO faces at the level of a company, and in some ways, it is even more nuanced than what a country leader confronts.[18]

The proposed head of an international institution is usually nominated by his or her country of origin. The authorities of the country campaign for the individual, often putting the full apparatus of foreign policy and pressure in play. The nomination often becomes an issue of national prestige, with a successful nomination being viewed as a national achievement.

Yet, once the nominee assumes the leadership of the international institution, he or she is "expected" to put the multilateral cause ahead of the interest of the country of origin. Indeed, the treatment of all countries is expected to be governed by the "uniformity principle." Needless to say, many have questioned whether these expectations play out fully in the real world.

There is a sense today that, more than ever before, the community of nations is more open to shifting to a more transparent, merit-based approach to selecting the heads of the international institutions. Indeed, two recent appointees—Strauss-Kahn of France for the IMF and Zoellick of the United States for the World Bank, both of whom assumed their positions in 2007 following the early departures of their predecessors—have talked about this issue. Both have appropriately positioned themselves as reform-oriented leaders committed to helping their institutions' regain legitimacy, respect, and relevance in the global economy.

Time will tell whether these two leaders will succeed in uniting a diverse group of "political masters" behind reforming and more effective institutions. Fortunately, the key items of the reform agenda are clear and have already been subject to protracted discussion. It is also clear that, while the implementation challenge is significant, failure to progress would result in a lose-lose situation for the global economy, including member countries that foolishly guard entitlements that were granted to them by historical considerations and are now inconsistent with the world of today and even more so with the world of tomorrow.

With time, some of the industrial countries that have (and are) resisting a reform-induced erosion in their historic entitlements will realize that they actually have more to lose by opposing change. Indeed, they would be well advised to take note of what Stanley Fischer, the MIT professor who served as the IMF's first deputy managing director and is now governor of the Bank of Israel, said in a recent interview when discussing the international response to the 1994 Mexican crisis: "The United States tried to handle the crisis on its own, and then realized that it couldn't. It is much harder for one country to impose conditions on another than for an international organization to have one of its members sign up to those conditions."[19] While the notion of industrial countries' imposing economic conditionality on emerging nations is becoming less relevant on account of numerous considerations, industrial countries will realize that multilateral institutions offer the best avenue for interacting productively with emerging economies in today's rapidly changing global economic system.

Where Does this Leave Us?

This and the previous chapter detailed some of the steps that can be taken by different market participants in order to benefit from the new secular destination. In the process, they will also be reducing the risk of ending up with obsolete investment strategies, ineffective business approaches, inefficient policy responses, and weak institutional set-ups at the national and multilateral levels.

Several of the proposed steps involve difficult choices, tricky retooling efforts, and complicated changes in the configuration of entitlements and empowerments. As such, they are not easy to implement. Yet the costs of not persisting with this difficult task are high and consequential.

At the level of the individual firms, they entail the risk of business disruptions and institutional casualties; at the level of the national economy, they involve the risk of subpar growth, financial instability, and growing internal inequities; and at the level of the global economy, they carry the risk of negative systemic shocks and protectionist forces.

Having discussed the needed adaptations for the new secular destination, let us now turn to how best to navigate the bumpy journey ahead—one that is full of potholes and tempting, but costly, diversions. Remember, a destination is only attractive if you can get there in one piece!

CHAPTER 8

IMPROVED RISK MANAGEMENT

The importance of enhanced risk management cannot be overstated, especially when talking about how best to navigate the journey to the new secular destination. Consider the insights of the disciplines and tools I used earlier in the book to explain the nature and consequences of the ongoing structural transformations:

- Insights from traditional economics and finance suggest that structural transformations inevitably lead to asymmetrical reactions and challenge the robustness of exiting activities and institutions. As such, market failures can and do occur.
- Nassim Taleb's work is consistent with the hypothesis that the transformations increase the probability of "Black Swans" for which market participants are already ill equipped to deal with, in part because they are largely underinsured against "fat tail" events. Indeed, his work illustrates the excessive way in which the traditional probabilistic approach to mapping outcomes is blinded by the median and, therefore, underestimates the tails.

- Meanwhile, behavioral and neuroscience research suggest that the transformations can easily accentuate existing biases, including by confusing the "analytical" part of the brain and allowing the "emotional" part to take over in governing market-related activities.

Ultimately, success in risk management boils down to achieving a single objective through a process that has an appropriate level of predictability, responsiveness, and impact: minimizing the left tail—namely, reducing one's vulnerability to the extreme of the distribution that induces intolerable pain for each group of market participants. In the case of investors and corporations, this pain would be felt in very large losses; for national and international policy makers, it would involve an inability to promote sustained economic growth in the context of low inflation and financial stability.

Interestingly, in our daily lives we all engage in attempts to minimize the left tail. The question we face in doing so often boils down to this: How much of the tail do we want to cut off and at what cost? We go through this exercise whenever we buy insurance for our cars and homes. We have to decide on how much to insure and what deductible to use. We also go through the same methodology as parents when deciding how much freedom to give our children when it comes to running around the neighborhood, staying out late at night, or engaging in any other risky endeavors.

A History of Asymmetrical Risk Postures

Recent history points to some asymmetry in the way investors and policy makers have approached this issue. Indeed, there is a whole group of people who believe that this asymmetry is connected—namely, that excessive readiness by the official sector to react to systemic risk has reduced the private sector's willingness to self-insure.

As detailed below, investors have shown a general reluctance to pay insurance premiums that are sufficient in relation to the potential (and now fatter) left tail. Part of this reluctance is a reflection of some of the incentives inherent in the fee structure charged by the fastest-growing investment vehicles out there (that is, hedge funds and private equity); part is a reflection of the unusually benign risk environment that prevailed until the summer of 2007; part is a reflection of the old nemesis of hubris; and part of it is a reflection of the complexity of the risks that renders comprehension and hedging harder.

By contrast, national policy makers have shown little hesitancy in trying to take action to restore market calm. This has been most notable in the domain of monetary policy through which the Federal Reserve has reduced interest rates and, along with the European Central Bank (ECB) and other central banks, provided the market with liquidity in response to various market and liquidity dislocations. It has also been illustrated by the bipartisan adoption by the U.S. Congress of a $170 billion stimulus package in early 2008, which entailed the mailing of checks to a large part of the population in an attempt to sustain spending.

The behavior of the Federal Reserve has been such that the market has coined a term in the last few years for its reactive approach: the "Greenspan Put." If my recollection is correct, the term first appeared in 1998 when the Federal Reserve undertook emergency cuts in interest rates to stop and reverse a breakdown in market liquidity occasioned by Russia's default and, more importantly, the collapse of the Long-Term Capital Management (LTCM) hedge fund. This rate cutting reinforced the action the Fed took in 1987—very early in Alan Greenspan's tenure—when the Fed reacted to the stock market collapse on "Black Monday" (October 19, 1987). The market's notion of the "put" has now been transferred to the Bernanke Fed, albeit with less conviction, after the way it reacted to the turmoil that started in the summer of 2007.

The notion of the put, which relates to the ability of an investor to avoid the costly implications of a market downturn by selling a specified position at a higher predetermined price, captured the perception that monetary authorities would protect the investors' downside. And this is where the "moral hazard" crowd gets all excited.

The Moral Hazard Debate

As I touched on earlier, "moral hazard" refers to the notion that insurance arrangements can, in themselves, change people's behavior.[1] The example usually cited is that of a driver's becoming less careful because his or her vehicle is insured. Put another way, the availability of insurance alters the risk-mitigating steps that the driver would otherwise take. Such steps could include something as simple as not locking the car. As such, the greater the amount of insurance, the less optimal the behavior of the entity being insured.

Moral hazard is a tough issue to be principled about in practice. As Xavier Freixas noted in the paper he presented at the September 2007 conference organized by the Federal Reserve

Bank of Chicago and the International Monetary Fund (IMF), the role of the lender of last resort is invaluable at the macrolevel but it is often problematic at the microlevel.[2] It is an inevitable part of emergency responses to situations in which there are information asymmetries and failures; but its availability could well end up promoting the types of behavior that ultimately trigger systemwide malfunctioning subsequently.

As an example, consider a fire truck responding to a fire. In a perfect world, the fire brigade would have the time to "debrief" the occupants fully before pinpointing the hoses at the key fire areas. In this way, they would respond to the fire without causing excessive water damage to areas that are not in the front line. Yet that almost never happens—not because firefighters are not interested in information and are keen to overreact; rather, it is because the cost of waiting is high, especially if the fire has the potential to spread to other buildings.

In financial circles, the most-often-heard concern is that repeated attempts by officials to "bail out" markets eats away at the integrity and credibility of mechanisms of market discipline. You will hear the concern that the attempts to rescue investors from their foolish investments will simply encourage them to take even more thoughtless risk in future; insuring deposits at banks will weaken the incentive for depositors to carry out an adequate level of due diligence; and providing official emergency lending to countries and companies will encourage others to assume excessive indebtedness in the knowledge that they will be rescued from their foolish decisions.

These considerations are valid, and, to some degree, they are partially inevitable in a modern financial system. Indeed, some of the actions that give rise to moral hazard concerns are motivated by important systemic considerations—for example, to minimize the risk of collateral damage for those who have been behaving appropriately. It is just that certain widely used instruments of economic intervention are not refined enough to distinguish the good investors and lenders from the bad ones.

My characterization of the journey suggests that issues of moral hazard will continue to come up. Officials will face difficult choices when asked to react to the consequences of newly enabled market activities that go beyond the capacity of the financial system to accommodate and sustain them. This type of challenge, which will increasingly be faced by policy makers, was vividly highlighted in the insightful discussion by Krishna Guha, the Washington-based journalist for the *Financial Times*, ahead of a Federal Open Market Committee (FOMC) meeting being held in the midst of the market disruptions in the summer of 2007.

Guha described the situation as follows: "While all policy makers are committed to acting as 'needed' to prevent the market turmoil from causing serious damage to the real economy, there remains considerable dispersal of views within the Federal Open Market Committee. Some of the most influential Fed officials appear increasingly sure it will prove necessary to cut rates in order to guard against the tail risk of a sharp housing-led downturn. . . . By contrast, a number of regional Fed presidents appear encouraged by the lack of evidence so far of the spillover effects."[3]

The policy dilemma was even more acute in the United Kingdom. As noted earlier, the British authorities were forced to intervene to save the Northern Rock bank notwithstanding their initial public expressions of concerns about moral hazard risk.

This policy path potentially leads to even more controversial bank nationalization, as was the case in Sweden in the 1990s.

In confronting these and a host of other uncertain policy alternatives, it is likely that officials will continue to err on the side of overreaction. After all, the national and international consequences of overreacting often appear less than those of underreacting. And this will continue until at least one of three things discussed in the previous chapter becomes evident: Officials develop more refined and targeted policy tools; the private sector retools sufficiently so that it can sustain the range and magnitude of newly enabled activities; and/or the influence of endogenous liquidity declines.

As unpleasant as this may taste, the prospects are thus for a continuation of the willingness by the official sector to minimize the cost of systemic disruptions. But this does not mean that companies and investors need not worry about their ability to manage the changing configuration of risk occasioned by the structural transformations. On the contrary. Official action does not and will not protect all participants. Moreover, there is a real question as to whether the official sector's *willingness* will be matched by its *ability and effectiveness*. After all, the official sector is also operating with policy instruments that were built for the world of yesterday and not the world of tomorrow.

The question here goes well beyond that of collateral damage. Indeed, the jury is still out as to whether the official sector can sustainably cut off the left tail of the distribution for the system as a whole and, within this, for many private companies and investors. *Investors are well advised to assume greater responsibility for risk management in today's world where the conditions of yesterday are colliding with those of tomorrow.* Indeed, as I concluded a July 2007

Op Ed in the *Financial Times*, "Those that did best the last few years were those who bought liquid assets and levered up. The next few years will belong to those who prudently manage risk."[4]

Overcoming a Natural Hesitancy

The natural inclination of investors—especially retail investors—is to essentially avoid the direct execution of risk management operations. Instead, the common practice is to outsource the function to the professional managers that they have chosen to manage their funds. After all, these are well-paid professionals, with access both to complicated tools and to sophisticated counterparties on Wall Street.

While this mindset is understandable, it is inadvisable for a number of reasons. Most importantly, it is undermined by what economists call "agency problems"—that is, the misalignment of incentives between principals and agents.

While at the Harvard Management Company (HMC), and because of the "Harvard brand," I had the privilege of interacting with some of the world's most famous money managers running hedge funds, mutual funds, and private equity and real estate firms. This group of managers truly constituted a "best in breed." I also had the opportunity to sit in on many meetings during which other money managers were pitching for new business. Some of these managers have been around for a long time, and others have just started out or are looking to do so.

I repeatedly observed in these meetings that because insurance is costly, only a handful of managers pursued the issue with as much vigor as they showed when chasing opportunities for alpha. This is not a particularly surprising outcome when you think about it. The only thing that is certain about buying protection is that you have a contractual obligation to make the payments on the insurance premiums. Most managers hate this concept of "negative carry"—that is, the certainty of persistent payments that "bleed" the portfolio. As such, their desire is to minimize the use of insurance in many, if not most, states of the world. This tendency is reinforced by human and institutional factors. As John Maynard Keynes explained, the worst thing for you the investor is to be wrong on your own. Given the way things are judged in this world, you are better off being wrong with the majority.

Institutional factors also act to counter optimal levels of portfolio insurance in some cases. This is particularly the case for investment vehicles that are subject to performance-based fees and that have weak clawback mechanisms.[5] This structure poses a significant "principal-agent problem": Typically, the investment manager owns an important part of the upside in performance while the end investor underwrites the bulk of the downside. It is also the case for the manager who hugs the index. Under all these circumstances, it is likely that the managers will persistently underinsure the portfolio.

The Example of Argentina

My first encounter with this phenomenon came early on in my investing career on the emerging markets bond desk at PIMCO. Having been heavily influenced by the fundamental analysis we undertook during my 15 years at the IMF and working at a firm that is serious about risk management, there were times when we would have a rather strong view about the absolute prospects of a country. Such an episode occurred in 1999 to 2000 when we felt that Argentina would not be able to avoid an economic and financial crisis notwithstanding the pronounced support it had from the IMF and the World Bank.

Our views, which were documented in a regular PIMCO publication *Emerging Markets Watch*, were influenced by three distinct considerations: First, the economic system that Argentina had in place limited the authorities' ability to deal with the country's mounting problems; second, even if they were able, the authorities showed little willingness to make the difficult decisions that were needed; and third, the regional and global environment rendered things even more difficult for Argentina.[6]

Argentina represented over a fifth of the EMBI—that is, the index against which most emerging market bond managers were measured.[7] Increasingly, fund managers were running an "underweight" in Argentina as the country's economic and financial prospects were dimming. Yet no one seemed to be willing to go as far as we did at PIMCO in having no long exposure to Argentina.

Our thinking at PIMCO in selling all our Argentine exposure was simple: The country faced a notable probability of a crisis that, given market prices, would translate into significant losses for investors. Therefore, the right thing to do for our clients was to hold no Argentine long exposure in their portfolios. And we told our clients this.

In eliminating all our long Argentine positions, we were also conscious of the possibility, no matter how small, that the economy could recover (what we called internally "the immaculate recovery," a phrase coined by Paul McCulley). To this end, we used the internal correlations of emerging markets—and, in particular, the instruments issued by other countries that displayed strong *technical* upward comovements with Argentina—to de facto build a portfolio overlay that would capture some of the upside should an Argentine recovery materialize.

At the time, this approach triggered a high degree of skepticism on the part of other fund managers and some analysts on Wall Street. The thinking ran as follows: Since Argentina had such a high weight in the index, it was "irresponsible" to sell all the exposure. Instead, it sufficed to underweight the name (that is, allocate some 15 to 18 percent of the fund to Argentina as opposed to the 20 percent plus in the index).

At the end of the day, it boiled down to the balance between capital preservation and what is known in the industry as "tracking error" (that is, the deviation from the index). We felt strongly that the right thing to do was to avoid what we felt was a high probability of loss even if this meant keeping only a partial claim on an Argentine upside; others preferred to underweight the name but still maintain large absolute exposures given index-related considerations.

Argentina defaulted in December 2001. The Argentine component of the EMBI index lost 65 percent of its value that year, dragging the whole index to a negative 1 percent performance for the year. Argentina was the only country in the index to experience a negative year (and what a negative year). Indeed, had you simply invested in the index minus Argentina, you would have returned around 20 percent that year.

Beyond Traditional Principal-Agent Issues

Economists will tell you that these types of principal-agent problems are prevalent in what inevitably constitute ill-defined investment management contracts. They are ill defined in that it is virtually impossible to fully align incentives ex ante. They, and others, will remind you that this speaks to the cost-benefit calculations that third-party investment managers (the agents) make in the presence of an index. In order to maximize the chances of being retained by the investor (the principal), it is better for the agent to position the portfolio for neutral or outperformance (that is, relative to the index) even if this comes with a higher probability of realizing absolute losses on the capital.

Now, suppose that you are one of the few who happen to be investing with managers who worry adequately about both their clients' absolute upsides and their clients' absolute downsides. While you are in a good position, you are not yet in the clear. For I learned something else at HMC: The rational and well-intentioned decisions of individual managers may not necessarily add up properly at the overall portfolio level. Indeed, portfolio-wide reconciliation is one of the trickiest parts of investment management—an issue that I also alluded to in Chapter 6's discussion of individual asset classes.

Institutional investors are able to address these challenges through the active use of overlays and the management of a fat tail insurance program. And it is important to think of them as distinct elements. Retail investors are less fortunate. They currently have to rely on the blunter instrument of asset allocation. In particular, as I discussed in Chapter 6, they need to place a greater emphasis on capital preservation instruments such as government bonds and cashlike instruments.

Over time, it is likely that the financial industry will provide retail investors with a broader array of instruments. I can imagine a day when they will benefit from a larger offering of holistic asset allocation funds that refine the asset allocation process and combine it with more sophisticated approaches to risk management. Both steps would constitute a significant improvement on what is currently available.

I can also imagine other investors' being better able to achieve a similar outcome through a building block approach that provides them with greater control. The evolution will be similar to that which has already resulted in the gradual emergence of funds to short various segments of global markets.[8] Specifically, these investors will be able to combine actively managed funds and various varieties of passively managed index funds with a larger set of focused risk management offerings.

Overlays

Overlays are aimed at ensuring that the overall portfolio remains in line with the risk tolerance of the institution. In such situations, the portfolio requires a high-frequency monitoring of the betas—that is, the sensitivity of the portfolio to the key market risk factors (for example, equity, interest rate duration, currency, and credit risk). Such monitoring goes from the simple (essentially correlation exercises) to the complex and sophisticated (for example, the factor decomposition of the portfolio). While sophistication is naturally desirable, the reality is that one ends up living in a world of second best. My own recommendation for institutional investors is to start by monitoring the betas using simple techniques and to do so at a high-frequency level.

It is important to stress that the idea is *not* to tweak the overlay continuously. Rather, it is to develop a mental time series that provides a "feel" for how the portfolio reacts in different states of the world. Indeed, I found it useful to play a little game with myself: see how well I can predict likely movement in the portfolio's overall value based on inputs pertaining to how various segments of the market did the previous day and the previous week.

To emphasize the point regarding "the world of second best," this exercise was carried out at Harvard on the part of the overall endowment invested in liquid markets—that is, it excluded the private equity, timber, and real estate segments. Yet, despite this partial coverage occasioned by the incomplete availability of higher-frequency data, we found the exercise useful in signaling time periods in which major adjustments were required in overlay strategies. A couple of these adjustments were subsequently covered in the media, including after the market sell-off of late February 2007.[9] Ex post, the repositioning appeared to some observers as enlightened "market timing"; in reality, it was part of a risk-mitigating strategy that sought to maintain the endowment within prudent risk tolerance levels.

Overlays are best implemented using liquid instruments that speak directly to one of the risk factors mentioned above. They normally take the form of dampening the portfolio's exposure to one or more of the following categories of risk:

equities (which can be monitored using such composites as the S&P, the EAFE for international exposures, and the EEM for emerging markets); interest rate durations (which can be monitored using either target bond maturities or the host of exchange-traded fund [ETF] indexes); currencies (which can be followed by focusing primarily on the G-3 pairs among the euro, yen and U.S. dollar); and credit (which can be followed by using the Dow Jones CDX indexes).

Tail Insurance

Simply put, a tail insurance program aims at cutting off what market participants refer to as the "extreme left tail of the distribution." This program, which also goes by the more mundane name of "Armageddon protection," recognizes that there is a probability, albeit small, that certain elements of the inevitably bumpy journey facing investors could turn into something more sinister that cannot be adequately handled by "self-insurance." The issue is not that the probability is small; it is. But the consequences are huge.

In the marketplace, this situation goes by the label of "Pascal's Wager." It refers to the argument set out by Blaise Pascal, a French seventeenth-century mathematician and physicist, who deliberated about the costs and benefits of whether to believe in God in the context of an inevitable lack of proof as to whether God exits (given that God is "infinitely incomprehensible" to mortals).[10] In a "reasoned defense of Christian belief," Pascal pointed out that, because of the consequences of potentially being wrong, the expected value (probability times consequences) of believing in God always exceeded that of not believing.

In essence, Pascal's Wager applies to a situation in which there is a small probability of an event that has an enormous consequence. Think of the earthquake risk in California. If people believed that the probability of the "big one" was high, they would not live in California. Yet, because the probability is nonzero and the consequences are so severe, it makes sense to consider earthquake insurance, especially if the market is providing it cheaply.

Since no two crises ever look the same, especially if they are severe, it is important to think of the tail insurance program as using a basket approach to considering risks. Ideally, rather than focus on just one instrument, it is advisable to design and implement a combination of instruments that covers the key characteristics of the fat tail events—for example, the event that there is a severe economic downturn that is accompanied by either deflation or inflation or the event that there are significant geopolitical disruptions that disrupt the supply of oil.

The availability of cheap tail insurance has been a notable feature of the world that we have been living in. It reflected people's infatuation with returns—that is, people seeking to leverage whatever carry they can find. As a result, until the spread of the disruptions that started in the summer of 2007, it was possible to construct a basket of tail insurance for which the premiums were very low—especially if the approach was to resort to buying protection on the senior tranches of corporate indexes, through interest rate floors, and so on.

The cost of running tail insurance programs can be alleviated but not eliminated by various strategies. At their core, these strategies typically involve "funding" part of the purchase of tail insurance through exploiting structural hedging opportunities in the belly of the risk curve. By definition, the funding offset will likely be partial, if not minuscule. An example of this could be the sale of very short dated protection on credit names that have insignificant debt servicing coming up. Particularly in the case of emerging market sovereigns, such protection usually trades well above its fundamental value (in terms of basis points) because it is used by other investors to partially (and imperfectly) hedge long positions on related entities that are lower in the country's capital structure. As such, the return to the seller of the short-dated sovereign protection is considerably higher than what is warranted by sovereign creditworthiness considerations.

Having shared with you the obvious attributes of a tail insurance program, let me now focus on three additional twists that are often less visible to investors. All three serve to enhance the role that such a program plays in portfolio construction.

First, while most tail insurance instruments are meant to provide protection against a significant economic disruption, they also assume substantial value in the event of a liquidity disruption. As an example, the cost of the 15 to 30 tranche of five-year protection on the investment-grade corporate index in the United States jumped from 4 to 6 basis points in the year prior to the summer market turmoil of 2007 to some 55 to 65 basis points later in the year. Note that this huge jump occurred notwithstanding the fact that there was no material change in the incidence of defaults in the universe of investment-grade companies. Yet the buyers of protection experienced a significant mark-to-market appreciation in their insurance positions, which faced them with an interesting dilemma: whether to treat the protection as a "trade" and unwind it at considerable profit or to keep it as part of a long-dated tail insurance program that had significantly repriced.

This sensitivity to liquidity conditions comes from the manner in which the underlying risk is leveraged and from the extent of co-ownership. In the case of the 15 to 30 tranche, the protection is bundled and sold in the form of a highly leveraged note that carries an AAA rating by the agencies in view of the high default attachment point. It often ends up in portfolios that emphasize leveraged carry trades and, as such, own other positions that are highly correlated. These portfolios typically experience significant stress during periods of intense liquidity disruptions. This can force liquidations that impact the value of the underlying instruments even though there has been no change in the default rates.

Second, the attraction of tail insurance programs goes beyond limiting the potential negative impact on the portfolio of major economic and liquidity dislocations. It also facilitates the ability of investors to shift from defense to offense in portfolio positioning when the situation warrants such a shift. (Those who follow American football will also recognize the intermediate phase of "special teams" during which the focus is on pockets of value among high-quality instruments whose prices have been unduly depressed by contagion effects—that is, the application of the insights from the market-for-lemons literature discussed in Chapter 3.)

Tail insurance programs can minimize the risk of undue paralysis when it comes time to "bottom fishing." As the behavioral finance literature has demonstrated—and as experienced observers of investor behavior will confirm—too many long-term investors can become paralyzed at the very point when their capital attributes call for them to make a decision that is likely to serve them well for many years. This typically happens at the bottom of a market cycle when price overshoots offer significant value but at the same time also impose large mark-to-market losses on existing holdings. When this happens, investors who should be adding positions are frequently inhibited from doing so because of the prevailing market valuations of their holdings. By limiting the severity of the mark-to-market losses in such circumstances, the tail insurance program can enhance the probability that the correct investment reaction will actually materialize. Indeed, along with periodic scenario analyses, it can serve to reduce the risk of undue (and eventually) costly paralysis among long-term investors at the bottom of a market cycle.

Third, tail insurance programs can help investors appropriately capture what I call "the elusive center" during times when analysts are split among competing corner solutions. I first wrote about this in November 2003, using the analogy of a little book that had a significant influence on me during my undergraduate years at Cambridge University.[11]

This little Penguin paperback (*Cooking in a Bedsit*)[12] was far from being a classic. It was a rudimentary cookbook that allowed the reader to reconcile the need for regular sustenance with the reality of a student's budget constraints. If I recall correctly, the book had two distinct sections: "Cooking to Survive" and "Cooking to Impress." The first contained brutally simple recipes that allowed you to eat cheaply and in bulk. The second section spoke to the preparation of more sophisticated dishes. This approach explicitly ruled out the middle ground. After all, you either survived or impressed. It is similar to what occurs when analysts are pushed to extremes in market debates.

In the recent past few years, this phenomenon has played out in many areas. It has been evident in the debates on global imbalances and in the tug-of-war that has played out in the markets between fear and greed. It also includes pronounced differences of views in the markets on the outlook for the U.S. economy (namely, a V- or U-like return to trend growth as opposed to a protracted recession that would look more like a 1 or an L or even a two-phase recovery such as a W); on the prospects of a global credit crunch (prolonged and expanded dislocations versus a quick policy-induced healing); and, of course, on the global consequences of the U.S. economic and financial difficulties ("decoupling" for the rest of the world versus disruptive contagion).

Tail insurance programs provide investors with an important additional degree of freedom when it comes to portfolio construction in the context of uncertainty about corner solutions. Specifically, they release investors from the suboptimal alternative of having to use large asset allocation decisions as the main instruments to express a view about uncertain extremes. Instead, a combination of these programs and asset allocation adjustments can help investors refine their positioning over time, including capturing the elusive middle in terms of portfolio construction; that is, they can help investors retain a claim, albeit less than 100 percent, on the upside while also protecting against the downside.

Scaling Issues and Circuit Breakers

Great portfolio managers have a knack for scaling their trades. In doing so, they combine the right degree of insurance with a manageable cost.

Needless to say, an important consideration here relates to the effectiveness of the circuit breakers that come with today's global economic and financial conditions. Indeed, the analysis in this book speaks to more than the dominant secular themes for the next few years. It also sheds light on the way in which certain aspects can help ensure that the inevitable bumps (including those that pertain to the potential policy mistakes and market accidents detailed in Chapter 5) do not completely derail the journey.

The global economy is fortunate at this time to benefit from three circuit breakers that reduce, but not eliminate, the probability of individual dislocations contaminating the long-term economic well-being:

- First, policy makers seem willing to intervene in an attempt to safeguard the smooth functioning of the international financial system and the robustness of economic growth; in the process, they are willing to underwrite the inevitable risk of moral hazard.

- Second, there is considerable fresh capital on the sideline able and willing to step in; in the case of the patient funds held by the SWFs, this is starting from a position of significant absolute and relative underexposure to risk assets.

- Third, the breakout phase of economic growth in key emerging economies provides the global economy with a degree of resilience that it has generally lacked in the past.

Investors would be well advised to maintain a careful check on the strength and lag structure of these three circuit breakers, whose effectiveness also depends on the potential duration of the technical dislocation (itself a function of the degree to which existing institutions have gotten themselves offside and, therefore, need to delever and reduce balance sheet). The greater (lower) the robustness, the smaller (larger) the appropriate scaling of the tail insurance program for a given unit cost of protection. Moreover, the greater (lower) the robustness, the stronger (weaker) the case for investors to consider selling index volatility in various market segments (particularly stocks and bonds) as a supplement to the expected returns from their equilibrium asset allocation.

Some Concluding Wisdom from the Harvard Management Company

The discussion of overlays and tail insurance would not be complete without mentioning a story that Peter Dolan, HMC's head of private equity, shared with me some time ago. It relates to what professionals call "manager risk"—that is, the possibility of facing loss on account of a deterioration in the quality of portfolio management services.

Peter warned of the potentially harmful cycles that some investment managers can go through if they are not subject to an internal culture that appreciates the potential of markets to humble any investor. In an e-mail that drew on what he had been told by others, Peter reminded me of the need to guard against the following sequence: "The psychological process begins with a person who possesses arête ('excellence' or 'striving for excellence'). Great arête leads to hubris ('feeling of excessive pride in oneself'), which in turn leads to ate ('blind recklessness'), when an individual loses his or her sense of human limitations and indulges in behavior that is rash or imprudent. Ate, in turn, leads to nemesis ('retributive justice') because the person who acted imprudently is punished by others."

Peter went on to describe how this scenario influenced his team's decision to walk away from certain investment managers at particular moments: "We are constantly on the lookout for those investor managers who after having demonstrated arête subsequently become imbued with hubris only to be destroyed by nemesis."

Investors would be well advised to follow Peter's insights when undertaking the periodic assessment of their investment vehicles. Bumpy journeys have a way of tripping up investment managers whose hubris results in excessive overconfidence and insufficient appreciation of the challenges that lie ahead.

CHAPTER 9

CONCLUSION

During my time at the International Monetary Fund (IMF), I had the great fortune of working with David Coleman, a management coach. The fund's Administration Department, as it was called at the time, hired David to help the institution better manage its human talent. Thus he met regularly with SPMs (senior personnel managers) to assist them with human resource matters in their departments.

Like many other institutions, the IMF promoted its staff members mainly on the basis of technical expertise and achievements. As such, many of the senior staff had to develop a knowledge base for human capital management. No wonder several colleagues did their utmost to avoid significant people management functions, especially when it came in the form of the SPM job. But no matter how hard they tried, some were inevitably given these responsibilities. They were asked to manage and oversee the activities of hundreds of staff members as well as undertake their own tasks. Thus the need for experts like David.

It has been almost 15 years since I worked with David as my management coach, yet I remember many of the tools he

Figure 9-1 A Simple Management Framework

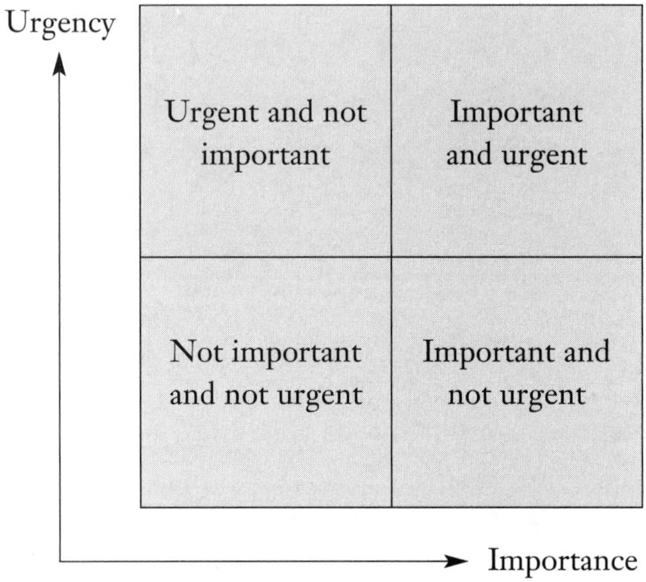

Urgency

Urgent and not important	Important and urgent
Not important and not urgent	Important and not urgent

Importance

conveyed to me during our weekly meetings. One of my favorites remains the importance of never losing sight of how urgency and importance interact.

David made the point through a simple but powerful matrix. One axis specifies the urgency of the task; and the other specifies its importance. In its purest form, the matrix has the four combinations detailed in Figure 9.1.

David noted that most people were pretty good at recognizing what is important and urgent, and they reacted accordingly. They also tended to be able to identify and avoid the not important and not urgent. It is the other two boxes that separated success from average or mediocre performance.

The successful managers never lost sight of the important and not urgent. These tasks are highly deterministic when it comes to positioning oneself for sustained future excellence. The others got diverted by the urgent and not important tasks. Most of these end up claiming an enormous amount of time and effort but have little material impact on the longer-term success of an endeavor.

Important and Urgent

In this book, I have argued that it is important and urgent to understand the nature and implications of the anomalies that have appeared in the global economy. Rather than constituting noise with little information content—and therefore dismissing them as not important and not urgent—they signal that the global economy is in the midst of a fundamental structural transformation.

The ways in which the drivers of the transformation are unfolding (that is, the influence of what we called the new actors, instruments, and products) have caught many market participants by surprise. Accordingly, the activities that have been enabled by this ongoing change have clearly outpaced the current system's capacity to accommodate and sustain them. The result has been, and will continue to be, costly dislocations for individuals, institutions, and countries.

This outcome is not surprising. It is a repeated feature in the history of significant innovation and structural change. It is equally not surprising that too many market participants missed the signals that were within the noise: The natural temptation is to do so, as illustrated by the insights of many disciplines such as economics, finance, and behavior and neuroscience.

Ongoing transformations alter in previously unthinkable ways the configurations of risk and return. They necessitate adjustments on the part of market participants that, counterintuitively, may also involve deviating even further from what was previously deemed conventional wisdom.

As a result of this, it is important and urgent for market participants to internalize the fact that some long-established strategies and entities will face sudden operational difficulties that were previously unimaginable. Inadvertently, the world has embarked on a fundamental set of changes with a plumbing system (including the regulatory structures, mindsets, policies, and risk management strategies) that is more suitable to the realities of yesteryear than to those of the future. As a result, the markets of yesterday have been colliding with those of tomorrow and will continue to do so.

At the heart of all this is the gradual unfolding of an economic, financial, and technical realignment of the global system. The main drivers include the emergence of a new set of systemically important countries, a significant cross-border transfer of wealth to entities that are yet to adjust fully to their new circumstances, and the proliferation of new instruments and products that dramatically alter barriers to entry and exit, change correlations, and turbocharge the influence of endogenous liquidity.

Over time, a new secular destination will emerge that will involve greater elements of stability. A faltering U.S. engine of global growth will be replaced by several emerging market engines. The global imbalances will recede as countries adjust. Highly concentrated portfolios will be allocated to a broader set of asset classes. And the inevitable improvement in the policy and market infrastructure will better accommodate the new and complex interactions of products and investors.

It is critical for market participants to recognize and act on the likelihood that the new secular destination will be attained via what is likely to be a rather bumpy journey. Indeed, I would argue that this is inevitable pending the needed retooling of systems, people, policies, and processes to ensure that the international economy can adequately accommodate and sustain the new realities. It also reflects the challenge to policy makers occasioned by a gradual change in price dynamics as the tailwind of global disinflation, enabled by the large-scale entry of cost-effective labor into the global workforce, gives way to a headwind occasioned by several factors, including continued price pressures on commodities.

The journey has already been characterized by institutional excesses, market overshoots, and institutional debacles. Even some basic parameters of normal market functioning—such as confidence in valuations, price discovery, visibility, and property rights—have come under pressure. Worse yet, already pressured balance sheets have been harder to define given the new and uncertain nature of contingent liabilities.

Not surprisingly, the results have included (and will continue to include) periodic breakdowns in the functioning of markets. Buyers and sellers are no longer able to iterate smoothly to market-clearing outcomes; trust among counter-parties has declined, forcing each firm to retrench and preserve its balance sheets; certain market segments have been subjected to sudden stops in liquidity; and policy makers have been thrown into a crisis management mode, having to undertake emergency interventions that address the immediate liquidity dislocations but at the cost of gradually undermining the long-term efficient functioning of markets.

Not Important but Urgent

How about the not important but urgent? The main risk for market participants lies in the inevitable diversions that populate the journey to the new secular destination. Such diversions can consume a significant amount of resources without any concurrent long-term welfare enhancements.

The risks here are material. They are led by the temptation to act in a manner that treats the growing host of aberrations as requiring no strategic reorientation. This results in a reaction function that is ad hoc, and essentially consists of a series of temporary and ultimately ineffective responses. The outcome is a much higher probability of market accidents and policy mistakes as market participants continue with backward-looking strategies.

There is also the temptation to react to just one of the three structural transformations without giving adequate attention to how it interacts with the other two. Such partial adaptation does not necessarily translate into an overall improvement and, indeed, could actually distort the adjustment process.

Important and Not Urgent

This leads to what may appear to many as "important and not urgent"—namely, how to position oneself for the new secular destination that will transpire over a number of years. It is seemingly "not urgent" because this change pertains to the world of tomorrow—one that is still unfamiliar and runs counter to habits formed by past experience. Moreover, some elements of this destination conflict with the journey that must be navigated first. Yet it is "important" as it represents a response to a sustainable long-term shift.

David taught me that what appears today as "important and not urgent" will, most likely, separate in the future the strong performers from the average and mediocre ones. Accordingly, *When Markets Collide* has attempted to propose the basic components of an action plan for each of three major sets of market participants: long-term investors, government officials, and international institutions. Inevitably, the particulars of the individual action plan involve revisiting elements of conventional wisdom. Some imply a change in mindset; others a retooling of institutional and organizational parameters. As such, they are not easy to implement. And they involve risks. But these difficulties pale in comparison to the consequences of not adjusting.

For investors, the to-do list includes the ability to target long-term asset allocations that will play out over time as the new secular realities assert themselves in market prices. In the process, investors should also go back and test the robustness of their investment vehicles, risk mitigation, and institutional set-ups to ensure that they are consistent with the ongoing structural changes. Critically, they should be open in particular to supplement the traditional (and too often badly implemented) outsourcing of risk management with a greater use of overlays and tail insurance protection programs.

For policy makers, the to-do list includes being willing to seek new sources of policy-related information and to improve their policy instruments and approaches accordingly. And for multilateral institutions, the list includes updating their governance and operational approaches that are being suffocated by outmoded entitlements and feudal mindsets.

By adapting the action plan to their particular circumstances, individual market participants will be in better positions to both navigate the journey and benefit from the new destination. They will realize a greater potential to exploit opportunities and manage the new configurations of risk. And the impact will be felt on the size and time profile of their bottom lines.

The Public Good

So far, the discussion has been about the self-interest of each group of market participants. However, there is another reason for hoping that all will respond appropriately—the need to safeguard the growth and poverty-alleviation potential of the global economy.

As an aggregate, the global economy is navigating structural changes at a time of considerable fragility. Certain balance sheets are stretched, particularly in the United States; not all segments of the population benefit from the new global realities; the challenge of global climate change is real and as yet unaddressed; and political cycles are increasingly deviating from economic ones, raising the risk of disruptive protectionism and "beggar-thy-neighbor" policies.

Indeed, the global economy is in the midst of a tug-of-war. On the one side, we have pockets of financial excesses, over-leverage, resource pressures, and inequalities—all of which serve to undermine the sustainability and beneficial impact of globalization and integration. On the other side, the coming onstream of more balanced growth led by emerging economies and the deployment of their excess savings act as stabilizers and provide a meaningful potential for a new wel-fare-enhancing phase for globalization, economic growth, and poverty alleviation.

There is a lot at stake, and the challenges are considerable and multifaceted. There are also critical coordination and inter-dependency issues.

Even if it were feasible and desirable, the official sector is in no position to lead the private sector to an orderly adjustment path. The private sector must assume this responsibility. The best that the official sector can do is to help encourage a potentially more orderly process by making much-needed progress on its own set of urgent reform priorities. Indeed, for the private sector to get it right, it needs support in the form of concurrent adjustments in the parameters that govern important aspects of market behavior, including those in the regulatory and policy channels at both the national and multi-national levels.

The hope is that, in classic Adam Smith manner, global wel-fare will be enhanced by each group of market participants simultaneously pursuing their self-interest in response to the ongoing structural transformations—thereby reinforcing the potential incentive alignments and feeding the virtuous ele-ments of the adjustment process. The danger is that differences in the willingness and ability to adapt will further complicate the journey and make the global economy more vulnerable to growth slowdowns, protectionist forces, liquidity sudden stops, and financial market dislocations.

It is time for investors and policy makers to take measures. By acting in a decisive and timely manner, they will shift the balance away from the dynamics of a vicious cycle toward those of a virtuous cycle. The resulting gains will go well beyond superior investment performance and good policy implementation. They will also be reflected in the ability to make this age of global economic change consistent with high global growth, declining poverty, and relative financial stability.

NOTES

Preface

1. Steven D. Levitt and Stephen J. Dubner, *Freakonomics: A Rogue Economist Explores the Hidden Sides of Everything*, HarperTorch, New York, 2006.
2. Nassim Nicholas Taleb, *Fooled by Randomness: The Hidden Role of Chance in Life and the Markets*, Random House, New York, 2005; and Nassim Nicholas Taleb, *The Black Swan: The Impact of the Highly Improbable*, Random House, New York, 2007.
3. Peter L. Bernstein, *Capital Ideas Evolving*, Wiley, Hoboken, N.J., 2007.
4. Richard L. Peterson, *Inside the Investor's Brain: The Power of Mind Over Money*, Wiley Trading, Hoboken, N.J., 2007.
5. This quote is popular among certain universities marketing their economics courses.

Introduction

1. As noted in a paper by Columbia University Professor Guillermo Calvo published by the IMF (Guillermo Calvo, "Explaining Sudden Stop, Growth Collapse, and BOP Crisis: The Case of Distortionary Output Taxes," *IMF Staff Papers*, vol. 50, 2003), the term "sudden stop" was coined by the MIT economist Rudi Dornbusch in 1995 (Rudiger Dornbusch, Ilan Golfajn, and Rodrigo O. Valdes, "Currency Crises and Collapses," *Brookings Papers on Economic Activity*, 1995). It was popularized by Calvo in the context of the emerging market crises of the 1990s.
2. David Enrich, Robin Sidel, and Susanne Craig, "World Rides to Wall Street's Rescue: Citigroup, Merrill Tap Foreign Aid Lifelines; Damage Tops $90 Billion," *Wall Street Journal*, January 16, 2008, p. A-1.
3. *Financial Times*, "US Banks Get $21 Billion Foreign Bail-Out," January 16, 2008, p. 1.

4. *The Economist*, "Invasion of the Sovereign Wealth Funds," January 19–25, 2008, front cover.
5. The rationale for this was detailed in Mohamed A. El-Erian, "Development and Globalization: Friends or Foes," *Emerging Markets Watch*, PIMCO, March 2002.
6. The *Emerging Markets Watch* publication, which I had the privilege of authoring from December 1999 until I left PIMCO for HMC in early 2006, was taken over by my two PIMCO colleagues Michael Gomez and Curtis Mewbourne. The articles are available on www.pimco.com. The columns that appeared in the *Financial Times* and *Newsweek* are available on www.ft.com and www.newsweek.com.
7. See the related discussion in Chapter 1 that refers to the February 16, 2005, testimony of Chairman Alan Greenspan before the Committee on Banking, Housing, and Urban Affairs of the U.S. Senate. Available on www.federalreserve.gov/boarddocs/hh/2005/february/testimony.htm.
8. Stephen Barrow, the CIO of Ironbridge Capital Management in London, put it in the following way in an interview that appeared in the August 20 edition of *Barron's*: "Wealth is not created by financial engineering. Financial engineering tends to be a transfer of wealth."
9. Ben White and David Wighton, "Credit Squeeze Costs Banks $18 Billion," *Financial Times*, October 6, 2007, p. 1.
10. Christine Harper, "Goldman Doesn't Plan Significant Mortgage Writedowns, CEO Blanfein Says," *Bloomberg News*, November 13, 2007.
11. Mohamed A. El-Erian, "Foreign Capital Must Not Be Blocked," *Financial Times*, October 2, 2007.
12. For an early discussion of SWFs, refer to the papers contained in Jennifer Johnson-Calari and Malan Rietveld, *Sovereign Wealth Management*, Central Banking Publications, London, 2007.
13. See, for example, Berkshire Hathaway *Annual Report 2002*.

Chapter 1

1. L.K. Jha Memorial Lecture by Lawrence H. Summers, "Reflections on Global Account Imbalances and Emerging Markets Reserve Accumulation," delivered on March 24, 2006, at the Reserve Bank of India, Mumbai, India. Available on www.president.harvard.edu/speeches/2006/0324_rbi.html.
2. Gillian Tett and Steve Johnson, "New Zealand Finance Chief Says Rush into Currency Is 'Irrational,'" *Financial Times*, September 7, 2006.
3. There is no single definition for the group of "emerging economies." For the purposes of our analysis, we will use the IMF/World Bank definition.
4. Martin Wolf, "Questions and Answers on a Sadly Predictable Debt Crisis," *Financial Times*, September 5, 2007.
5. Alan Greenspan, *The Age of Turbulence: Adventures in a New World*, Penguin Press, New York, 2007.

6. The argument is set out in his remarks: "The Global Saving Glut and the U.S. Current Account Deficit," Remarks by Governor Ben S. Bernanke at the Sandridge Lecture, Virginia Association of Economics, Richmond, Va., March 10, 2005: www.federalreserve.gov/boarddocs/speeches/2005/200503102/default.htm. (Governor Bernanke presented similar remarks with updated data at the Homer Jones Lecture, St. Louis, Mo., on April 14, 2005.)

7. Ben Bernanke, "The Economic Outlook," testimony before the Committee on the Budget, U.S. House of Representatives, January 17, 2007.

Chapter 2

1. International Monetary Fund (IMF), *The Managing Director's Report on the Fund's Medium-Term Strategy, September 15, 2005,* IMF, Washington, D.C. See also IMF, *The Managing Director's Report on Implementing the Fund's Medium-Term Strategy,* April 5, 2006, IMF, Washington, D.C.

2. Barry Eichengreen, "The IMF Adrift on a Sea of Liquidity," in *Reforming the IMF for the 21st Century,* edited by Edwin M. Truman, Peter G. Peterson Institute for International Economics (IIE), Washington, D.C., 2006.

3. Timothy D. Adams, "The IMF: Back to Basics," in *Reforming the IMF for the 21st Century,* edited by Edwin M. Truman, Peter G. Peterson Institute for International Economics (IIE), Washington, D.C., 2006.

4. Messrs. Lerrick and O'Neil are quoted in Christopher Swann, "Strauss-Kahn to Inherit IMF Job with Reduced Clout," *Bloomberg News,* August 31, 2007.

5. "Europe Is Wrong to Push Strauss-Kahn," *Financial Times,* August 28, 2007, p. 8.

6. As reported by Jude Webber and Richard Lapper, "It Won't be Easy . . . No Tears for the IMF as Feisty Argentina Awaits Its Next Evita," *Financial Times,* October 25, 2007.

7. For a summary discussion, refer to Mohamed A. El-Erian, "IMF Reforms: Attaining the Critical Mass," in *Reforming the IMF for the 21st Century,* edited by Edwin M. Truman, Peter G. Peterson Institute for International Economics (IIE), Washington, D.C., 2006.

8. For a description of the problem and potential solutions, see the International Monetary Fund (IMF), *Committee to Study Sustainable Long-Term Financing of the IMF, Final Report,* IMF, Washington, D.C., 2007. Available on http://www.imf.org/external/np/oth/2007/013107.pdf.

9. These issues are discussed in detail in the Peter G. Peterson Institute for International Economics (IIE) volume edited by Edwin M. Truman (2006). For further details, see also the following two op-ed articles that appeared in the *Financial Times*: Mohamed A. El-Erian and Michael Spence, "Refocus the IMF," *Financial Times,* August 6, 2007; and Mohamed A. El-Erian, "It's Time to End Feudal Selection Processes," *Financial Times,* March 29, 2005.

10. Data are derived from *IMF inFocus*, which is a supplement of the International Monetary Fund's *IMF Survey*, vol. 35, September 2006: www.imf.org/external/pubs/ft/survey/2006/090106.pdf.
11. Alexei Kudrin, "The Era of Empires Is Over for International Bodies," *Financial Times*, September 30, 2007.
12. Neil Unmack and Sebastian Boyd, "HSBC Will Take on $45 Billion of Assets from Two SIVs," *Bloomberg News*, November 26, 2007.
13. For background information, see the U.S. Securities and Exchange Commission, *Report on the Role and Function of Credit Rating Agencies in the Operation of the Securities Markets*, January 2003.
14. Gillian Tett, "Why Financiers Have Missed the New Monster," *Financial Times*, September 7, 2007, p. 22.
15. Michiyo Nakamoto and David Wighton, "Bullish Citigroup Is 'Still Dancing' to the Beat of the Buyout Boom," *Financial Times*, July 10, 2007.
16. Susanne Craig, David Reilly, and Randall Smith, "More Zeroes for Investors," *Wall Street Journal*, January 18, 2008.
17. See, for example, Irving Fisher, "The Debt-Deflation Theory of Great Depression," *Econometrica*, vol. 1, no. 4, October 1933.
18. Lawrence H. Summers, "Why America Must Have a Fiscal Stimulus," *Financial Times*, January 6, 2008.
19. Quoted from the letter of Meryvn King, the Bank of England's governor, to John McFall, chairman of the Treasury Select Committee of Parliament, as cited in Scheherazade Daneshkhu, "Bank Chief Defends Role in Northern Rock Crisis," *Financial Times*, September 21, 2007, p. 2.
20. Matt Ridley, Letters to the Editor, *Economist*, September 29, 2007, p. 19.
21. Martin Wolf, "The Bank Loses a Game of Chicken," *Financial Times*, September 21, 2007, p. 11.
22. See discussion in Xavier Freixas, "Systematic Risk and Prudential Regularities in the Global Economy," paper prepared for the joint Federal Reserve Bank of Chicago and the International Monetary Fund Conference on Globalization and Systemic Risk, Chicago, September 27–28, 2007.
23. Guillermo A. Calvo, Alejandro Izquierdo, and Luis-Fernando Mjia, "On the Empirics of Sudden Stops: ˙ ˙e Relevance of Balance Sheet Effects," National Bureau of Economic Research, Cambridge, Mass., 2004.
24. Charlie McCreevy, Official Opening Speech, Wachovia Bank International, October 26, 2007, p. 5. Available on ec.europa.eu/commission_barroso/mccreevy/docs/speeches/2007-1026/regulators_to_be_humble.pdf.

Chapter 3

1. John Mayard Keynes, *The General Theory of Employment, Interest and Money*, Macmillan, London, 1936.
2. Stuart Sim, *Manifesto for Silence: Confronting the Politics and Culture of Noise*, Edinburgh University Press, Edinburgh, 2007.
3. See, for example, Milton Friedman, *Essays in Positive Economics*, University of Chicago Press, Chicago, 1953. For a more holistic discussion, see Frank

Hahn and Martin Hollis, *Philosophy and Economic Theory*, Oxford University Press, New York, 1979.

4. Javier C. Hernandez, "Boston Tea Party Catches Fire Again," *Boston Globe*, August 28, 2007.

5. Amartya K. Sen, "Rational Fools: A Critique of the Behavioral Foundations of Economic Theory," *Philosophy and Public Affairs*, vol. 6, no. 4, Summer 1977.

6. Michael Douglas won the 1987 Oscar for best actor for this role. The movie was directed by Oliver Stone.

7. Thomas S. Kuhn, *The Structure of Scientific Revolutions*, University of Chicago Press, Chicago, 1962.

8. George A. Akerlof, "The Market for 'Lemons': Quality Uncertainty and the Market Mechanism," *Quarterly Journal of Economics*, vol. 84, no. 3, August 1970, pp. 488–500.

9. Nassim Nicholas Taleb, *The Black Swan: The Impact of the Highly Improbable*, Random House, New York, 2007, p. xviii.

10. As an example, see the many letters to the *Financial Times* editors sent in response to Taleb's op-ed: Nassim Nicholas Taleb, "The Pseudo-science Hurting Markets," *Financial Times*, October 24, 2007.

11. Howard Wainer, "The Most Dangerous Equation," *American Scientist*, May–June 2007, p. 250.

12. This is discussed in James J. Choi, David Laibson, and Brigitte Madrian, *Plan Design and 401(k) Savings Outcomes*, NBER Working Paper No. 10486, National Bureau of Economic Research, Cambridge, Mass., May 2004.

13. A detailed discussion may be found in Daniel Kahneman, and Amos Tversky, editors, *Choices, Values, and Frames*, Cambridge University Press, Cambridge, U.K., 2000.

14. Daniel Kahneman, "Maps of Bounded Rationality: A Perspective on Intuitive Judgment and Choice," Nobel Prize Lecture, Stockholm, Sweden, December 8, 2002.

15. The term was coined in Hersh Shefrin, and Meir Statman, "The Disposition to Sell Winners Too Early and Ride Losers Too Long: Theory and Evidence," *Journal of Finance*, vol. 40, no. 3, 1985, pp. 777–790.

16. See, for example, Baba Shiv and Alexander Fedorikhin, "Heart and Mind in Conflict: The Interplay of Affect and Cognition in Consumer Decision Making," *Journal of Consumer Research*, vol. 26, no. 3, December 1999, pp. 278–292.

17. John Y. Campbell, "An Interview with Robert J. Shiller," in *Inside the Economist's Mind: Conversations with Eminent Economists*, edited by Paul A. Samuelson and William A. Barnett, Blackwell Publishing, Malden, Mass., 2007.

18. Samuel M. McClure, David I. Laibson, George Lowenstein, and Jonathan D. Cohen, "Separate Neural Systems Value Immediate and Delayed Monetary Rewards," *Science*, vol. 306, October 15, 2004, pp. 503–507.

19. Drew Gilpin Faust, "Unleashing Our Most Ambitious Imaginings," Inauguration Speech, Harvard University, Cambridge, Mass., October 12, 2007.

20. See, for example, the work by Andrei Shleifer including Andrei Shleifer and Robert W. Vishny, "The Limits to Arbitrage," *Journal of Finance*, March 1997, pp. 35–55.

21. Ben S. Bernanke, "The Economic Outlook," testimony before the Committee on the Budget, U.S. House of Representatives, January 17, 2008.

22. For an example of such analysis, see Paul R. Masson, *Multiple Equilibria, Contagion, and the Emerging Market Crises*, International Monetary Fund (IMF) Working Paper No. 99/164, Washington, D.C., November 1999.

23. For a more detailed discussion, see Mohamed A. El-Erian, *Mexico's External Debt and the Return to Voluntary Capital Market Financing*, International Monetary Fund (IMF) Working Paper No. 91/83, Washington, D.C., August 1991.

24. For additional information, see Mohamed A. El-Erian, *Restoration of Access to Voluntary Capital Market Financing: The Recent Latin American Experience*, International Monetary Fund (IMF) Staff Papers 39, no. 1, Washington, D.C., March 1992.

25. Mohamed A. El-Erian, "How Investors Should Respond to the Boom in M&A Activity," *Financial Times*, May 30, 2007.

Chapter 4

1. This section draws heavily on Mohamed A. El-Erian, and Michael Spence, "Growth Strategies and Dynamics: Insights from Country Experiences," *World Economics*, vol. 9, no. 1, January–March 2008.

2. This insight comes from a discussion with Egypt's minister of finance, Youssef Boutros-Ghali during a 1995 conference on the country's economic prospects.

3. El-Erian and Spence,"Growth Strategies and Dynamics," p. 4.

4. El-Erian and Spence, "Growth Strategies and Dynamics," p. 7.

5. Dani Rodrik, *One Economics, Many Recipes: Globalization, Institutions, and Economic Growth*, Princeton University Press, Princeton, N.J., 2007.

6. Tim Callen, "Emerging Markets Main Engine of Growth," *IMF Survey Magazine*, International Monetary Fund (IMF), Washington, D.C., October 17, 2007.

7. *The Economist*, "Stronger China," September 29, 2007, p. 14.

8. For details, see Mohamed A. El-Erian, "Asia: Regionalism with an Outward Orientation," *Emerging Markets Watch*, PIMCO, Newport Beach, Calif., July 2004.

9. Lawrence H. Summers, "The U.S. Current Account Deficit and the Global Economy," The Per Jacobsson Foundation, Washington, D.C., October 3, 2004. Available on www.perjacobsson.org/2004/100304.pdf.

10. Michael Dooley, David Folkerts-Landau, and Peter Garber, *The Revived Bretton Woods System: The Effects of Periphery Intervention and Reserve Management on Interest Rates and Exchange Rates in Center Countries*, NBER Working Paper No. 10332, National Bureau of Economic Research (NBER), Cambridge, Mass., March 2004.

11. Nouriel Roubini and Brad Setser, "How Scary Is the Deficit?" *Foreign Affairs*, July–August 2005.

12. Chris P. Dialynas and Marshall Auerback, "Renegade Economics and the Bretton Woods II Fiction," PIMCO, Newport Beach, Calif., 2007.

13. Alan Greenspan, *The Age of Turbulence: Adventures in a New World*, Penguin Press, New York, 2007.

14. For example, India's labor force is still predominantly in the agricultural sector, and there is significant surplus labor to draw into the activities of the modern global economy.

15. Greenspan, *The Age of Turbulence*, p. 382.

16. International Energy Agency (IEA), *World Energy Outlook* (WEO), Paris, October 2007.

17. Aasim M. Husain, "Riding the Crest of the Oil Boom," *IMF Survey Magazine*, International Monetary Fund (IMF), Washington, D.C., October 30, 2007.

18. The four steps were initially set out in Mohamed A. El-Erian, "The Policy Challenge of Managing Success," *Emerging Markets Watch*, PIMCO, Newport Beach, Calif., January 2005. Further elucidation may be found in Mohamed A. El-Erian, "Asset-Liability Management in Emerging Economies," in *Sovereign Wealth Management*, edited by Jennifer Johnson-Calari, and Malan Rietveld, Central Banking Publications, London, 2007.

19. See, for example, Barry Eichengreen and Ricardo Hausmann, "How to Eliminate Original Sin," *Financial Times*, November 22, 2002. Available on www.ft.com.

20. Paul Blustein's January 2005 book on Argentina has a good discussion of this and related issues. See Paul Blustein, *And the Money Kept Rolling In (and Out): Wall Street, the IMF, and the Bankrupting of Argentina*, Public Affairs/Perseus, 2005.

21. McKinsey Global Institute (MGI), *The New Power Brokers: How Oil, Asia, Hedge Funds, and Private Equity Are Shaping Global Capital Markets*, MGI, San Francisco/McKinsey & Company, October 2007.

22. Norges Bank Investment Management, Oslo, Norway: www.norges-bank.no/.

23. Lee Kuan Yew, *From Third World to First—The Singapore Story: 1965–2000*, HarperCollins, New York, 2000, p. 97.

24. This category covers assets that would be expected to do well in an inflationary environment. In addition to real estate, this includes Treasury Inflation-Protected Securities (TIPS) and commodities.

25. Simon Johnson, "The Rise of Sovereign Wealth Funds," *Finance and Development*, September 2007, p. 57.

26. China Universal Asset Management Co. Ltd., Shanghai, China.

27. Bank for International Settlements (BIS), *Triennial and Semiannual Surveys on Positions in Global Over-the-Counter (OTC) Derivative Markets at End-June 2007*, BIS, Basel, Switzerland, 2007.

28. Darrell Duffie, "Innovation in Credit Risk Transfer: Implications for Financial Stability," paper presented at the Bank for International Settlements (BIS) Sixth Annual Conference, Financial System and Macroeconomic Resilience, Brunnen, Switzerland, June 18–19, 2007. Available on www.bis.org/events/brunnen07/duffiepres.pdf.

29. Two-thirds of subprime risk is said to have resided in structured finance instruments.

Chapter 5

1. *The Economist*, "Getting the Message, At Last," December 13, 2007.

2. Antoine van Agtmael, *The Emerging Markets Century: How a New Breed of World Class Companies Is Overtaking the World*, Free Press, New York, 2007.

3. These allocations are reflected in the evolution of the Policy Portfolio (or neutral asset mix) that is set out on the Web site www.hmc.harvard.edu.

4. Data on asset allocations are available on the Harvard Management Company (HMC) Web site www.hmc.harvard.edu.

5. Mohamed A. El-Erian, "In the New Liquidity Factories, Buyers Must Still Beware," *Financial Times*, March 22, 2007.

6. Martin Wolf, "Questions and Answers on a Sadly Predictable Debt Crisis," *Financial Times*, September 5, 2007.

7. Kevin Warsh, "The End of History?" Speech to the New York Association for Business Economics, New York, N.Y., November 7, 2007.

8. Bryan Keogh and Shannon D. Harrington, "Citigroup Pushes Bank Borrowing Costs Above Companies," *Bloomberg News*, November 16, 2007.

9. Ben S. Bernanke, "Housing, Housing Finance, and Monetary Policy," Speech at the Federal Reserve Bank of Kansas City's Economic Symposium, Jackson Hole, Wyo., August 31, 2007. Available on www.federalreserve.gov/newsevents/speech/bernanke20070831a.htm.

10. For an early application of this view, see Mohamed A. El-Erian, "Symbiotic Parenting," *Emerging Markets Watch*, PIMCO, Newport Beach, Calif., June 2004.

11. Mohamed A. El-Erian, "A Route Back to Potency for Central Banks," *Financial Times*, January 17, 2007, p. 9.

12. Jim Cramer's outburst, Friday, August 10, 2007, may be seen on YouTube.com and www.cnbc.com.

13. Frederic S. Mishkin, "Monetary Policy and the Dual Mandate," Speech delivered at Bridgewater College, Bridgewater, Va., on April 10, 2007. The speech is available on www.federalreserve.gov/newsevents/speech/Mishkin20070410a.htm.

14. Roberto Cardarelli, Selim Elekdag, and M. Ayhan Kose, "Managing Large Capital Inflows," *World Economic Outlook*, International Monetary Fund (IMF), Washington, D.C., October 2007, ch. 3, p. 123.

15. Edwin M. Truman, "The Management of China's International Reserves: China and an SWF Scorecard," paper prepared for the Conference on China's Exchange Rate Policy, Peterson Institute for International Economics (IIE), Washington, D.C., October 19, 2007, p. 11. Available on www.petersoninstitute.org/publications/papers/truman1007.pdf. Also published in *Debating China's Exchange Rate Policy*, edited by Nicholas R. Lardy and Morris Goldstein, Peterson Institute for International Economics, Washington, D.C., 2008.

16. Jim VandeHei and Jonathan Weisman, "Republicans Split with Bush on Ports: White House Vows to Brief Lawmakers on Deal with Firm Run by Arab State," *Washington Post*, February 23, 2006, p. A01.

17. My remarks are contained in Mohamed A. El-Erian, "Towards a Better Understanding of Sovereign Wealth Funds," discussant comments on Peterson Institute Senior Fellow Edwin M. Truman's paper, "The Management of China's International Reserves," for the Conference on China's Exchange Rate Policy, Peterson Institute for International Economics (IIE), Washington, D.C., October 19, 2007. Available on www.petersoninstitute.org/events/event_detail.cfm?EventID=47.

18. *The Economist*, "The Invasion of the Sovereign-Wealth Funds," January 17, 2008, p. 11.

19. The transcript of the Democratic Debate in Las Vegas on January 15, 2008, as provided by the Federal News Service and reprinted in the *New York Times*, is available on www.nytimes.com/2008/01/15/us/politics/15demdebatetranscript.html?_r=2&pagewanted=all&oref=slogin&oref=slogin.

20. *The Economist*, "The Invasion of the Sovereign-Wealth Funds."

21. El-Erian, "Towards a Better Understanding of Sovereign Wealth Funds."

22. David Evans, "Public School Funds Hit by Defaulted SIV Debts Hidden in Investment Pools," *Bloomberg News*, November 15, 2007.

23. The members of the Group of Seven (G-7) are Canada, France, Germany, Italy, Japan, United Kingdom, and United States. The G-7 agreed in 1994 unofficially and in 1997 officially to include Russia in a new, mainly political forum, known as the Group of Eight (G-8).

24. Robert F. Bruner and Sean D. Carr, *The Panic of 1907: Lessons Learned from the Market's Perfect Storm*, Wiley, Hoboken, N.J., 2007.

Chapter 6

1. Jeremy J. Siegel, *Stocks for the Long Run: The Definitive Guide to Financial Market Returns & Long Term Investment Strategies*, 4th ed., McGraw-Hill, 2008, p. 4.

2. Mohamed A. El-Erian, "Waning Days of the Dollar," *Newsweek*, November 19, 2007.

3. David Swensen, *Unconventional Success: A Fundamental Approach to Personal Investment*, Free Press, New York, 2005.

4. For an interesting discussion on fundamental indexing, see Robert D. Arnott, Jason C. Hsu, and Philip Moore, "Fundamental Indexation," *Financial Analysts Journal*, vol. 61, no. 2, March/April 2005.

5. Marc Lifscher, "CalPERS Panel OKs Broader Mix," *Los Angeles Times*, December 18, 2007, p. C2.

6. For an early and comprehensive analysis of inflation-protected securities, see John Brynjolfsson and Frank J. Fabozzi, editors, *Handbook of Inflation Indexed Bonds*, Frank J. Fabozzi Associates, New Hope, Pa., 1999.

7. C.A.E. Goodhart, "Monetary Relationship: A View from Threadneedle Street," *Papers in Monetary Economics*, Vol. I, Reserve Bank of Australia, 1975.

8. Similar considerations have prompted the ongoing shift in company pension plans to automatic enrollment—that is, offering new hires the choice of opting out rather than opting in. This change has been shown to result in significant increases in the amount and speed of enrollment. See John Beshears, James J. Choi, David Laibson, and Brigitte C. Madrian, *The Importance of Default Options for Retirement Savings Outcome: Evidence from the United States*, CeRP Working Paper 43, Center for Research on Pensions and Welfare Policies (CeRP), Turin, Italy, 2003.

9. Mohamed A. El-Erian, "Decomposing Emerging Markets Bonds," *Emerging Markets Watch*, PIMCO, Newport Beach, Calif., September 2004.

10. William H. Gross, "Philosopher's Stone," *Investment Outlook*, PIMCO, Newport Beach, Calif., September 2004.

11. See, for example, Jasmina Hasanhodzic and Andrew W. Lo, "Can Hedge-Fund Returns Be Replicated? The Linear Case," August 16, 2006. Available at the Social Science Research Network (SSRN): http://ssrn.com/abstract=924565.

12. See, for example, Steven N. Kaplan and Antoinette Schoar, "Private Equity Performance: Returns, Persistence and Capital Flows," *Journal of Finance*, vol. 60, no. 4, 2005.

13. Oliver Gottschlag and Ludovic Phalippou, "The Truth about Private Equity Performance," *Harvard Business Review*, December 2007.

14. Josh Lerner and Antoinette Schoar, *The Illiquidity Puzzle: Theory and Evidence from Private Equity*, NBER Working Paper No. W9146, National Bureau of Economic Research (NBER), Cambridge, Mass., 2002.

15. Josh Lerner, Antoinette Schoar, and Wan Wong, *Smart Institutions, Foolish Choices? The Limited Partner Performance Puzzle*, NBER Working Paper No. 11136, National Bureau of Economic Research (NBER), Cambridge, Mass., February 2005.

16. Prashant A. Bhatia, *Chief Investment Officer Survey*, Citigroup Global Markets, September 25, 2007, 36 pages.

17. See, for example, Raghuram Rajan, "Bankers' Pay Is Deeply Flawed," *Financial Times*, January 8, 2008, p. 9.
18. Mohamed A. El-Erian, "Global Investor: Hedge Fund Truths," *Newsweek*, October 1, 2007.
19. David S. Scharfstein, and Jeremy Stein, "Herd Behavior and Investment," *American Economic Review*, vol. 80, no. 3, June 1990, p. 465.
20. The total pool of assets managed by HMC at the end of June 2007, which includes the endowment and related accounts, amounted to $41 billion.
21. Every December, Harvard University issues a press release detailing the compensation of the five top earners at the Harvard Management Company and that of HMC's CEO. This information is also contained in the tax statements of the university.
22. The sixth HMC spin-off, Convexity, which started investing in February 2006, raised over $6 billion up front. The amount constituted the largest initial capital raise-up for a hedge fund at that time.

Chapter 7

1. William H. Gross, "What Do They Know?" *Investment Outlook*, PIMCO, Newport Beach, Calif., October 2007.
2. International Monetary Fund (IMF), "Managing Large Capital Inflows," *World Economic Outlook*, IMF, Washington, D.C., October 2007.
3. Conference on China's Exchange Rate Policy, Peter G. Peterson Institute for International Economics (IIE), Washington, D.C., October 19, 2007. Truman's comments are reflected in his paper: Edwin M. Truman, "The Management of China's International Reserves: China and an SWF Scorecard." Also published in *Debating China's Exchange Rate Policy*, edited by Nicholas R. Lardy and Morris Goldstein, Peter G. Peterson Institute for International Economics (IIE), Washington, D.C., 2008.
4. For a more detailed discussion, see Mohamed A. El-Erian, "Towards a Better Understanding of Sovereign Wealth Funds," discussant comments on Peterson Institute Senior Fellow Edwin M. Truman's paper, "The Management of China's International Reserves," for the Conference on China's Exchange Rate Policy, Peter G. Peterson Institute for International Economics (IIE), Washington, D.C., October 19, 2007. Available on www.petersoninstitute.org/events/event_detail.cfm?EventID=47.
5. A detailed discussion may be found in Mohamed A. El-Erian, "Asset-Liability Management in Emerging Economies," in *Sovereign Wealth Management*, edited by Jennifer Johnson-Calari and Malan Rietveld, Central Banking Publications, London, 2007.
6. One example of these regulatory agencies is the U.S. Treasury's Committee on Foreign Investment in the United States (CFIUS).

7. U.S. Department of the Treasury, Office of Domestic Finance, "Who/What Is the Treasury Borrowing Advisory Committee (TBAC)?" See www.treas.gov/offices/domestic-finance/debt-management/who-is-tbac.shtml.

8. Thomas L. Friedman, *The World Is Flat: A Brief History of the Twenty-First Century*, Farrar, Straus and Giroux, New York, 2005.

9. As an example, see the recent survey article by Pinelopi K. Goldberg and Nina Pavcnik, "Distributional Effects of Globalization in Developing Countries," *Journal of Economic Literature*, vol. 45, no. 1, March 2007, pp. 39–82.

10. International Monetary Fund (IMF), "Globalization and Inequality," *World Economic Outlook*, IMF, Washington, D.C., October 2007, p. 49.

11. Ibid., p. 52.

12. See, for example, International Monetary Fund (IMF), *The Managing Director's Report on the Fund's Medium-Term Strategy, September 15, 2005*, and IMF, *The Managing Director's Report on Implementing the Fund's Medium-Term Strategy, April 5, 2006*, IMF, Washington, D.C.

13. See, for example, International Monetary Fund (IMF), *Committee to Study Sustainable Long-Term Financing of the IMF, Final Report*, IMF, Washington, D.C., January 31, 2007.

14. Edwin M. Truman, editor, *Reforming the IMF for the 21st Century*, Peter G. Peterson Institute for International Economics (IIE), Washington, D.C., 2006.

15. Mohamed A. El-Erian, "IMF Reform: Attaining the Critical Mass," in *Reforming the IMF for the 21st Century*, edited by Edwin M. Truman, Peter G. Peterson Institute for International Economics (IIE),Washington, D.C., 2006.

16. Richard P. Feynman, *Personal Observations on the Reliability of the Shuttle*, reprinted as Appendix A in *What Do You Care What Other People Think: Further Adventures of a Curious Character*, Norton, New York, 1988.

17. Mohamed A. El-Erian and Michael Spence, "Refocus the Fund," *Financial Times*, August 6, 2007.

18. Recall the CEO qualities that Jack Welch is fond of stressing: authenticity, vision, hiring ability, resilience, strategic mindset, and execution. For details, see Jack Welch and Suzy Welch, "Chief Executive Officer-in-Chief," *BusinessWeek*, February 4, 2008, p. 88.

19. Olivier Blanchard, "An Interview with Stanley Fischer," in *Inside the Economist's Mind: Conversations with Eminent Economists*, edited by Paul A. Samuelson and William A. Barnett, Blackwell Publishing, Malden, Mass., 2007.

Chapter 8

1. The impact of moral hazard, and the partly related phenomenon of adverse selection, is elegantly discussed in Joseph E. Stiglitz and Andrew

Murray Weiss, "Credit Rationing in Markets with Imperfect Information," *American Economic Review*, vol. 73, no. 3, June 1981, pp. 303–410.

2. Xavier Freixas, "Systemic Risk and Prudential Regulation in the Global Economy," paper prepared for the joint Federal Reserve Bank of Chicago and the International Monetary Fund (IMF) conference on Globalization and Systemic Risk, Chicago, September 27–28, 2007.

3. Krishna Guha, "Fed Ready to Act against 'Tail Risk,'" *Financial Times*, September 8/9, 2007, p. 5.

4. Mohamed A. El-Erian, "Sophistication in Managing Risk Is Part of the Regime Change," *Financial Times*, July 26, 2007.

5. Clawbacks seek to insure longer-term outperformance. They provide the owner of the capital with the ability to claw back performance fees from the investment manager should the record of outperformance not be sustained from a prespecified period of time.

6. Among the *Emerging Markets Watch* (EMW) issues that dealt with Argentina and that are available in the archive section of the PIMCO Web site (www.pimco.com), see "IMF Delivers Packages for the Holidays," December 2000; "Distracted by Reality," April 2001; "The Ant Trail," August 2001; "Cambia Todo Cambia," November 2001; and "To B Or Not to D.?," January 2002.

7. The Emerging Market Bond Index (EMBI) is maintained by JPMorgan Chase.

8. As an illustration, ProShares advertised on page M9 of the December 17, 2007 edition of *Barron's*, the weekly financial paper, that it was offering investors 29 short ETFs for the U.S. markets and was looking to introduce funds that short foreign markets.

9. See, for example, Geraldine Fabrikant, "Playing Hunches at Harvard," *New York Times*, March 15, 2007.

10. Blaise Pascal, *Pensées*, Penguin Classics, Penguin Books, London, 1995.

11. Mohamed A. El-Erian, "The Elusive Center," *Emerging Markets Watch*, PIMCO, Newport Beach, Calif., November 2003.

12. For those of you that have not come across this British concept, a "bedsit" is essentially what is labeled a "studio apartment" in the United States: It is a one-room abode that serves as both a bedroom and a living room.

Acknowledgments

1. I am taking the liberty here of drawing on the remarks I made to the October 4, 2006, Arab Bankers Association of North America (ABANA) Achievement Award Dinner (available on www.arabbankers.org).

REFERENCES

Akerlof, George A., "The Market for 'Lemons': Quality Uncertainty and the Market Mechanism," *Quarterly Journal of Economics*, vol. 84, no. 3, August 1970, pp. 488–500.

Arnott, Robert D., Jason C. Hsu, and Philip Moore, "Fundamental Indexation," *Financial Analysts Journal*, vol. 61, no. 2, March/April 2005.

Bank for International Settlements (BIS), *Triennial and Semiannual Surveys on Positions in Global Over-the-Counter (OTC) Derivative Markets at end-June 2007*, BIS, Basel, Switzerland, 2007.

Berkshire Hathaway, *Annual Report 2002*.

Bernanke, Ben S., "The Global Saving Glut and the U.S. Current Account Deficit," the Sandridge Lecture, Virginia Association of Economics, Richmond, Va. March 10, 2005.

———, "Housing, Housing Finance, and Monetary Policy," Speech at the Federal Reserve Bank of Kansas City's Economic Symposium, Jackson Hole, Wyo., August 31, 2007.

Bernstein, Peter L., *Capital Ideas Evolving*, Wiley, Hoboken, N.J., 2007.

Beshears, John, James J. Choi, David Laibson, and Brigitte C. Madrian, *The Importance of Default Options for Retirement Savings Outcome: Evidence from the United States*, CeRP Working Paper 43, Center for Research on Pensions and Welfare Policies (CeRP), Turin, Italy, 2003.

Bhatia, Prashant A., *Chief Investment Officer Survey*, Citigroup Global Markets, September 25, 2007, 36 pages.

Blustein, Paul, *And the Money Kept Rolling In (and Out): Wall Street, the IMF, and the Bankrupting of Argentina*, Public Affairs/Perseus, New York, 2005.

Bruner, Robert F., and Sean D. Carr, *The Panic of 1907: Lessons Learned from the Market's Perfect Storm*, Wiley, Hoboken, N.J., 2007.

Brynjolfsson, John, and Frank J. Fabozzi, editors, *Handbook of Inflation Indexed Bonds*, Frank J. Fabozzi Associates, New Hope, Pa., 1999.

Callen, Tim, "Emerging Markets Main Engine of Growth," *IMF Survey Magazine*, International Monetary Fund (IMF), Washington, D.C., October 17, 2007.

Calvo, Guillermo A., "Explaining Sudden Stop, Growth Collapse, and BOP Crisis: The Case of Distortionary Output Taxes," *IMF Staff Papers*, vol. 50, International Monetary Fund (IMF), Washington, D.C., 2003.

Calvo, Guillermo A., Alejandro Izquierdo, and Luis-Fernando Mjia, *On the Empirics of Sudden Stops: The Relevance of Balance Sheet Effects*, National Bureau of Economic Research (NBER), Cambridge, Mass., 2004.

Cardarelli, Roberto, Selim Elekdag, and M. Ayhan Kose, "Managing Large Capital Inflows," *World Economic Outlook*, International Monetary Fund (IMF), Washington, D.C., October 2007, ch. 3, p. 123.

Choi, James J., David Laibson, and Brigitte Madrian, *Plan Design and 401(k) Savings Outcomes*, NBER Working Paper No. 10486, National Bureau of Economic Research (NBER), Cambridge, Mass., May 2004.

Daneshkhu, Scheherazade, "Bank Chief Defends Role in Northern Rock Crisis," *Financial Times*, September 21, 2007, p. 2.

Dash, Eric, and Landon Thomas, Jr., "The Man in Citi's Hot Seat," *New York Times Sunday Business*, October 7, 2007, p. 1.

Dialynas, Chris P., and Marshall Auerback, "Renegade Economics and the Bretton Woods II Fiction," PIMCO, Newport Beach, Calif., 2007.

Dooley, Michael, David Folkerts-Landau, and Peter Garber, *The Revived Bretton Woods System: The Effects of Periphery Intervention and Reserve Management on Interest Rates and Exchange Rates in Center Countries*, NBER Working Paper No. 10332, National Bureau of Economic Research (NBER), Cambridge, Mass., 2004.

Dornbusch, Rudiger, Ilan Golfajn, and Rodrigo O. Valdes, "Currency Crises and Collapses," *Brookings Papers on Economic Activity*, 1995.

Duffie, Darrell, "Innovation in Credit Risk Transfers: Implications for Financial Stability," paper presented at the Bank for International Settlements (BIS) Sixth Annual Conference, Financial System and Macroeconomic Resilience, Brunnen, Switzerland, June 18–19, 2007.

The Economist, "Stronger China," September 29, 2007, p. 14.

The Economist, "Getting the Message, At Last," December 13, 2007, p. 18.

Eichengreen, Barry, and Ricardo Hausmann, "How to Eliminate Original Sin," *Financial Times*, November 22, 2002.

El-Erian, Mohamed A., *Mexico's External Debt and the Return to Voluntary Capital Market Financing*, IMF Working Paper No. 91/83, International Monetary Fund (IMF), Washington, D.C., August 1991.

———, *Restoration of Access to Voluntary Capital Market Financing: The Recent Latin American Experience*, IMF Staff Papers 39, no. 1, International Monetary Fund (IMF), Washington, D.C., March 1992.

———, "Sound Economics, Noisy Politics, and the Market for Lemons," *Emerging Markets Watch*, PIMCO, Newport Beach, Calif., June 2000.

———, "IMF Delivers Packages for the Holidays," *Emerging Markets Watch*, PIMCO, Newport Beach, Calif., December 2000.

———, "Distracted by Reality," *Emerging Markets Watch*, PIMCO, Newport Beach, Calif., April 2001.

———, "The Ant Trail," *Emerging Markets Watch*, PIMCO, Newport Beach, Calif., August 2001.

———, "Cambia Todo Cambia," *Emerging Markets Watch*, PIMCO, Newport Beach, Calif., November 2001.

———, "To *B* Or Not to *D*?" *Emerging Markets Watch*, PIMCO, Newport Beach, Calif., January 2002.

———, "Development and Globalization: Friends or Foes," *Emerging Markets Watch*, PIMCO, Newport Beach, Calif., March 2002.

———, "The Elusive Center," *Emerging Markets Watch*, PIMCO, Newport Beach, Calif., November 2003.

———, "Symbiotic Parenting," *Emerging Markets Watch*, PIMCO, Newport Beach, Calif., June 2004.

————, "Asia: Regionalism with an Outward Orientation," *Emerging Markets Watch*, PIMCO, Newport Beach, Calif., July 2004.

————, "Decomposing Emerging Markets Bonds," *Emerging Markets Watch*, PIMCO, Newport Beach, Calif., September 2004.

————, "The Policy Challenge of Managing Success," *Emerging Markets Watch*, PIMCO, Newport Beach, Calif., January 2005.

————, "Revisiting the Market for Lemons," *Emerging Markets Watch*, PIMCO, Newport Beach, Calif., May 2005.

————, "It's Time to End Feudal Selection Processes," *Financial Times*, March 29, 2005.

————, "IMF Reforms: Attaining the Critical Mass," in *Reforming the IMF for the 21st Century*, edited by Edwin M. Truman, Peter G. Peterson Institute for International Economics (IIE), Washington, D.C., 2006.

————, "Asset-Liability Management in Emerging Economies," in *Sovereign Wealth Management*, edited by Jennifer Johnson-Calari and Malan Rietveld, Central Banking Publications, London, 2007.

————, "In the New Liquidity Factories, Buyers Must Still Beware," *Financial Times*, March 22, 2007.

————, "How Investors Should Respond to the Boom in M&A Activity," *Financial Times*, May 30, 2007.

————, "Global Investor: Hedge Fund Truths," *Newsweek*, October 1, 2007.

————, "Foreign Capital Must Not be Blocked," *Financial Times*, October 2, 2007.

————, "Waning Days of the Dollar," *Newsweek*, November 19, 2007.

————, "Towards a Better Understanding of Sovereign Wealth Funds," discussant comments on Peter G. Peterson Institute for International Economics (IIE) Senior Fellow Edwin M. Truman's paper "The Management of China's International Reserves," for the Conference on China's Exchange Rate Policy, IIE, Washington, D.C., October 19, 2007.

El-Erian, Mohamed A., and Michael Spence, "Refocus the Fund," *Financial Times*, August 6, 2007.

El-Erian, Mohamed A., and Michael Spence, "Growth Strategies and Dynamics: Insights from Country Experiences," *World Economics*, vol. 9, no. 1, January–March 2008.

Evans, David, "Public School Funds Hit by Defaulted SIV Debts Hidden in Investment Pools," *Bloomberg News*, November 15, 2007.

Fabrikant, Geraldine, "Playing Hunches at Harvard," *New York Times*, March 15, 2007.

Faust, Drew Gilpin, "Unleashing Our Most Ambitious Imaginings," Inauguration Speech, Harvard University, Cambridge, Mass., October 12, 2007.

Feynman, Richard P., *What Do You Care What Other People Think?: Further Adventures of a Curious Character*, Norton, New York, 1988.

Financial Times, "Europe Is Wrong to Push Strauss-Kahn," August 28, 2007, p. 8.

Fisher, Irving, "The Debt-Deflation Theory of the Great Depression," *Econometrica*, vol. 1, no. 4, October 1933.

Freixas, Xavier, "Systemic Risk and Prudential Regulation in the Global Economy," paper prepared for the joint Federal

Reserve Bank of Chicago and the International Monetary Fund (IMF) conference on Globalization and Systemic Risk, Chicago, September 27–28, 2007.

Friedman, Milton, *Essays in Positive Economics*, University of Chicago Press, Chicago, 1953.

Friedman, Thomas L., *The World Is Flat: A Brief History of the Twenty-First Century*, Farrar, Strauss and Giroux, New York, 2005.

Goldberg, Pinelopi K., and Nina Pavcnik, "Distributional Effects of Globalization in Developing Countries," *Journal of Economic Literature*, vol. 45, no. 1, March 2007, pp. 39–82.

Goodhart, C.A.E., "Monetary Relationship: A View from Threadneedle Street," *Papers in Monetary Economics, Vol. I*, Reserve Bank of Australia, 1975.

Gottschlag, Oliver, and Ludovic Phalippou, "The Truth about Private Equity Performance," *Harvard Business Review*, December 2007.

Greenspan, Alan, *The Age of Turbulence: Adventures in a New World*, Penguin Press, New York, 2007.

Gross, William H., "Philosopher's Stone," *Investment Outlook*, PIMCO, Newport Beach, Calif., September 2004.

———, "What Do They Know?" *Investment Outlook*, PIMCO, Newport Beach, Calif., October 2007.

Guha, Krishna, "Fed Ready to Act against 'Tail Risk,'" *Financial Times*, September 8/9, 2007, p. 5.

Hahn, Frank, and Martin Hollis, *Philosophy and Economic Theory*, Oxford University Press, New York, 1979.

Harper, Christine, "Goldman Doesn't Plan Significant Mortgage Writedowns, CEO Blanfein Says," *Bloomberg News*, November 13, 2007.

Hernandez, Javier C., "Boston Tea Party Catches Fire Again," *Boston Globe*, August 28, 2007.

Husain, Aasim M., "Riding the Crest of the Oil Boom," *IMF Survey Magazine*, International Monetary Fund (IMF), Washington, D.C., October 30, 2007.

International Energy Agency (IEA), *World Energy Outlook* (WEO), Paris, October 2007.

International Monetary Fund (IMF), *The Managing Director's Report on the Fund's Medium-Term Strategy, September 15, 2005*, IMF, Washington, D.C.

———, *The Managing Director's Report on Implementing the Fund's Medium-Term Strategy, April 5, 2006*, IMF, Washington, D.C.

———, *IMF inFocus*, a supplement of the *IMF Survey*, vol. 35, September 2006.

———, *Committee to Study Sustainable Long-Term Financing of the IMF, Final Report*, IMF, Washington, D.C., January 31, 2007.

———, "Managing Large Capital Inflows," *World Economic Outlook*, IMF, Washington, D.C., October 2007.

———, "Globalization and Inequality," *World Economic Outlook*, IMF, Washington, D.C., October 2007.

Johnson, Simon, "The Rise of Sovereign Wealth Funds," *Finance and Development*, September 2007, p. 57.

Johnson-Calari, Jennifer, and Malan Rietveld, *Sovereign Wealth Management*, Central Banking Publications, London, 2007.

Kahneman, Daniel, "Maps of Bounded Rationality: A Perspective on Intuitive Judgment and Choice," Nobel Prize Lecture, Stockholm, Sweden, December 8, 2002.

Kahneman, Daniel, and Amos Tversky, "Prospect Theory: An Analysis of Decision Under Risk," *Econometrica*, vol. 17, 1979.

Kahneman, Daniel, and Amos Tversky, editors, *Choices, Values, and Frames*, Cambridge University Press, Cambridge, U.K., 2000.

Kaplan, Steven N., and Antoinette Schoar, "Private Equity Performance: Returns, Persistence and Capital Flows," *Journal of Finance*, vol. 60, no. 4, 2005.

Keogh, Bryan, and Shannon D. Harrington, "Citigroup Pushes Bank Borrowing Costs above Companies," *Bloomberg News*, November 16, 2007.

Keynes, John Maynard, *The General Theory of Employment, Interest, and Money*, Macmillan, London, 1936.

Kudrin, Alexei, "The Era of Empires Is Over for International Bodies," *Financial Times*, September 30, 2007.

Lardy, Nicholas R., and Morris Goldstein, editors, *Debating China's Exchange Rate Policy*, Peter G. Peterson Institute for International Economics (IIE), Washington, D.C., 2008.

Lerner, Josh, and Antoinette Schoar, *The Illiquidity Puzzle: Theory and Evidence from Private Equity*, NBER Working Paper No. W9146, National Bureau of Economic Research (NBER), Cambridge, Mass., 2002.

Lerner, Josh, Antoinette Schoar, and Wan Wong, *Smart Institutions, Foolish Choices? The Limited Partner Performance Puzzle*, NBER Working Paper No. 11136, National Bureau of Economic Research (NBER), Cambridge, Mass., 2005.

Levitt, Steven D., and Stephen J. Dubner, *Freakonomics: A Rogue Economist Explores the Hidden Sides of Everything*, HarperTorch, New York, 2006.

Lewis, K., "Trying to Explain Home Bias in Equities and Consumption," *Journal of Economic Literature*, vol. 37, June 1999, pp. 571–608.

Lifscher, Marc, "CalPERS Panel OKs Broader Mix," *Los Angeles Times*, December 18, 2007, p. C2.

Masson, Paul R., *Multiple Equilibria, Contagion, and the Emerging Market Crises*, IMF Working Paper WP/99/164, International Monetary Fund (IMF), Washington, D.C., November 1999.

McClure, Samuel M., David I. Laibson, George Lowenstein, and Jonathan D. Cohen, "Separate Neural Systems Value Immediate and Delayed Monetary Rewards," *Science*, vol. 306, October 15, 2004, pp. 503–507.

McCreevy, Charlie, Official Opening Speech, Wachovia Bank International, October 26, 2007, European Commission, p. 5.

McCulley, Paul, "Teton Reflections," *Global Central Bank Focus*, PIMCO, Newport Beach, Calif., August/September 2007.

McKinsey Global Institute (MGI), *The New Power Brokers: How Oil, Asia, Hedge Funds, and Private Equity Are Shaping Global Capital Markets*, MGI, San Francisco/McKinsey & Company, October 2007.

Mishkin, Frederic S., "Monetary Policy and the Dual Mandate," Speech delivered at Bridgewater College, Bridgewater, Va., April 10, 2007.

Nakamoto, Michiyo, and David Wighton, "Bullish Citigroup Is 'Still Dancing' to the Beat of the Buyout Boom," *Financial Times*, July 10, 2007.

Pascal, Blaise, *Pensées*, Penguin Classics, Penguin Books, London, 1995.

Peterson, Richard L., *Inside the Investor's Brain: The Power of Mind Over Money*, Wiley, Hoboken, N.J., 2007.

Ridley, Matt, Letters to the Editor, *The Economist*, September 29, 2007, p. 19.

Rodrik, Dani, *One Economics, Many Recipes: Globalization, Institutions, and Economic Growth*, Princeton University Press, Princeton, N.J., 2007.

Roubini, Nouriel, and Brad Sester, "How Scary Is the Deficit?" *Foreign Affairs*, July/August 2005.

Samuelson, Paul A., and William A. Barnett, *Inside the Economist's Mind: Conversations with Eminent Economists*, Blackwell Publishing, Malden, Mass., 2007.

Scharfstein, David S., and Jeremy Stein, "Herd Behavior and Investment," *American Economic Review*, vol. 80, no. 3, June 1990, p. 465.

Sen, Amartya K., "Rational Fools: A Critique of the Behavioral Foundations of Economic Theory," *Philosophy and Public Affairs*, vol. 6, no. 4, Summer 1977.

Shefrin, Hersh, and Meir Statman, "The Disposition to Sell Winners Too Early and Ride Losers Too Long: Theory and Evidence," *Journal of Finance*, vol. 40, no. 3, 1985, pp. 777–790.

Shiller, Robert J., *Irrational Exuberance*, Princeton University Press, Princeton, N.J., 2000.

Shiv, Baba, and Alexander Fedorikhin, "Heart and Mind in Conflict: The Interplay of Affect and Cognition in Consumer Decision Making," *Journal of Consumer Research*, vol. 26, December 1999, pp. 278–292.

Shleifer Andrei, and Robert W. Vishny, "The Limits to Arbitrage," *Journal of Finance*, March 1997, pp. 35–55.

Siegel, Jeremy J., *Stocks for the Long Run: The Definitive Guide to Financial Market Returns & Long Term Investment Strategies*, 4th ed., McGraw-Hill, New York, 2008.

Sim, Stuart, *Manifesto for Silence: Confronting the Politics and Culture of Noise*, Edinburgh University Press, Edinburgh, 2007.

Simon, Scott, "Scott Simon Discusses PIMCO's Views on the U.S. Housing Market," PIMCO, Newport Beach, Calif., December 2006.

Stiglitz, Joseph E., and Andrew Murray Weiss, "Credit Rationing in Markets with Imperfect Information," *American Economic Review*, vol. 73, no. 3, June 1981, pp. 303–410.

Summers, Lawrence H., "Reflections on Global Account Imbalances and Emerging Markets Reserve Accumulation," L.K. Jha Memorial Lecture delivered on March 24, 2006, at the Reserve Bank of India, Mumbai, India.

Swann, Christopher, "Strauss-Kahn to Inherit IMF Job with Reduced Clout," *Bloomberg News*, August 31, 2007.

Swensen, David, *Unconventional Success: A Fundamental Approach to Personal Investment*, Free Press, New York, 2005.

Taleb, Nassim Nicholas, *Fooled by Randomness: The Hidden Role of Chance in Life and the Markets*, Random House, New York, 2005.

———, *The Black Swan: The Impact of the Highly Improbable*, Random House, New York, 2007.

———, "The Pseudo-Science Hurting Markets," *Financial Times*, October 24, 2007.

Tett, Gillian, "Why Financiers Have Missed the New Monster," *Financial Times*, September 7, 2007, p. 22.

Truman, Edwin M., editor, *Reforming the IMF for the 21st Century*, Peter G. Peterson Institute for International Economics (IIE), Washington, D.C., 2006.

———, "The Management of China's International Reserves: China and an SWF Scorecard," paper prepared for the Conference on China's Exchange Rate Policy, Peter G. Peterson Institute for International Economics (IIE), Washington, D.C., October 19, 2007. Also published in *Debating*

China's Exchange Rate Policy, edited by Nicholas R. Lardy and Morris Goldstein, IIE, Washington, D.C., 2008.

Unmack, Neil, and Sebastian Boyd, "HSBC Will Take on $45 Billion of Assets from Two SIVs," *Bloomberg News*, November 26, 2007.

van Agtmael, Antoine, *The Emerging Markets Century: How a New Breed of World Class Companies Is Overtaking the World*, Free Press, New York, 2007.

VandeHei, Jim, and Jonathan Weisman, "Republicans Split with Bush on Ports: White House Vows to Brief Lawmakers on Deal with Firm Run by Arab State," *Washington Post*, February 23, 2006, p. A01.

Wainer, Howard, "The Most Dangerous Equation," *American Scientist*, May–June 2007, p. 250.

Warsh, Kevin, "The End of History?" Speech to the New York Association for Business Economics, New York, N.Y., November 7, 2007.

Webber, Jude, and Richard Lapper, "It Won't be Easy . . . No Tears for the IMF as Feisty Argentina Awaits Its Next Evita," *Financial Times*, October 25, 2007.

Welch, Jack, and Suzy Welch, "Chief Executive Officer-in-Chief," *BusinessWeek*, February 4, 2008.

White, Ben, and David Wighton, "Credit Squeeze Costs Banks $18 Billion," *Financial Times*, October 6, 2007, p. 1.

Wolf, Martin, "Questions and Answers on a Sadly Predictable Debt Crisis," *Financial Times*, September 5, 2007.

———, "The Bank Loses a Game of Chicken," *Financial Times*, September 21, 2007, p. 11.

Yew, Lee Kuan, *From Third World to First—The Singapore Story: 1965–2000*, HarperCollins, New York, 2000.

INDEX

ACKNOWLEDGMENTS

This book has been influenced by many people who have touched my life and enriched it by their generosity and insights.

The book would not have seen the light of day were it not for the catalytic role played by Jeanne Glasser at McGraw-Hill. She was instrumental in encouraging me to put pen to paper (or, more accurately, fingers to a keyboard), and she and her colleagues readily answered the questions that came up.

Francesc Balcells, Mike Spence, and Ramin Toloui were kind enough to read an early draft of the entire manuscript and provide extremely useful comments.

Several of the ideas contained in this book benefited from discussions in seminars and conferences. I learned a lot from the interactions with students and faculty at the Harvard Business School, the Harvard University Department of Economics, and the John F. Kennedy School of Government. I also benefited from comments received at gatherings organized by Allianz; the Bank for International Settlements (BIS); the Council on Foreign Relations; the Federal Reserve Bank of Chicago; the Federal Reserve Bank of New York; 100 Women

in Hedge Funds; the Grant Fall Forum; the International
Finance Corporation (IFC); the International Monetary Fund
(IMF); the Kuwait Investment Authority (KIA); the Massachusetts Institute of Technology (MIT); the National Bank of
Kuwait (NBK); the Peter G. Peterson Institute for International Economics (IIE); the Technical University of Munich;
and the World Bank.

If nothing else, this book illustrates how lucky I have been
in my life. I have been exposed to many interesting professional opportunities, I've learned from brilliant teachers and
colleagues, and I've been surrounded by a supportive family
and wonderful friends. There is simply no way that I can do
justice to all this through a traditional "acknowledgment." So,
at the risk of inadvertent omissions, I would like to thank a
number of individuals.

In sharing their insights and experiences, my colleagues at
the Harvard Management Company (HMC), the International Monetary Fund (IMF), the Pacific Investment Management Company (PIMCO), and Salomon Smith Barney/
Citigroup were instrumental in teaching me how the real
world operates.

In the two enjoyable years I spent at HMC, I benefited
from interactions with talented colleagues, including Joe
Auth, Francesc Balcells, John Bergen, John Campbell, Peter
Dolan, Graig Fantouzzi, John Galanek, Glenn Hutchins, Rob
Kaplan, Dan Kelly, Marty Leibowitz, Jay Light, Kate
Murtagh, Hilda Ochoa-Brillembourg, Don Rich, Jim Rothen-
berg, and Andy Wiltshire. These interactions were greatly
enhanced by numerous spontaneous and illuminating investment discussions that I had on the trade floor, in particular

with Steve Alperin, Stephen Blyth, Elise McDonald, Karen Parker, Craig Szeman, Marc Seidner, and Stan Zuzic.

Many people helped and influenced me during my 15-year stay in Washington, D.C., while I worked at the IMF. Special thanks go to Mark Allen, Caroline Atkinson, Fred Bergsten, Jack Boorman, Andrew Crockett, Said El-Naggar, Stan Fischer, Morris Goldstein, Jacque de Larosiere, Malcolm Knight, Alessandro Leipold, the late Tom Leddy, Claudio Loser, Adan Mazarei, Mike Mussa, Moises Naim, Gumersindo Oliveros, Klaus Regling, Shakour Shaalan, Ernie Stern, Ted Truman, Max Watson, John Williamson, and Muhammad Yaqub.

PIMCO provided me with a professional and intellectual home that most people can only dream of. I am particularly grateful to Bill Gross who inspired me and many others through his disciplined approach to investment, his insights, his openness to new ideas, and his commitment to getting it right in different market cycles and policy conditions. I also benefited from interactions with others on PIMCO's Investment Committee, including Chris Dialynas, Pasi Hamalanian, Paul McCulley, Bill Powers, and Changhong Zhu. To outsiders, our discussions might appear to be rough verbal wrestling matches, but we know that they are precious attempts to get to the truth in the context of a high degree of mutual intellectual and personal respect. These discussions were enriched by interactions with many other PIMCO colleagues including Andrew Balls, Rich Clarida, Michael Gomez, Dan Ivacsyn, Jay Jacobs, Scott Mather, Curtis Mewbourne, Saumil Parikh, Mark Porterfield, Steve Rodosky, Scott Simon, Bill Thompson, Ramin Toloui, Dick Weil, and Lori Whiting. I also had the benefit of interesting exchanges in Munich. Special thanks go to Paul Achleitner, Michael Diekmann, Joachim Faber, Helmut Perlet, and other members of the Allianz Group.

My time at Salmon Smith Barney/Citigroup marked an important transition from the policy world to the daily realities of the marketplace. I managed this transition because of the guidance of colleagues such as Rafael Biosse-Duplan, Amer Bisat, Edward Cowen, Jim Faroese, Mark Franklin, Desmond Lachman, Tom Maheras, and Kim Schoenholtz.

My professional career would not have been as much fun as it was if I had not been able to draw on the academic world. Here, I would like to thank colleagues at Cambridge, Harvard, and Oxford who taught me a lot through interesting discussions and debate. Particular thanks go to Rawi Abdelal, Derek Bowett, Randy Cohen, Andy Cosh, Joy de Beyer, John Eatwell, Drew Faust, Frank Hahn, Jim Herzog, the late John Hicks, Jakub Jurek, Nick Knight, Robert Mabro, Murray Milgate, Andre Perolt, Ken Rogoff, the late Joan Robinson, Bob Rowthorne, Eytan Shapiro, Ajit Singh, Frances Stewart, Larry Summers, Luis Vicera, and Jeff Weir. I would also like to thank Lloyd Blankfein, Gary Cohn, Alan Greenspan, Ken Griffin, Seth Klarman, Adam Lerrick, Vikram Pandit, and Mike Spence who have been wonderful intellectual catalysts.

Over the years, I have had the privilege of publishing op-eds that have helped me sharpen and better define my views. I am particularly grateful to colleagues at the *Financial Times* and *Newsweek* such as Lionel Barber, Thorold Barker, Rana Faroohar, Chrystia Freeland, Brian Groom, Krishna Guha, Roula Khalaf, Gwen Robinson, Tony Tussell, Martin Wolf, and Fareed Zakaria.

Finally, and most importantly, none of the above would have materialized were it not for my amazing family and friends.[1] My parents instilled in me from a very early age the importance of education and inquiry. Despite his modest academic (and then civil servant) salary, my father never shied away from sending his children to the best schools in Egypt, Europe, and the United States. He encouraged us to excel while remaining faithful to our roots and never losing sight of the special opportunities being afforded to us. My mother continued this tradition after our father passed away suddenly in 1981. Throughout all this, I received wise counsel from them and from many friends—and usually with a healthy dose of good humor.

No mention of family support would be even somewhat complete without a special mention of my amazing wife, Jamie, and our wonderful daughter. I am so privileged in this regard. They have surrounded me with an incredible amount of love. They have created, on a daily basis, the conditions that allow me to function well.

For weeks, my family tolerated my coming home after a day at the office, or several days on the road, and then sitting at the computer in the kitchen to write this book. They put up with many weekends of my working on this book while our dog lay on the floor next to me keeping me company. They even tolerated my writing during our already too infrequent family holidays. Without my family's support, I would not have been able to write this book.

ABOUT THE AUTHOR

Mohamed A. El-Erian is co-CEO and co-CIO of the Pacific Investment Management Company (PIMCO), one of largest and most-respected investment management companies in the world with over $700 billion in assets under management (as of December 2007). Prior to assuming these positions when he rejoined PIMCO in January 2008, Dr. El-Erian was president and CEO of the Harvard Management Company (HMC), the entity that manages Harvard University's endowment and related accounts. Dr. El-Erian also served as a member of the faculty of Harvard Business School and as deputy treasurer of the university.

After completing his undergraduate degree in economics at Cambridge University in England, Dr. El-Erian obtained masters and doctorate degrees in economics from Oxford University. He spent 15 years at the International Monetary Fund (IMF) in Washington, D.C., where he participated and headed negotiating missions to countries in Africa, Asia, central Europe, Latin America, and the Middle East. During his IMF tenure, he served as the advisor to the first deputy managing director and as deputy director. Dr. El-Erian left the public sector in December 1997 to join the private sector. He initially worked at Salomon Smith Barney/Citigroup in London where he was a managing director heading the emerging markets research group. He subsequently joined PIMCO in Newport Beach, California. In his first seven-year tenure at PIMCO, Dr. El-Erian served as a senior portfolio manager, a member of the firm's Investment Committee, and a member of its Partner Compensation Committee.

Dr. El-Erian has served on several boards and committees, including the Emerging Markets Traders Association (EMTA) and the IMF's Committee of Eminent Persons. He was a member of the U.S. Treasury Borrowing Advisory Committee, and he is currently a board member of Cambridge in America, the International Center for Research on Women, and the Peterson Institute for International Economics (IIE). He is also a member of the IMF's Capital Markets Consultative Group and the International Advisory Committee for the National Bank of Kuwait. He chairs Microsoft's Investment Advisory Committee.

Dr. El-Erian has published on a range of economic and financial issues. He has been profiled by *Barron's*, *Bloomberg*, CNBC, *Euromoney*, *Forbes*, the *Financial Times*, and the *New York Times*, to name a few. He has won a number of investment awards from Lippers and Global Investors. In 2004, he was named by *Fortune* as a member of its eight-person Mutual Fund Dream Team. *Latin Finance* named him as one of its 50 Most Influential People in Latin America, while the *Financial News* included him in its list of the Ten Most Influential Europeans in America.

Dr. El-Erian is married to Jamie, a lawyer. They have one daughter.